T5-CVQ-223

Conflict Resolution and Peacebuilding in Laos

Using the case study of Laos, a small landlocked country in Southeast Asia that has seen some of the world's most brutal forms of poverty and violence, this book examines the power of traditional and indigenous conflict resolution systems as a tool for social justice. It explores how the conflict resolution mechanisms build infrastructures that support social harmony and address larger-scale conflicts within communities, nations, and international arenas.

The book discusses how over centuries, foreign powers have polarized and used the ethnic groups of Laos to support their own agendas, and how in spite of this, the Lao people have consistently managed to re-create the peace and harmony that support their social relationships, whether that is within groups or between many distinct groups. Through the development and use of appropriate grassroots conflict resolution structures that do not require a formal court system and that exist outside the political arena, they have been successful in resolving conflicts within and across cultural groups. The book shows that the conflict resolution systems of Laos are embedded in the fabric of ordinary, everyday life and operate independently of the hierarchical structures that dominate governing institutions.

Highlighting how peace continues to work its way into existence through elaborate mediation systems and rituals that bring people together, this book will be of use to students and scholars of Southeast Asian politics, peace studies and war, and conflict studies.

Stephanie Phetsamay Stobbe is a faculty member in the Department of Conflict Resolution Studies at Menno Simons College, a College of Canadian Mennonite University and affiliated College of the University of Winnipeg, Canada.

Routledge Contemporary Southeast Asia Series

Conflict Resolution and Peacebuilding in Laos

Perspective for today's world

Stephanie Phetsamay Stobbe

LONDON AND NEW YORK

First published 2015
by Routledge

2 Park Square, Milton Park, Abingdon, Oxon OX14 4RN
711 Third Avenue, New York, NY 10017, USA

Routledge is an imprint of the Taylor & Francis Group, an informa business

First issued in paperback 2016

Copyright © 2015 Stephanie Phetsamay Stobbe

The right of Stephanie Phetsamay Stobbe to be identified as author of this
work has been asserted by her in accordance with sections 77 and 78 of the
Copyright, Designs and Patents Act 1988.

All rights reserved. No part of this book may be reprinted or reproduced or
utilised in any form or by any electronic, mechanical, or other means, now
known or hereafter invented, including photocopying and recording, or in
any information storage or retrieval system, without permission in writing
from the publishers.

Notice:
Product or corporate names may be trademarks or registered trademarks,
and are used only for identification and explanation without intent to infringe.

British Library Cataloguing in Publication Data
A catalogue record for this book is available from the British Library

Library of Congress Cataloging-in-Publication Data
Stobbe, Stephanie Phetsamay, author.
  Conflict resolution and peacebuilding in Laos : perspective for today's
world / Stephanie Stobbe.
    pages cm. — (Routledge contemporary Southeast Asia series ; 73)
    Includes bibliographical references and index.
  1. Conflict management—Laos. 2. Peace-building—Laos. 3. Social
justice—Laos. 4. Laos—Civilization. I. Title.
    HN700.4.Z9C7376 2015
    303.6'909594—dc23
    2015001189

ISBN: 978-1-138-77476-6 (hbk)
ISBN: 978-1-138-63352-0 (pbk)

Typeset in Times New Roman
by Apex CoVantage, LLC

To my family, who played an important role in encouraging and supporting me in this project, through years of research, travel, and interaction in Laos and elsewhere. To my mother, Pinkham, who used all of her extraordinary gifts helping our family survive, persevere, and thrive, and her strong endorsement of educational values. To my husband, Karl, who has been exceptional in his support, as a caregiver for our children during my research trips, as a sounding board for ideas, and in technical assistance. Our heritage could not be more different, yet his voice and perspective have contributed significantly to my world. To my wonderful children, Katherine and Matthew, who gave me the hardest gift that any mother could ask of their children – time.

Contents

Illustrations

Figures

Tables

Permissions

Bounyavong, O. (1999). Wrapped-Ash Delight. In O. Bounyavong, *Mother's Beloved Stories from Laos* (pp. 93–103). Seattle: University of Washington Press. Reprinted with permission by University of Washington Press, August 5, 2014.
   The "Wrapped-Ash Delight" story is located on pages 31–34.

Preface

The field of conflict resolution (peace and conflict studies) has seen intensive growth over the last twenty-five years. Starting with a single university graduate program twenty-five years ago, there are now over 400 well-established programs across North America and numerous other university programs around the world. Most of these programs are situated in developed countries in the West that have focused on alternative dispute resolution (ADR) processes of formal interest-based mediation and arbitration, alongside recognized rule-of-law–type legal systems. Unfortunately, these systems are largely unfamiliar and impractical for much of the world's population and are incapable of providing social justice in those contexts.

There are still significant philosophical and practical gaps in the peace and conflict world. I have long been interested in informal and non-professional justice systems, looking at traditional, indigenous conflict resolution mechanisms as a way of promoting positive relationships and overall peace in simple communities as well as the international arena. With a large population that still prefers a grass-roots-style conflict resolution system, Laos seemed like an opportune place for research, especially considering my Lao heritage and linguistic fluency. (Note: The use of the word "traditional" has several meanings in conflict resolution. I use it in reference to the conflict resolution system customarily used by the Lao people. For the purposes of this book, the words "grassroots," "indigenous," and "traditional" have slightly different meanings, but share a reference to historical cultural practices.)

I left Laos at the age of seven with my family and did not return to the country until I was an adult. Upon my first visit, I was immediately drawn back to its culture, history, and worldviews. I began working with local non-governmental organizations (NGOs) in Laos and some government-related entities as I looked into conflict resolution, Lao style. I developed connections in the country and started travelling to villages and other places that would help me learn more about what traditional, grassroots conflict resolution had to offer. Initially, I had no intention of writing a book about it, but that changed during a trip to a fairly remote village in the summer of 2008. With appropriate permissions in order, I brought a group of ten Lao researchers with me, asking people in the village about what systems they used to resolve conflicts in their family, workplace, and community.

I was out for a walk in the village when I looked over and saw an older man working over a fire underneath his house built on stilts. He had two granddaughters watching him work as he crouched over, fanning the flames of an open fire to generate heat. I watched for a minute, noticing that he was using old missile casings and other war junk as tubes and pipes to force air to the fire and used the heat to forge metal into tools and other useful items. War junk is not an uncommon site in Laos, and I had seen it used for many creative things – as part of a fence, as a beam or post to support a shed or small living space, and as decorative ornaments in other places. I had known that there were people who were crafting and building with it, but this was the first time I had seen this in person. I walked over to the man's house where he was working underneath the main living area. I asked him if he could explain what he was doing, and he informed me that, today, he was making knives – the type one would use for farming.

He invited me to sit at the small table in the yard and we continued our conversation. Eventually he told me many stories of his experience in the war and his experience searching for and finding the leftover scraps with which he could scrape out a living. His positive demeanor, gracefulness, and gentleness struck me, considering he could easily have been bitter and ruined from the tragedies he had endured. But he did not harbor ill will and asked me what I was doing in their village and how my research was going so far. His openness to talk and share his invaluable experiences and stories was powerful and enriching for me. I began to realize that although Laos had very little to offer the world in an economic sense, the richness of its culture and people was an offering that deserved an audience, an export that had real meaning for the world.

The intended audience for *Conflict Resolution and Peacebuilding in Laos: Perspective for Today's World* is both academic and non-academic, as the book's topics are relevant to multidisciplinary studies (conflict resolution, peace studies, cultural studies, Asian studies, anthropological studies) and occupations (mediators, lawyers, professors, students, business people, humanitarian workers, peacekeepers, development workers, non-profit organizations). Traditional, indigenous conflict resolution systems is an area that is still significantly understudied, especially in relation to the tremendous diversity of groups in Southeast Asia. Using stories and narratives to gain insight into the conflict resolution world of Laos and offering, by extension, insight into other global conflict situations, this book develops a holistic, multidimensional concept of conflict resolution that will contribute to our understanding of conflicts everywhere, and especially to those working with the displaced, marginalized, and oppressed people of the world.

December 2014
Stephanie Phetsamay Stobbe, PhD
Menno Simons College, a College of Canadian
Mennonite University and affiliated College of University of Winnipeg
Winnipeg, Manitoba

Acknowledgements

I would like to say a big "thank you" to all the people, NGOs, and other organizations that have been a part of my Lao life. Their help with organizing trips and introducing me to the many people who assisted me with my research made this book possible. Their enthusiasm, support, and knowledge of Laos were invaluable to me, and I hope that our friendship will continue for many years. Also, tremendous thanks to all the people in Laos who contributed their wisdom, knowledge, and private details about their own lives and conflicts. I hope that this book properly salutes you, your families, your communities, and your world and celebrates the beauty and humanity you bring to our globe. And I especially thank my Lao friends for allowing me to be a part of so many wonderful ceremonies and rituals, to watch your conflict resolution system at work. Allowing me to enter your lives has deeply changed my life.

Note on transliteration

The transliteration of the Ethnic Lao language presents significant problems. There is no official or standard system of anglicization that I am aware of. Clearly, other authors have had similar issues, as reading different English interpretations of Lao can sometimes feel like very different languages. For example, the Lao city and district of Huay Xai has been spelled by some authors as Houayxai, Houayxay, Housai, Houxai, Housei, and so forth. I have seen at least three different spellings listed in passports. There are, of course, Lao-English dictionaries but, unfortunately, they are also rarely consistent with each other. The complicating factor seems to be the highly tonal nature of the Lao language, something that the English alphabet cannot readily convey.

In trying to write down Lao terms, it seemed the most efficient approach would be to translate them as I hear them, based on the Luang Prabang dialect of Lao, translated into the Western Canadian English that I speak. Most regions of Laos will have slightly different pronunciations and connotations for various terms. For example, the word *fan* (or *phan*) translates to "friend" in Vientiane, whereas in Luang Prabang it translates to "romantic friend." This is understandable, considering the two regions have different dialects. There are, in fact, five basic dialects of the Ethnic Lao language within Laos.

In my transliteration, I tried to be as consistent as possible. Lao words that have been anglicized are written in italics. Some are used with their English translations, whereas some of the more important words are only translated the first time. A glossary of the Lao terms is included as an appendix.

Figure p.1 Map of Laos

About the author

Stephanie Phetsamay Stobbe is an associate professor in conflict resolution studies at Menno Simons College (a college of Canadian Mennonite University), affiliated with the University of Winnipeg. As an active educator, trainer, and Alternative
Dispute Resolution (ADR) practitioner with a PhD in peace and conflict studies,
she has worked and conducted research in Canada, United States, South America,
and Southeast Asia. In 2006, she was invited to work with local citizens in the
development of the first peace program in Laos, leading to a full research project
on traditional mediation and conflict resolution rituals between 2007 and 2011. In
2013, she co-facilitated a series of seminars and workshops for political leaders in
Myanmar (Burma) on institutional designs in conflict resolution, peacebuilding,
and reconciliation as the country transitions to democratic governance.

In 2011 Stephanie co-edited a book, *Critical Aspects of Gender in Conflict Resolution, Peacebuilding, and Social Movements* (2011) for Emerald Publishing's
series on Research in Social Movements, Conflicts and Change. Although not a
lawyer, in 2012 she was invited to join the American Bar Association team of
experts to discuss "Gender-Responsive Peacebuilding: Implementing the Secretary-
General's Report on Women's Participation in Peacebuilding" and provide recommendations to the United Nations Development Programme, Peacebuilding
Support Office as they address UN Security Council Resolutions 1325 and 1889.
In that same year, she also served as a visiting professor/researcher at the Matsu-
naga Institute for Peace and Conflict Resolution at the University of Hawaii. Her
current research projects include *A History of Refugee Families in Manitoba and
Abroad: Intergenerational Oral History, Digital Storytelling, and Conflict Resolution Among Refugees in the Diaspora Since the 1970s.*

Introduction

In the period during and after the Vietnam War (1960–1975), the country of Laos gained the distinction of being subjected to "some of the heaviest aerial bombardment in the history of warfare" (Stuart-Fox, 1997, p. 139). US aircraft dropped almost 2.1 million tons of bombs on Laos, an amount approximately equal to the total tonnage dropped by the United States air forces during all of World War II, in both the European and Pacific theatres (Cummings, 1994). Had the bombing been spread out evenly throughout the country, there would have been almost nine tons of bombs per square kilometer. In the most densely bombed part of the country, Xieng Khouang Province, an "estimated 300,000 tons of bombs were dropped, equaling more than two tons per inhabitant . . . [while] 25% of the country's villages remain severely contaminated [with unexploded ordinance]" (MCC, 2000, p. 1). Between 1964 and 1973, the Americans dropped the equivalent of one B-52 planeload of bombs in Laos every eight minutes, twenty-four hours a day, seven days a week (Eberle, 2008). By the end of the war, Laos had become the most heavily bombed country per capita in the history of the world.

It seems impossible that this war could have been a secret. After all, the United States spent US$7.2 billion on this war, the equivalent of US$2 million a day for nine years (Lonely Planet, 2014). However, according to historian Stuart-Fox (1997), "for most of the decade from the renewed outbreak of fighting in 1964 to the cease-fire of 1973, the true extent of the war in Laos remained largely hidden from the outside world by deliberate American deception" (p. 136). The secrecy surrounding the war, including to the American Congress, led to a situation with almost no oversight and very few rules of engagement. The second biggest city in Laos was then Long Cheng, which the Americans built entirely from scratch in the middle of the jungle. It could not be found on any maps of the world because it was populated with people who were not supposed to be there. Its airport was one of the busiest in the world, with some 400 flights per day arriving and departing. Still, the city remained unclassified (Eberle, 2008). This was a secret city, the "hub and nerve center of the clandestine war in the Other Theater" (Robbins, 2005, p. 55). By early 1973,

Almost all of the 3,500 villages under Pathet Lao control had been partly or wholly destroyed . . . 200,000 dead and twice that number of wounded . . .

as many as three-quarters of a million people, a quarter of the entire population had been driven from their homes to become refugees in their own
country . . . The war placed intolerable strains on upland Lao society, weak-
ened the Lao state, corrupted the morality of public life, and set back the
cause of national unity and reconciliation.

(Stuart-Fox, 1997, p. 144)

Of course, the "Secret War" was an abject failure. The only victory the United
States could claim was in having kept it a secret so that they did not have to admit
yet another military loss after the Vietnam War.

I was born in Laos in the midst of this "Secret War," and so my knowledge of
the country, its culture, and issues result from both birthright and intense study.
My birth occurred during a particularly volatile time in the early 1970s, in a part
of Laos with highly diverse multi-ethnic interactions. I am not trying to be evasive
about my age, but I do not actually know my birthdate. At the time, there was no
infrastructure in place to gather and keep track of such vital statistics. My mother
was so preoccupied with the war and with keeping her family safe that she either
did not know the date I was born or simply forgot as the passage of time began to
blur into the misty haze of panic that is the unfortunate reality for many people
caught in the dregs of war and violence.

Even today, few people understand the full ramifications of the Vietnam War
and its effect throughout Southeast Asia. When I was born, the war in Vietnam
was nearing its end, yet in Laos it was just hitting its peak of violence and would
eventually cause almost 10 percent of the Lao population, including my family,
to flee to refugee camps in Thailand. Although I was not born in the most dangerous area, the violence searched us out, and we would often move from place to
place, trying to stay just ahead of it. My mother was a smart businesswoman and
always managed to find us places to stay. There were always holes dug in the
ground underneath the house for those times when the war caught up with us too
quickly.

One of my earliest memories is of fleeing to safety in one of those caverns,
where my mother tried to keep my sister and I quiet as we spent a night underneath
our house in a small, dug-out hole. Somehow it provided just enough protection
for us to survive. Bullet casings and shells would sometimes rest on our beds in
the morning. My father was a ranking officer in the war, and therefore a worthy
target for the other side. My mother tells me that he was often away fighting in the
war, and shortly after my birth, he did not return at all.

Ironically, Laos is a place of serene calm and beauty. I was born in the northwestern part of the country in the region infamously known as the "Golden Tri-
angle," the area where the Lao, Thai, and Burmese borders all converge along the
Mekong River. For most of the twentieth century this area was central to the
world's opium trade. I grew up in the lowlands, surrounded by majestic mountains
that engulfed the lime-green rice fields in the valleys. The tropical jungle was rich
and vast, consuming everything that was not regularly tended to. The bamboo trees
in the dense forests grew rapidly, reaching up to fifteen feet in a year.

Though the effects of the war, death, and resettlement have affected every aspect of my life, I still remember the beauty of the land, the people I grew up with as a child, and the people still living there whom I now know as an adult. These people are caring, gentle, and peace loving. Their genuine smiles, life stories, and ready acceptance of others are etched in my memory. I have always been drawn back, emotionally and intellectually, to the complexity of my birthplace – a place where community, inclusivity, peace, and harmony in relationships are highly valued, but at the same time, a place that has witnessed some of the most brutal forms of violence ever seen in history. There is no better experience of this contrast than to take an early morning walk to the old temple on top of Mount Phousi, quietly and elegantly presiding over the slumbering streets of Luang Prabang, only to be reminded of the dark side of Laos by the presence of a rusty, old anti-aircraft gun just ten steps away from the temple foundations.

The strength and resilience of my mother and our family's personal experiences of war and resettlement have shaped my interest in Laos, our country of birth. The streets of Luang Prabang are full of the sights, smells, and sounds of Laos: monks in their bright orange garments, the smells of food over coal-fired ovens, the elegance of elders watching over the streets, children laughing, and the beautiful flowers and plants adorning the shops – planted in old missile casings (see Figure 0.1). This image defines the heart of conflict resolution, namely, taking the very instrument of destruction and turning it into a foundation for beauty, growth, and new life. Examples of this perfect metaphor abound in Laos.

Figure 0.1 An excellent use of old missile casings from the war

© Stephanie Phetsamay Stobbe 2009

One of the biggest buildings in all of Laos is the Patuxai in Vientiane, a memorial to those who died in pre-revolutionary wars, built from concrete donated by the United States for building a runway to aid in the war (Cummings & Burke, 2005).

My study and practice of conflict resolution, multiple trips back to Laos, and the passage of time have helped me come to terms with the trauma of my past. In turn, reflecting on the images and complexities of Laos continues to shape my interest and thought processes about conflict resolution. In that regard, what I have learned about conflict resolution in the West has sometimes contrasted with those experiences. Western practice has often assumed superiority over other models of conflict resolution and imposed values of mediator neutrality and professional third parties in dispute resolution systems. This book is an effort to acknowledge the valuable contributions to conflict resolution theory and practice made by other cultural groups.

It seems somewhat ironic that Laos, officially named the Lao People's Democratic Republic (Lao PDR), is the backdrop for a book about conflict resolution, about the human capacity for peace. But Laos is an important case for peace and conflict studies. The people of Laos have seen violence and have been victims of hatred, injustice, and ignorance. They have been pawns of powerful outsiders and subject to political agendas that are irrelevant to the vast majority of their population. Yet as we will see, the Lao people know peace. It exudes from their temples, from the streets, from the paddy rice farms in the lowlands, and from the swidden rice fields in the hills.

Laos is part of what anthropologist James C. Scott (2009) terms "Zomia," an area of about 2.5 million square kilometers with 100 million minority peoples of extraordinary ethnic and linguistic diversity. Zomia refers to lands at altitudes above 300 meters that include Thailand, Burma, Laos, Cambodia, Vietnam, and four provinces of China. Some of the ethnic minorities living in these countries would share similar cultural backgrounds, having occupied the area long before the borders were put into place. Through cross-border migration activities, several of these groups occupy areas that transcend borders. Within Laos, its forty-nine official ethnic groups (Government of Lao PDR, 2006) have historically had relatively few conflicts, usually finding ways to reinvent the peace and harmony that outside third parties have disturbed. Through centuries of interaction, conflict resolution structures have developed that promote positive relationships within and across ethnic groups.

This book provides greater understanding and appreciation of the contributions from diverse groups of people who are working every day to establish positive relationships, constructive and appropriate conflict resolution systems, and overall peace in their world. It demonstrates where peace can be found in difficult situations, among people who care little for political agendas but care a great deal about existing harmoniously with others in their communities in order to mutually raise their quality of life. As we shall see, the conflict resolution systems of Laos are embedded in the fabric of grassroots, ordinary, everyday life, and operate independently of the hierarchical structures that dominate governing institutions.

In fact, Laos is a place without an effective court system. The Lao people view the court system as unfamiliar and incapable of providing social justice. Taking a case to court is seen as a loss of face and destructive to relationships. Given this context, I examine how people across ethnic and cultural divides find appropriate conflict resolution processes for maintaining healthy, positive, and interdependent relationships.

In order to explore those dynamics, this book uses the traditional conflict resolution practices of Laos, including mediation, rituals, and cross-cultural processes, as a case study to help us answer the following questions: (1) How can culturally specific conflict resolution processes at the grassroots level be used to promote equality, justice, and freedom in places where formal legal systems are unfamiliar, undeveloped, and are not a compelling force in promoting social justice?; (2) How can traditional conflict resolution processes and rituals assist in the maintenance and reparation of relationships between parties in conflict?; and (3) How can these processes be used and adapted in cross-cultural conflict resolution to establish relationships between groups?

As will become evident, grassroots peace-building processes, ranging from simple, everyday interactions between individuals, to formal mediation, can lead to commonalities in conflict resolution systems and rituals that bond people together. Looking carefully at these structures, I identify ten themes that I see as the mechanics of the Lao conflict resolution system and suggest that they are the principles on which successful conflict resolution operates.

This book is a culmination of life experiences, several trips to Laos over the last twenty years, and research projects conducted between 2006 and 2011. As a professional, I have worked with non-government organizations (NGOs), university students, the Lao National Science Council for Research and Development, and others in exploring peace building in Laos. I have always been intrigued by the complexity of my birthplace, particularly in the peaceful and relaxed people that I have come to know, contrasted with the brutal violence of their past. Understanding how the Lao people have managed to build a shared cultural identity that encompasses at least forty-nine different ethnic groups gives me hope that this can happen elsewhere.

Chapter 1 – *Background and historical context of Laos* describes the background and historical context to frame the discussion of the Lao conflict resolution system. It briefly summarizes the eventful 700-year history of Laos, its culture, religion, economics, legal system, and ethnic and national identities to allow for informed discussions on their cultural conflict resolution processes. Understanding the history of violence and peace in the region, the "Secret Lao War" and Vietnam War, and other background information is important for developing the theme of Lao conflict resolution. These contexts shape how Lao people conceptualize conflict and pursue conflict resolution.

Chapter 2 – *Face and eyes: understanding conflict through metaphor* examines the Lao cultural view of conflict and conflict resolution, often expressed in metaphors, through the concepts of conflict avoidance and saving face. Through various Lao metaphors, knowledge of the Lao worldview emerges that sheds light on the topic of conflict and conflict resolution. The Lao story of "Wrapped-Ash Delight" is used to illustrate the importance of avoidance and saving face in conflict situations and the creative conflict resolution processes endorsed by the village leaders and the community. The use of metaphors, stories, and folk tales teach people about saving face, maintaining face, preventing a loss of face in conflict resolution, and preserving relationships.

Chapter 3 – *Op-lom: the language of conflict resolution* provides an overview of the important concept of *op-lom*. The Lao word *op-lom* is only used in reference to conflict and conflict resolution. It refers to a process of listening, discussing, educating, teaching, reminding, and advising parties to resolve disputes constructively. Conflicts are resolved through *op-lom* within a continuum of progressive levels of mediation. These mediation levels are organized into a "Lao Conflict Resolution Spectrum," from informal private third parties to the more formal public committees of the *Neoy Gai Geer*, a Lao village mediation committee. Through these processes, there is an understanding of how *op-lom* and the Lao Conflict Resolution Spectrum interact to create an effective conflict resolution process.

Chapter 4 – *Rebuilding through rituals* broadens our understanding of Lao cultural conflict resolution practices by discussing the *soukhouan* and *soumma* rituals associated with private and public conflict resolution and reconciliation processes. The rituals and symbols are connected to cultural practices and the Buddhist and animist religions. Both of these cultural activities provide an opportunity to restore the "face and eyes" of people, family, and community in conflict. The ceremonies reflect the importance of relationship building in their conflict resolution structures, evidenced by a metaphoric connection to spiritual completeness and their linguistic use of the word *chai* (heart) in referring to conflict resolution.

Chapter 5 – *Cross-cultural conflict: from micro to macro* explores the value of mediation processes and rituals in conflict resolution between the different ethnic groups in Laos, particularly in addressing intergroup dispute resolution. Beginning with a general discussion on culture, it seeks to fully understand the similarities and connections between inter-ethnic conflict resolution mechanisms, theorizes as to how these parallels in conflict resolution processes and rituals may have developed, and explains how these systems have had a hand in maintaining relationships between groups even through the violence and war of their collective histories.

Chapter 6 – *Grassroots conflict resolution: building from the ground up* develops the topic of conflict resolution embedded in grassroots relationships, mediation, and rituals. Laos demonstrates that effective conflict resolution, whether interpersonal or criminal, is not reserved for formal, expensive, and cumbersome legal systems. It begins with an overview of the Lao conflict resolution system, based on grassroots third parties and processes, and starts to examine the effects of grassroots mediation in other parts of the world and how they relate to more formal legal systems. It explores how these two different conflict resolution systems interact and provide balance in conflict resolution that meets the needs of different groups.

Finally, Chapter 7 – *Tenets of conflict resolution* brings together some of the themes that have developed in looking at the Lao conflict resolution system and begins a discussion centered around whether these characteristics are actually principles, a necessity for the many different forms of conflict resolution that aim to provide social justice. In looking at the fundamentals of conflict resolution, the discussion identifies tenets of conflict resolution that are found on multiple levels in Lao conflict resolution, suggesting that these principles might be inherent in other successful systems. If so, these tenets might be an effective way of evaluating and designing other conflict resolution systems.

This book is about supporting effective conflict resolution processes apart from a formal, "rule of law" system. Too often, these "grassroots" systems have been overlooked, neglected, and perceived as substandard in searching for true justice. In Laos we find that, in certain contexts, these grassroots systems are far more capable of providing justice than the professional systems espoused by Western developed countries. In that, it challenges our traditional attitudes toward conflict, development, and justice in both the world's impoverished nations and its wealthiest.

Bibliography

Cummings, Joe. (1994). *Laos*. Hawthorn: Lonely Planet Publications.

Cummings, Joe, & Burke, Andrew. (2005). *Laos*. Victoria: Lonely Planet.

Eberle, Marc. *The Most Secret Place on Earth – CIA's Covert War in Laos*. Directed by Marc Eberle .Germany: Gebrueder Beetz Filmproduktion, 2008.

Government of Laos PDR. (2006). Lao People's Democratic Republic: Northern Region Sustainable Livelihoods Development Project. *Indigenous Peoples Development Planning Document*, 15. Retrieved May 20, 2010, from www.asianlii.org.

Lonely Planet. (2014). *Laos*. Retrieved August 12, 2014, from www.lonelyplanet.com/laos/history.

MCC. (2000). Clusters of Death. Retrieved February 26, 2009, from http://mcc.org/clusterbombs/resources/research/death/laos_appendix.html

Robbins, Christopher. (2005). *The Ravens: Pilots of the Secret War of Laos* (3rd ed.). Bangkok: Asia Books Co. Ltd.

Scott, James C. (2009). *The Art of Not Being Governed: An Anarchist History of Upland Southeast Asia*. New Haven: Yale University Press.

Stuart-Fox, Martin. (1997). *A History of Laos*. Cambridge: Cambridge University Press.

1 Background and historical context of Laos

> Culture, whether born of a minority group, a people or a nation, must not be restricted to a specific geographical area. It belongs to the universal heritage of humankind.
>
> (Peltier, 2000, p. Preface)

On the surface, Laos seems like an improbable place for a study of conflict resolution. Politically speaking, for the 700 or so years of its existence, its longest period of peace lasted approximately fifty-seven years. During its history, it has been under constant threat from various neighbours – from Thai, Burmese, Vietnamese, and Khmer empires, and the international presence of the French, Americans, Chinese, and Soviets. Religious artifacts have been stolen and re-stolen, monarchs starved and murdered, and monetary tribute has flowed from its coffers to pay off powerful neighbours, sometimes even warlords. Still, as a nation that has been living under occupation, poverty, and general military and economic weakness for the past 300 years, it has somehow managed to survive, and is even beginning to show signs of health and strength. Even if the Vietnam War stripped it of its status as a kingdom, there is still a very strong Lao identity that delineates it from its Thai ethnic and linguistic family, and the Vietnamese political system to which it has such strong ties.

What is so interesting about Laos is that, in spite of the political turmoil that has plagued its existence, its extremely complex social structure and diverse population have largely been peaceful and respectful. The people of Laos consider themselves to be a multi-cultural society with multiple groups of different ethnic heritages, incorporated into a common national identity. Different political powers through Southeast Asian history have managed to wage wars for every imaginable reason, from ideology to resource expansion, but the diverse groups seem to find peace with each other relatively easily. Why here and, equally importantly, why not elsewhere?

Many consider Laos to be the last vestige of ancient Asia. The way of life, customs, rituals, religion, and social and civic organization have remained largely unchanged since the great Thai and Khmer empires dating back 1,000 years. Indeed, Luang Prabang holds United Nations Educational, Scientific and Cultural

Organization (UNESCO) World Heritage status because it is one of the best preserved cities to still retain its social and architectural organization; an organization
that was at one time the norm through most of East and Southeast Asia. Some of
its temples have been operational since the sixteenth century, and its organization
of *ban*, or villages surrounding a temple structure within a context of a larger city,
is still in use today. Dating before the kingdoms of Laos, the mysterious Plain of
Jars gives us clues about highly organized civilizations dating back to 500 BCE–
800 BCE (UNESCO World Heritage, 2014), and current archeological studies provide evidence of ancient nomadic groups occupying this region some 50,000 years
before that (Demeter *et al.*, 2012).

Since 1975, Laos has been officially called the Lao People's Democratic Republic (Lao PDR), a small, landlocked country in Southeast Asia which borders China
to the north, Vietnam to the east, Cambodia to the south, Thailand to the west, and
Myanmar (Burma) to the northwest. Being landlocked, it depends very much on
its neighbors for trade and access to the sea. Much of Laos is very mountainous
and densely forested. Sedentary agriculture is mostly limited to the Mekong Plains.
Laos covers an area of 91,400 sq. mi. (234,804 sq. km) (Leibo, 2003). The country's capital city is Vientiane, located along the Mekong River, near the border with
Thailand.

Laos has an extremely diverse population of 6.6 million. The number of ethnic
groups living in Laos ranges from 49 to 240, depending on which statistics are
used. The largest ethnic groups are the Ethnic Lao, Khammu, and Hmong (CIA,
2009). Major centers see these groups co-habitating, but many smaller villages are
still chiefly occupied by single ethnicities.

Since December 2, 1975, Laos has been governed by an authoritarian one-party
Communist state, the Lao People's Revolutionary Party (LPRP). It was modeled
on existing Communist regimes, specifically the Soviet Union, Vietnam, and China
(Stuart-Fox, 2008). Laos is divided into sixteen provinces (*kwang*) with a number
of districts or cities (*muang*) that are further divided into villages (*ban*). Villages
do not necessarily refer to rural areas of settlement, but also communities, neighbourhoods, or sub-divisions. Traditionally, a temple exists in the center of a village
and serves as a focal point of village life. Within a city, there can be many villages composed of a number of families that form different communities. Some
villages consist of only a few families, whereas others include several hundred. A
village chief or village leader (*nei ban*) manages each village. All ethnic groups
have villages as their basic social and economic unit. There are more than 11,000
villages in Laos (Stuart-Fox, 2008).

Brief history

Based on various historical and anthropological sources (Leibo, 2003; Magocsi,
1999; Savada, 1995; Stuart-Fox, 1997, 2006, 2007, 2008; Stuart-Fox & Kooyman,
1992), the following section provides a summary of the history of Laos. The history of a unified Laos can be broken down into three different periods: (1) kingdom
of Lan Xang, from 1354–1779; (2) Occupational and Colonial Rule, from

1779–1953; and (3) Modern Laos, from 1953 to the present, which is marked by the struggle for independence and renewed strength. In order to understand the patterns of violence and peace in Laos, it is important to have a brief understanding of each of these periods.

The kingdom of Lan Xang (the Land of a Million Elephants) represents the creation and foundation of the Lao identity in which the present country of Laos is rooted. As the first unified Laos, the kingdom of Lan Xang, was founded in 1354 by Fa Ngum, a prince of Muang Sua (modern-day Luang Prabang). As a child, Fa Ngum was sent to the Khmer Empire of Angkor, where he was educated as a prince and given a Khmer princess as his bride. By all accounts, he impressed the Angkor elite, who saw considerable potential in him as a leader and an ally. The great Khmer Empire was in decline and was being threatened on several fronts, notably by a growing Thai population, including the Lanna and Sukhothai empires in the north, and a smaller but powerful group to the south that would eventually form the Ayutthaya Kingdom (Coe, 2005; Wyatt, 2003).

The death of Fa Ngum's grandfather led to a power dispute in Muang Sua, and Angkor recognized an opportunity to establish a buffer state between itself and the growing Thai threat. They gave Fa Ngum an army with the hope that he would be able to take control of a large region of Southeast Asia that the Khmer regime no longer had the strength to control (Coe, 2005). The campaign was very successful, and the kingdom of Lan Xang was established. It would soon become one of the largest and most dominant forces in Southeast Asia.

Lan Xang was a major contributor to Southeast Asian arts, including literature, medicine, law, music, and dance. Buddhists throughout Southeast Asia flocked to its cities to study the Theravada Buddhist traditions. Monasteries and other education centers wielded considerable cultural and political power, and their influence extended across political borders. As a whole, Lan Xang had significant military strength, a very capable government and political structure, a powerful *sangha* (religious clergy), and a strong economy (Stuart-Fox, 1997).

Nevertheless, there was a continual rotation between periods of peace and periods of war between Lan Xang and its neighbours. As a powerful player in Southeast Asia, Lan Xang was involved in violent wars against the Vietnamese Empire of Dai Viet between 1448 and 1479, the Thai kingdom of Ayutthaya between 1540 and 1560, and successive Burmese empires between 1565 and 1590. The so-called "Golden Age" of Lan Xang culminated around King Sourigna Vongsa (1637–1694), and Lan Xang experienced a period of peace lasting fifty-seven years, its longest-ever peaceful period (Ivarsson, 2008).

King Vongsa's death in 1694 left no clear heir to the throne, and a struggle for power ensued. By 1713, Lan Xang was split into three Lao kingdoms: (1) Luang Prabang, the ancient royal capital to the north; (2) Vientiane, the business capital in central Lan Xang; and (3) Champasak, the former territory of the Khmer Empire in the south (Viravong, 1964). The three kingdoms frequently feuded with each other, contributing to their decline. By 1779, these kingdoms were too weak to exist independently, and each was forced into a suzerain relationship with its more powerful neighbours. Between 1779 and 1953, the various sections of ancient Lan Xang were subject to financial, artistic, and human plundering from Thailand, France, Japan, and Vietnam. There were several attempts at repelling the colonizing forces during this time, but none had any real measure of success. One particularly notable attempt was quelled in 1828, when Thailand finally had enough of Lao rebellions for independence. The Siamese-Lao War of 1826–1828 left Vientiane completely plundered, destroyed, and uninhabitable (Askew, Long, & Logan, 2007). The Thais resettled a large population of Lao people into an area known as Isan.

It would be difficult to overstate the significance of this resettlement. The political ramifications have had lasting effects even today. At the time of the resettlement, the entire area was under Thai control as an occupying force. But the political realities were becoming increasingly complex as the French began taking a significant interest in Southeast Asia. By the late 1850s, the French had a significant military presence in Vietnam, and by the 1880s had established an official protectorate over the empires in Vietnam and the kingdoms of Cambodia and Luang Prabang. The French continued to advance in Southeast Asia, resulting in the Franco-Siamese War of 1893. The next thirty years saw continual feuds between the Thais and the French, until they agreed to treaty terms in 1929. Part of the Franco-Siamese treaty established a border between Laos and Thailand, which once settled upon, incorporated the area of Isan into Siam, or modern-day Thailand (Savada, 1995; Stuart-Fox, 1997).

In essence, the Thais forced resettlement of Lao people from the east to the west of the Mekong River would eventually see those people being absorbed into modern-day Thailand. The area of Isan is now Thailand's largest region, home to 21 million people. The majority of the Isan population are direct descendants of this resettlement, referred to as Thai Isan, Thai-Lao, or Lao Isan, and account for some 19 million people. The main language of Isan is a dialect of Lao, and the Isan people hold to their Lao cultural traditions, including cuisine, folk music, and celebratory rituals, many of which will be discussed later. Essentially, there are close to triple the number of Lao people living in the Isan area of Thailand as there are in all of Laos (Cummings, 1992; National Statistical Office, 2004).

It would be impossible to speculate how the Lao resettlement and subsequent border demarcation changed the future of Southeast Asia. Had Laos had the additional population, the upcoming Indochina Wars could have played out very differently. In Thailand, the recent political instability between the red-shirts (United Front for Democracy against Dictatorship – UDD), composed of rural farmers and the urban working class, and the yellow-shirts (People's Alliance for Democracy – PAD), composed of royalists, ultra-nationalists, and the urban middle class, has been intensified by Isan support of the red-shirt movement, the largest ethnolinguistic group to support the Thaksin family (BBC News, 2012). This, however, is a topic for another book.

Ironically, for all the trouble the French went to in occupying Laos, they actually took very little interest in it. Partly due to Laos' remoteness and lack of natural resources, the French did virtually nothing to develop it during its occupation between 1893 and 1945. Just like the Khmer Empire of the 1300s, the French saw

Laos as a buffer zone between its interests in Vietnam and the strong, aggressive Thai kingdom of Siam, which had links to Great Britain.

The seeds of the Indochinese Wars were planted at the end of World War II, as the Japanese withdrew their presence from Southeast Asia. After their withdrawal, the French came back to Southeast Asia to reclaim Vietnam, Laos, and Cambodia as French colonial protectorates. Three royal Lao brothers, Princes Rattanavongsa, Souvanna Phouma, and Souphanouvong, founded a nationalist movement called *Lao Issara,* or "Free Laos," to rid themselves of the French colonists who were trying to recapture Laos after the Japanese withdrawal. The movement was fledgling at best, and the French quickly retook Laos, which resumed its status as a French colony. Still, the princes would play a major role in shaping and re-shaping Lao politics (Conboy & Morrison, 1995; Stuart-Fox, 1997).

The French chased the three brothers out, with each going a different way, searching for outside help to advance their cause. In 1947, Lao King Sisavang Vong declared Laos an independent nation within the French Union and began building the Royal Lao Army. Prince Phetsarath Rattanavongsa was invited back to resume his duties as the king's viceroy. Prince Souvanna Phouma also returned to Laos and eventually became the prime minister. Prince Souphanouvong went to North Vietnam and allied himself with Ho Chi Minh and the Communist movement. He became the head of the Communist Pathet Lao army and was heavily involved in growing this group from a small guerilla operation into a well-funded, disciplined, professional army (Savada, 1995; Stuart-Fox, 1997, 2008).

The French were far less successful in reclaiming Vietnam as a French colony. The first Indochina War (1946–1954) occurred between the French and North Vietnamese, who fought for control over Vietnam. By 1954, the French presence in Vietnam was tenuous and the North Vietnamese could smell victory. After the Battle of Dien Bien Phu, just 10 km away from the Lao border, the defeated French lost all hope of ever gaining stability in Vietnam. Without Vietnam, French interest in Southeast Asia entirely evaporated, and they withdrew their army and official presence from all of Southeast Asia. North Vietnam, South Vietnam, Cambodia, and Laos all declared their independence (Dommen, 2001; Lonely Planet, 2014; Stuart-Fox, 1997, 2008).

The United States quickly moved into Southeast Asia to replace the French. The US involvement was ideological. Specifically, Laos must be saved as a buffer zone to prevent the advance of Communism from China and North Vietnam. The United States knew that the Pathet Lao had strong backing from the North Vietnamese, who were promoting Communist ideology and heavily recruiting military muscle. Thus began the Second Indochina War, a phase which would feed the minds and imaginations of conspiracy theorists the world over. The United States had no public mandate to go into Laos, and had even signed treaty documents forbidding such activities. However, they knew that unless they could control the flow of goods between North and South Vietnam that ran through Laos along the "Ho Chi Minh Trail," Communism would surely take over all of the previous French colonies (Dommen, 2001; Lonely Planet, 2014; Stuart-Fox, 1997).

In declaring its independence, Souvanna Phouma, who controlled the neutralist Royal Lao Army, and his brother, Souphanouvong, who controlled the Communist Pathet Lao, as well as several smaller, right-wing conservative factions, attempted to merge their respective groups into one government. The Americans believed that the best way to justify involvement in Laos was to destabilize the coalition government, thereby gaining access on the pretext of trying to stabilize a civil war. Essentially, they would intervene to stabilize a situation that they had intentionally destabilized. Officially, the United States supported Souvanna Phouma, providing training and weapons to his neutralist forces and the Royal Lao Army. Secretly, however, the Central Intelligence Agency (CIA) was also supplying and training the conservative, right-wing forces (Eberle, 2008). During this same time, the US Embassy told the Lao government that having Communists in the government would be a significant barrier to receiving US foreign aid. The Royal Lao regime depended on the United States economically, militarily, and politically. In truth, US aid was not primarily for economic development, but for "economic, cultural, and political domination" (Stuart-Fox, 1997, p. 154). Obviously, the coalition fell apart, and the civil war began in earnest.

Between 1960 and 1962 there were coups and counter-coups. Coalitions were formed and broken, and the CIA consistently fed weapons to different militia groups and provided intensive training to them, hoping that eventually they would join together to fight against the Pathet Lao. Often, they fought against each other. In fact, a relatively lasting coalition during that period was between the neutralist and Communist forces, an alliance that would see US and Soviet weapons fighting side by side against the conservative forces that were trained and supplied by the CIA (Eberle, 2008; Stuart-Fox, 1997).

Both Cold War superpowers got nervous about the whole operation in 1962 and forced the competing factions into another coalition. A tentatively united Laos again declared its independence mid-year. As stipulated by the Geneva Agreements of 1962, foreign military technicians were required to withdraw from Laos soil. The withdrawal was symbolic, as the Pathet Lao remained heavily supplemented by the North Vietnamese and the Americans were still training and supplying almost anyone who was not Communist. By mid-1964 the players were set for the main part of the Second Indochina War. The coalition had fallen apart, pitting the right wing and neutralists against the Communists. The left-leaning neutralists split up, some siding with the Pathet Lao and some with the Royal Lao Army. The Americans provided training, supplies, and money to a wholly ineffective Royal Lao Army and also to the much more reliable ethnic guerilla units under the leadership of General Vang Pao. Whenever required, the Americans would provide massive air strikes in hopes of bombing the Communists into submission. The Soviets supplied weapons to the Pathet Lao, who were significantly bolstered with man-power from the North Vietnamese (Stuart-Fox, 1997, 2008).

For nine years Laos was immersed in "Secret War" operations, torn apart by foreign powers that divided the country into opposing factions and used it as a battleground for Cold War politics that meant nothing to an impoverished population. Once again, Laos was only valuable as a buffer zone between the free-market, western-aligned Thailand, and the Communist, Soviet-aligned Vietnam. The three coalition governments during the Thirty-Year Struggle were in response to international pressures and eventually led to the victory of the Pathet Lao Communist party (Stuart-Fox, 1997, 2008). The Communist victories in Cambodia and Vietnam, the establishment of the Lao PDR in 1975, and fear of persecution caused people to flee to various refugee camps (Leibo, 2003; Magocsi, 1999). The ruling monarchy was abolished and mostly killed, and the long-time leader of the Pathet Lao, Prince Souphanouvong, became the president of Laos (Leibo, 2003).

The after-effects of the war were devastating. Unexploded ordinance (UXO) ravaged the population, taking some 50,000 lives. Even now, forty years after the war, UXOs are still present in every province of Laos, claiming thirty to forty lives annually. Since 1975, about 10 percent of the population has left the country: 66.5 percent of those for the United States, 14.5 percent for France, 8.7 percent for Canada, and 4.9 percent for Australia (Cummings, 1994). Twenty years after the war ended, an estimated 60,000 refugees still remained in Thai camps (Savada, 1995), which aimed to close by 2000. However, even in 2009, the United Nations (UN) voiced concerns when 4,689 ethnic Hmong asylum seekers were forcibly repatriated back to Laos (BBC News, 2014; Unrepresented Nations and Peoples Organization, 2012).

However, in spite of those grim statistics, Laos has seen a deeply needed time of peace since the end of the war, and with the help of foreign investment, tourism, and most of all stability, the pace of development is rapidly increasing throughout the country. It has an astonishingly low crime rate, a high level of gender egalitarianism, and is tolerant of sexual orientation. For example, in comparison to similarly sized cities in the United States, Vientiane is considered a relatively safe city with non-confrontational crimes against foreigners consisting of pick-pocketing, thefts, and residential burglaries. Physical assaults are relatively rare in comparison to many major centers (OSAC, 2012). The United Nations Office on Drugs and Crime (UNODC) (2014b) reports that transnational trafficking of amphetamine-type stimulants, heroin, and other illicit drugs increased during the 1990s, resulting in a temporary rise of drug abuse, domestic crime, and violence. However, the Lao government has since effectively reduced opium production and cultivation through various law enforcement agencies and coordinated efforts, bringing crime rates back down. Ethnic Lao women have considerable social and cultural status due to a cultural practice of matriolocality. Since 1957 women have had the right to vote, with full citizenship rights. Today, according to the World Bank (2013), 30 to 40 percent of private-sector entrepreneurs are women, and cross-border markets of textiles and handicrafts are mainly produced by women. Currently, 25 percent of the members of the National Assembly are women, one of the highest in the area (UN Women, n.d.). However, as in most places in the world, women continue to struggle with equal participation in the political arena and need an increased voice in local and national decision-making processes. Homosexuality is legal in Laos, although same-sex marriage is unrecognized.

Its ethnically diverse population is mostly respectful, inclusive, and shares numerous inter-relationship activities. The 2003 constitution of the Lao PDR stresses the multi-ethnicity of the population and "unity and equality" among all ethnic groups who have the right to "protect, preserve, and promote the fine customs and cultures of their own tribes and of the nation" (Pholsena, 2006, p. 5). Its multi-ethnic culture and diverse traditional dispute-resolution processes make it an excellent case study to examine how such approaches can be used to resolve larger conflicts. The different ways in which ethnic groups resolve conflicts are still used today, and we will need to understand these groups further to get a firm grasp on how this is possible.

Cultural groups

As a major geographical intersection for countries with Buddhist, Christian, Hindu, and Islamic religions, Laos is rich in culture (Ladouce, 2007). The government of Laos recognizes forty-nine distinct ethnic groups in a population of approximately 6.6 million. During French colonization, for simplicity of administration, ethnographers and colonial rulers were looking for homogenous units that linked tribes to territories (Pholsena, 2006). The tripartite categorization of the population – Lao Loum, Lao Theung, and Lao Soung – originated in an 1899 report on Laos and has (for better or worse) become the accepted terminology (Evans, 1999). As a way of understanding the ethnic cultures of Laos, this categorization is massively simplified, especially considering that some of the cultures occupying the same category have almost nothing to do with each other.

The classification of the three Lao groups was based on the elevation of the traditional habitats they lived in, from the lowest plains to the highest mountain ranges (Savada, 1995). These classifications are problematic in that they generalize some very distinct groups into these three broad categories. For example, two different ethnic groups considered part of the Lao Soung could be living hundreds of kilometers apart, separated by impassable mountain ranges, speak completely different languages, and never have any contact with each other. Clearly their cultures are vastly different, yet they are categorized together in the same group.

That said, the more populous ethnic groups in Laos have had significant interaction and, in reality, many people in Laos are the genetic product of unions and intermarriage between different groups, learning the languages of parents and grandparents as is necessary for their family and business lives. Despite some of the concerns with the tripartite categorization, it is still the most used categorization of ethnic groups in Laos, and understanding it in a general way is probably a requirement of any study of Laos. It is important to remember, though, that the categorizations are flawed, and the structure of the categories is not necessarily rigid.

The Lao Loum (Lowland), which include the Ethnic Lao, make up the majority of the population at 68 percent; the Lao Theung (Upland), which include the Khammu, comprise the largest minority group at 22 percent; the Lao Soung (Highland), which include the Hmong, are 9 percent of the population; and the Vietnamese/Chinese are 1 percent (CIA, 2008; Savada, 1995; US Department of State, 2008). These groups all have distinct native languages, many of which have descended from very different linguistic groups. Currently, there are eighty-four individual languages listed for Laos (Lewis, 2009). However, the official language in Laos is Lao, which "has successfully become the lingua franca (a universally understood linking language) between all Lao and non-Lao ethnic groups" (Cummings & Burke, 2005, p. 289).

Lao Loum

The Lao Loum ("Lao of the Plains" or "Lowland") subgroup consists of six different ethnic groups, including the Ethnic Lao, who moved from the north into the Southeast Asian peninsula about 1,000 years ago (Savada, 1995). Modern scholars believe the Tai people originated in the mountainous southern border regions of China, northwestern Vietnam, and northern Laos, and began to expand between the eighth and thirteenth centuries into the northern parts of the Khmer Empire (Chao Phraya, Mekong River, Shan highlands in Burma) (Stuart-Fox, 2008; Stuart-Fox & Kooyman, 1992).

The Lao Loum subgroup, specifically the Ethnic Lao, have been the dominant group numerically, politically, and economically since the founding of the kingdom of Lan Xang in the fourteenth century (Savada, 1995). The Lao Loum's cultural patterns are considered the norm in designing policy or establishing development priorities. They speak the *Tai-Kadai* languages. The Ethnic Lao language is the only official language in Laos that has a traditional written script. The group tends to live near lowland rivers and streams, and is primarily involved in wet paddy rice cultivation in lower altitudes (Evans, 1999; Leibo, 2003).

In 1422, the structure of early Lao society consisted of four categories: aristocracy, free peasants or commoners, slaves, and non-Ethnic Lao at the bottom (Pholsena, 2006). In the pre-colonial period, the Ethnic Lao's control of the government did not try to assimilate the upland population, as "systematic and institutionalized policies were not enforced to draw the upland peoples into a unitary culture" (Pholsena, 2006, p. 21). The Lao kingdom was in fact based on a system of village autonomy (Pholsena, 2006; Robbins, 2005), and there were economic contacts and exchanges between groups.

Lao Theung

The Lao Theung ("Lao of the Mountain Slopes" or "Upland") subgroup is composed of thirty distinct ethnic groups, of which the largest is the Khammu. They are of Austroasiatic origin and considered the autochthonous inhabitants of Laos, having migrated northward in prehistoric times (Savada, 1995). The Khammu speak dialects of Austroasiatic languages, also known as the Mon-Khmer languages. Their population is currently estimated to be 614,000, an increase of some 200,000 in fifteen years (Savada, 1995; Stuart-Fox, 2006, 2007). Lao Theung are socially, economically, and politically the most marginalized group of the three ethnic classes. The Lao Theung have been traditionally classified as "*Kha*" which refers to slave-like, primitive, or inferior status in a system of ethnic hierarchy

(Evans, 1999; Pholsena, 2006). In post-war Laos, this term is more of a pejorative one (Evans, 1999).

During the "Secret Lao War" (Second Indochina War), many Lao Theung supported the Lao Patriotic Front (LPF), the political party of the Pathet Lao, who would eventually win the war. At the end of the war, some Lao Theung received mid-level positions in government but were later replaced by Ethnic Lao with more experience. The Khammu were traditionally scattered throughout northern Laos, from Xiangkhoang to Bokeo provinces along the mountain slopes, and relied on swidden, or slash-and-burn cultivation, as the staple of their farming and dietary practices (Leibo, 2003; Savada, 1995).

Since the end of the war, the Lao PDR government has relocated large numbers of ethnic minorities, particularly the Lao Theung, from their homes in the mountains to lowland plains and restricted their traditional practice of swidden cultivation. Traditional swidden farming is changing due to government policies, population increases, and the resettling and consolidation of villages (Sodarak, 2005; Thongmanivong & Vongvisouk, 2006). Increasing economic development, cash crop production, and intensive agricultural practices have changed the landscape of Laos. These activities are creating conflicts for ethnic minorities who have for centuries relied on the natural environment for food, traditional medicine, and basic livelihood.

Lao Soung

The Lao Soung ("Lao of the Mountain Tops" or "Upland") are composed of six primary hill-tribe ethnic groups who practice slash-and-burn agriculture in altitudes above 1,000 meters (Savada, 1995; Stuart-Fox, 2008). The Lao Soung are probably the most diverse of all the ethnic groups in Laos, with multiple dialects of languages descending from several different language groups, including the Hmong-Mien and Sino-Tibetan languages (Cummings, 1994; Stuart-Fox, 2008). Most historians consider them to be the most recent inhabitants of the area, migrating from various places within the last 300 to 400 years (Savada, 1995). The largest group is the Hmong (also referred to as Miao or Meo), with a population of approximately 200,000. In an effort to provide a living for their families and communities, the Hmong produced much of Lao's black-market opium cash crop (Cummings & Burke, 2005). The Hmong are mostly found in the northern provinces and in Bolikhamsai in central Laos.

During the Vietnam War in the 1960s and the "Secret Lao War," the Hmong were recruited by the CIA to help fight against the Communist Pathet Lao Army. The Hmong, who "gathered critical intelligence, rescued downed U.S. aircrews, and protected intelligence/navigational sites . . . and observed and sabotaged the Ho Chi Minh Trail complex in Laos" (Hamilton-Merritt, 1995, p. 1), were considered one of the best US allies during the Vietnam War. Upon the Pathet Lao victory in 1975, about a third of the Hmong fled to resettle in countries such as the United States, Canada, France, and Australia, while a small number of soldiers fled to the jungles of Laos to launch armed resistance against the government.

A few Hmong resistance groups are still believed to exist in the mountains of Xieng Khuang and Sainyabuli provinces (Amnesty International, 2007a, 2007b; Cummings, 1994). Some believe that they no longer pose a military threat against the Lao government and only organize "bandit-like" attacks to procure money and valuables. Living with their families in small groups, they struggle to survive, unable to meet their basic human needs as the Lao military forces them to constantly relocate and denies them any human rights (Amnesty International, 2007a, 2007b, 2007c). Other reports state that as the Hmong fighters become more dissatisfied with the current government, they are resorting to attacks on corrupt leaders and those involved in unpopular resettlement policies from the highlands to the plains (Economist, 2000; UN Committee on the Elimination of Racial Discrimination, 2006). Many Hmong have settled within mainstream Lao society.

Over the past three decades, Thailand has been host to some 7,500 Lao Hmong asylum seekers in the northern Phetchabun Province (Amnesty International, 2008, 2009a, 2009b, 2010; Medecins Sans Frontieres, 2007). The repatriation of Lao people back to Laos began with the 1989 Comprehensive Plan of Action (CPA) for Hmong veterans and their families, the 1991 Luang Prabang Tripartite Agreement by the United Nations High Commissioner for Refugees (UNHCR), Lao and Thai government support (with US political and financial support) for other Hmong and Lao refugees, the 1996 bilateral agreement between Thailand and Laos, and the UNHCR's Memorandum of Understanding with the Lao government on repatriation and reintegration operations (Ballard, 2002; Hamilton-Merritt, 1995; Nanuam, 2006).

Upon taking power, the Communist government began promoting a new national identity as part of its propaganda machine, trying to recognize diversity and equality between different ethnic groups. By giving every group equal recognition, the goal was to eliminate the ethnic issue in Laos, especially after the struggles of the civil war. Nevertheless, ethnic conflicts have not been eliminated over the last thirty years, and the Lao sense of belonging continues to center around a multiple identity platform that somehow binds different ethnic histories into a larger national entity (Pholsena, 2006). Politically, some of the ethnic groups feel they have gained some recognition under the Communist government, but admit that they have not obtained equal status.

Education

Prior to 1975, only the Ethnic Lao had formal education and written script. Much of the education was based in Buddhist temples called *wat*, where the monks taught novices and boys Lao and Pali scripts, basic arithmetic, and other religious and social subjects, but only those who were ordained had access to advanced education (Savada, 1995). Traditionally, girls were taught at home and had lower literacy rates. Crafts and skills were learned from parents or through an apprentice system (Stuart-Fox, 2008). During the colonial period, the French established an education system, and French became the language of instruction after the second grade. Secondary education instruction was limited to elites, who completed their education in Hanoi, Saigon, or Phnom Penh (Savada, 1995; Stuart-Fox, 2008).

After the establishment of the Lao PDR in 1975, there was universal compulsory education. Unfortunately, limited resources meant a lack of trained teachers, teaching materials, and poorly constructed buildings. From 1992 to 1993, estimated enrollment in primary school was 603,000, or 65 percent, and 130,000 in secondary school, or 15 percent (Savada, 1995). At the tertiary level, those Communist party members with financial means sent their children for further education in Vietnam, China, and the Soviet Union. Those numbers have been steadily increasing, and opportunities for post-secondary education are becoming more available within Laos and, with new freedoms to travel, opportunities for foreign education have vastly increased. Overall, literacy rates have jumped some 20 percent since 1995, and current estimates in 2013 suggest a literacy rate of about 85 percent. Unfortunately, many of these statistics are taken from urban centers – literacy rates suffer significantly in rural settings. Generally, the minority groups tend to live in more rural settings, and therefore seem to have somewhat less access to education than the majority Ethnic Lao. Still, overall literacy and education continue to be priorities for the Lao government, and that work seems to be paying off.

Religion

In prehistoric times, the people in Laos practiced animism, the worship of nature spirits. During the Chenla period (a Southeast Asian kingdom during the sixth to ninth centuries which would eventually morph into the Khmer Kingdom of Angkor), Indian influence brought Hinduism and Buddhism to Southeast Asia. Mon monks began to spread Theravada Buddhism, which originated in Sri Lanka, as they made contact with various groups. When Fa Ngum founded the Lao Kingdom in the fourteenth century, he brought his Buddhist education with him and recognized Buddhism as the state religion. Buddhism is still a dominant aspect of daily existence, and the *wat*, the Buddhist temple or monastery complex, is central to village life, being the site of major festivals which occur several times a year. Many of these festivals have descended from the old traditions of southern Theravada Buddhism (Leibo, 2003).

Savada (1995) describes Theravada Buddhism as a tolerant religion – one that is inclusive, flexible, and non-authoritative in its attitude toward its members and other religions. The essence of Buddhism lies in Four Noble Truths. These truths are born directly out of wisdom. They are (1) *Dukkha* – suffering exists; (2) *Samudaya* – cause of suffering is desire; (3) *Nirodha* – cessation of suffering is possible; and (4) *Magga* – the way to end suffering is through the Eightfold Path that leads to permanent peace. The Eightfold Path consists of right understanding, right intention, right speech, right action, right livelihood, right effort, right mindfulness, and right concentration (McConnell, 1997, 2001; National Identity Board, 1993; Savada, 1995; Senghaas, 2002).

Buddhism teaches that conflict is caused by greed, hate, and delusion, and encourages its members to control these impulses. Through self-awareness and right-mindfulness one can overcome the destructive and harmful effects that conflicts pose to social harmony. Just as ending suffering is possible, so also is the peaceful resolution of conflict. This is done through active thought, such as detachment, hatelessness, and clarity of mind. The psychological processes that produce suffering can be transformed into processes that lead to health and enlightenment. Therefore, conflict is seen as an opportunity for peacemaking and, to fulfill the endeavor to end suffering, peace must become central in one's life.

Buddhist philosophy provides hands-on approaches to resolving conflict. In conflict situations, it is important to see the truth, be conscious of one's own motives, act in ways that do not harm others, live in ways that do not damage others, cultivate thought and sentiments, and be conscious of emotional and mental processes through meditation training (Senghaas, 2002). Individual goals are valued as long as they do not interfere with the goals of others. The Buddhist principles teach the self-reliance, love of freedom, and pragmatism that are characteristics of Thai and Lao cultures.

In an interesting intermingling of historical religious perspectives, animist beliefs are still widespread among the entire population, and these ancient spirit cults have been largely incorporated into the Buddhist belief system. According to Evans (1999), "in Laos, the spirit cults are to a comparatively large degree incorporated into the official 'religion,' and they are highly relevant to issues of national and ethnic identity" (p. 195). In fact, many Buddhist temples (wat) have a small spirit hut that is associated with the beneficent spirit of the monastery (*phi khoun wat*) built in one corner of the grounds.

Animism is a religious practice oriented toward protective or guardian spirits commonly associated with places or the family ancestors (e.g., *phi ban* or village protective deity). It is centered on the belief in spirits (*phi*) connected with heaven, earth, fire, and water. House spirits (*phi hern*), village spirits (*phi ban*), and forest spirits (*phi pba*) are common, along with sacrifices of chicken, water buffalo, and other offerings to the spirits. All of the major ethnic groups in Laos have some combination of these two religious practices, although most ethnic minority groups tend to concentrate more heavily on animist beliefs, whereas the Lao Loum belief system leans more towards Buddhism (Savada, 1995). Generally, ethnic minorities' religious life revolves around various spirits associated with natural phenomena (Stuart-Fox, 2008).

For example, the *phi* cult is strong among the tribal Tai, especially the Tai Dam, who believe the *phi then* are earth spirits that preside over plants, soils, and entire districts. They also believe in the thirty-two souls and shamans who can propitiate and exorcise spirits during festivals and ceremonies. The Khammu tribes also have similar *hrooi* spirits associated with guardianship of house and village. The Hmong are animists, although some have now converted to Christianity through Protestant and Roman Catholic missionaries. Traditionally, they believe the spirits are the cause of illnesses and conflicts. Most Hmong villages do not have a central religious building such as a temple or *wat*. Hmong are more individualistic in looking after the well-being of their household before considering the welfare of the village (Savada, 1995).

As a general rule, most Lao are relatively uninterested in the theological intricacies of their spiritual belief system, and an interesting intermixing of faith traditions and religious practices is often the reality of their individual spiritual lives. This multi-faith incorporation and inter-relationship between Buddhism and animism, and its different manifestations between different ethnicities, will become very important later on as we discuss the ceremonies and rituals of conflict resolution.

The other major religious institutions also have a foothold in Laos, although not to the same extent as Buddhism and animism. Islam was likely introduced in Laos in the sixteenth century through Muslim merchants. Christianity was introduced in the early seventeenth century by Catholic missionaries, but did not have much impact until the arrival of the French in late nineteenth century. Today, Buddhism continues to be widespread and a central component of Lao national identity (Stuart-Fox, 2008).

Family and kinship

The Ethnic Lao follow a pattern of bilateral kinship, with descent traced through both the maternal and paternal sides of the family (Hockings, 1993; Magocsi, 1999). Kin groups are defined by choice: siblings, immediate maternal and paternal relatives, and distant relatives close to the family. Kinship relationships are recognized and reinforced through sharing of goods and produce, labor reciprocity, and participation in family and religious rituals.

In earlier generations, Ethnic Lao marriages may have been arranged by the families, but since the 1960s, most couples have been free to make their own choices (Hockings, 1993; Savada, 1995). Marriage partners may be proposed either by parents or the young people, but parents of both must approve in order to begin traditional marriage negotiations. Bride-price varies greatly, but usually includes gold, one or more animals, and cash. A Brahmanic/animist marriage ceremony takes place at the bride's family home (Hockings, 1993). Residence is ideally matrilocal after marriage, as husbands join their wives' households (Magocsi, 1999; Savada, 1995). The groom helps the bride's family with farming for several years until the couple is economically ready to establish their own household. Patrilocal residence is less common. There is a tendency for the youngest daughter to live with her parents to care for them in old age. Divorce is discouraged, but may be initiated by either party (Hockings, 1993; Savada, 1995).

According to Savada (1995), most of the ethnic minority groups in both the Lao Theung and Lao Soung categories follow a patrilineal line. The average Khammu household is between six and seven persons, but may be as large as twelve or fourteen persons, including parents and children, wives of married children, and grandchildren. When a couple decides to marry, their parents must negotiate a bride-price. Married sons may then have to live and work with the wife's parents to pay off that bride-price. Although the taking of multiple wives is legally forbidden, polygyny is traditionally allowed in Khammu custom, as long as one can afford a second wife. A widow may marry her husband's brother, and the brother is responsible for support whether they marry or not. Typically in the non–Ethnic Lao cultural groups, gender roles are more differentiated. Khammu men take care of finances and trade, and the women take care of the household duties and children. In rural settings, men hunt and women gather roots, shoots, and wild vegetables. Both men and women work the land, weed the fields, and gather the harvest (Savada, 1995).

The Hmong groups are also patrilineal and recognize fifteen or sixteen patrilineal exogamous clans that are traced to a common mythical ancestor. The Hmong are divided according to features of traditional dress (e.g., White Hmong, Striped Hmong, and Green Hmong). Their languages vary, but are mutually comprehensible. Each village has at least two clans, and a wife lives with her husband's family. Traditionally, marriages are arranged by go-betweens and, if the union is accepted, a bride-price is negotiated. Two wedding celebrations take place: one at the bride's house and another at the groom's house. Young men may sometimes "steal" a bride with the help of their friends and, as a result, parents are obliged to accept a lower bride-price. Most are not actual abductions, but elopements. Divorce is less common in the Hmong culture, although it is possible and can be initiated by either men or women. The Hmong have strong gender role differentiation where the women are responsible for all household chores and the children. The patrilocal residence, subordination to the mother-in-laws and deference for men and elders can sometimes make it difficult for the daughter-in-laws (Savada, 1995).

Economics

According to the United Nations Development Programme (UNDP) Global Human Development Index (HDI), Lao PDR continues to be one of the least developed and most rural countries in the world, and is currently ranked 138th out of 177 countries (UNDP, 2009). In Laos, 31 percent of the population earn less than US$1 a day, whereas 77 percent earn less than US$2 a day (Bertelsmann, 2006). With figures like that, it is no surprise that poverty continues to be a major source of conflict. In the study *Country Strategy: Laos 2004–2008*, the Swedish Ministry for Foreign Affairs stated that Laos' national poverty line decreased from 46 percent in 1992–1993 to 32 percent in 2002–2003, but the income gap has grown between lowland and upland households, majority and minority populations, and urban and rural areas (Ministry for Foreign Affairs, 2004)

Droughts and famines have a tremendously devastating impact on Laos, a poor, landlocked country with inadequate infrastructure and an unskilled workforce. Agriculture, mostly subsistence rice cultivation, dominates the economy and employs 78 percent of the population, producing 43.4 percent of the gross domestic product (GDP). The terrain of Laos is mountainous with a few plateaus and plains. Arable land accounts for 4 percent of the country's land use, and permanent crops account for less than 1 percent. Considering that only 4 percent of the land is arable and 78 percent of the population is employed in agriculture, land is a valuable commodity (CIA, 2008; Savada, 1995). Other forms of economic development in Laos rely heavily on foreign aid and loans. Donor-funded programs accounted for 14 percent of GDP and 70 percent of the capital budget in 2006, with an estimated foreign debt of $3.2 billion (US Department of State, 2008).

During the pre-colonial period, the economy of Laos was based on subsistence agriculture of wet rice (paddy) or swidden farming. Under the French, rapid economic development in plantation agriculture did not occur, except in the area of coffee production. After independence, a thirty-year civil war slowed down an economy that only stayed afloat with American aid. The formation of Lao PDR in 1975 caused the artificial economy to collapse and led to a socialist transformation of the economy, where industry, commerce, and finance were nationalized and agriculture collectivized. Agricultural collectivization was later abandoned (Stuart-Fox, 2008).

In 1986, the Lao government introduced the New Economic Mechanism (NEM) to increase private-sector and open-market activities. Under the NEM, free-enterprise initiatives included decentralized decision making, deregulation of pricing and financial systems, and promotion of domestic and international trade and foreign investment (Huso, 2008; Savada, 1995; Stuart-Fox, 2008). As part of this process, farmers were urged to make the transition from subsistence-based production to cash crops.

The government promoted agricultural intensification and cash crop production (e.g., rice, maize, and soy beans) and industrial tree planting (e.g., teak, eucalyptus, and rubber) to improve the livelihoods of rural people and develop its national economy (Thongmanivong & Vongvisouk, 2006). The recent increased demand for cash crops in China is rapidly transforming the upland landscape in northern Laos. Rural farmers are producing cash crops such as sugar cane, maize, and rubber. Also, Chinese farmers and small-scale entrepreneurs from southern Yunnan Province are establishing themselves in northern Laos and contributing to agricultural intensification (Thongmanivong & Vongvisouk, 2006). In fact, in northern Laos many businesses, streets, and highways are using signs written in Chinese alongside the Lao.

As economic development continues to grow, new types of conflict are emerging between businesses and local communities, particularly over land, forest, and other natural resources. Land that had valuable hardwoods was expropriated from farmers and communities to preserve the wood for commercial extraction. This has had significant effects on upland villages (Evans, 1999; Leibo, 2003; Savada, 1995). There, farmers had very little experience with cultivating new types of cash crops. Some of these groups were resettled into lowland locations suitable for paddy rice cultivation. Again, many of these groups did not easily adapt to the farming techniques needed for lowland farming. Land expropriation and relocation are common problems for rural villages, where people are commonly being relocated in the lower plains, forcing them to adjust to a new way of life and livelihood (Stobbe, 2006, 2008; Stuart-Fox, 2006, 2007).

The government's NEM discourages swidden cultivation, a method indigenous to the Khammu and other ethnic minorities, as it negatively affects agricultural productivity by exhausting the soil and the forest environment. Many minority groups are semi-migratory, who relocate when swidden lands are exhausted. Plots of land require at least four to six years of fallow for soil rejuvenation (Geertz, 1963; Savada, 1995). According to Geertz (1963), swidden agriculture has four distinctive features: (1) it takes place in very poor tropical soils; (2) it represents an elementary agricultural technique; (3) it is marked by a low density of population; and (4) it involves a low level of consumption. Long fallow periods can limit soil degradation, weed competition, and pest damage. In practice, shorter bush fallow systems of agriculture have replaced long fallows. However, the length of cropping periods remains the same, or even increases, during short fallows, thereby leading to declining productivity and making the land unsuitable for further cultivation. Also, the re-growth of secondary forest fallow vegetation is made slower or destroyed completely (Sodarak, 2005). Traditional swidden farming is changing due to government policies, population increase, and the resettling and consolidation of villages (Sodarak, 2005; Thongmanivong & Vongvisouk, 2006).

At the same time the government was promoting a move to cash crops, they were under severe international pressure to curtail one of the few cash crops that the Lao Theung and Lao Soung farmers had experience with – opium production. Poppy cultivation in Laos was a common practice of Hmong farmers and other ethnic minorities. According to the UNODC (2005), Laos' poppy cultivation has been declining rapidly and Laos is no longer a world supplier of illegal opiates. The opium currently produced is mostly consumed by the 20,000 opium smokers in Laos. Fifty-two percent of the addicts grow their own crops for personal and medicinal use, and 48 percent sell them to obtain cash or buy food. Government efforts to rid Laos of opium cultivation have had a significant effect on farmers. The government has struggled to help farmers develop other kinds of cultivation, as officials and villagers lack expertise in this area (UNODC, 2005). The government is trying to address infrastructure issues, but progress has been slow.

The Asian economic crisis had a great impact on the Lao economy in the late 1990s, where the kip lost more value than any other currency in the region. Direct investments in 1997 were US$113 million, with two thirds of that in hydroelectric projects, hotels and tourism, and transport and communication. Currently, it is anticipated that revenues will increase due to hydroelectricity sales, mining dues, agricultural productivity, the service sector, development of natural resources, and economic integration with Southeast Asia. However, the industrial sector will remain weak due to competition associated with the Association of Southeast Asian Nations Free Trade Agreement and membership in the World Trade Organization in 2010 (Stuart-Fox, 2008).

Overall, the type of massive development that is needed in Laos does not come easily. Nevertheless, in the last twenty years I have witnessed significant development in Laos. The morning markets are increasingly colourful, offering diverse goods, quality food, and other products necessary for daily life. Urban streets are clean and bustling, and services are improving. Many Lao people, particularly in the more urban areas, are enjoying a rising standard of living. Economic progress is occurring, but clearly it is not without its problems. Finding balance between economic growth and the preservation of traditional ways of life is an issue for many in Laos, and adapting to new economics has been harder on some than on others. We all continue to hope that the economic policymakers and businesses that drive the Lao economy forward will respect that balance, being mindful and generous to those who struggle to find their place in an ever-developing economy.

Legal system

During the kingdom of Lan Xang, codes of laws were developed by founding king Fa Ngum and later monarchs, which stipulated punishments for banditry, murder, theft, adultery, and damage to property, as well as conditions for debt slavery and fair trial. A hierarchy of officials administered the law, but the king was the final arbiter in conflict situations. Punishment included execution, imprisonment, flogging, and fines. The laws reflected traditional practices and Buddhist moral precepts that prohibit adultery, theft, murder, lying, and drunkenness. The division of Lan Xang in the early eighteenth century led to less rigorous and more arbitrary enforcement of laws. During the French colonial administration, law and order were imposed to enhance tax collection and social order. The Royal Lao government retained the framework of French laws, but corruption grew among those in authority. In 1975, the Lao PDR established socialist law to replace the old legal system. Under the LPRP, "people's tribunals" carried out "revolutionary justice" by applying arbitrary rules. All regime opposition was suppressed, and corruption among authorities became widespread (Stuart-Fox, 2008).

Currently, the judicial branch of Laos includes the People's Supreme Court, the appellate (appeals) courts, the people's provincial courts and city courts, the people's district courts, and the military courts. Since 1975, the court system has been under constant review and revision, both within Laos and with international help, to make it a more functional system and a compelling force in promoting social justice. In fairness, changes and improvements have been made. Unfortunately, many scholars still cite a culture of corruption and patronage appointments as inhibiting the pace of legal reform.

Development and freedoms are slowly seeing their way into the Lao formal legal system. According to the Lao Constitution, which was revised in 2003, there are conflict resolution mechanisms for its citizens. Article 41 (Government of Lao PDR, 2003) states

> Lao citizens have the right to lodge complaints and petitions and to propose ideas to the relevant State organisations in connection with issues pertaining to the public interest or to their own rights and interests. Complaints, petitions and ideas of citizens must be examined and resolved as provided by the laws.
>
> (p. 8)

However, Laos historian Stuart-Fox (2006, 2008) argues that many of the new laws are unknown to the wider public and are applied ineffectively, especially outside the capital city, and interference and bribery continue to undermine rule of law. The rule of law is inconsistently applied across the country, depending largely on the political leaders' interpretations (Stuart-Fox, 2006). The legal system has become a tool that promotes corruption and power inequity.

The Lao government, under the auspices of nationalism, suppresses any mass protests and does not allow for multi-party electoral competition. As there are very few civil societies or social organizations distinct from the government, there are no movements against social injustice, crony capitalism, and official corruption. On a positive note, according to the Swedish Ministry of Foreign Affairs, the government of Laos recently adopted a new law that would allow operations of civil society within the country (Ministry for Foreign Affairs, 2010). Hopefully this will bring a higher level of accountability to the political and legal systems in place now. In the meantime, Laos is developing its legal system, with a goal of a state with rule of law by 2020 (Vientiane Times News, 2012), although it is unclear exactly what that will look like.

The legal profession is tenuous, with fewer than 100 lawyers available for a population of 6.6 million. A rule of law system and its required expertise are not strong (UNODC, 2014a). With its extremely underdeveloped legal system, there is a lack of basic understanding and considerable absence of any consistently enforced, formal infrastructures for justice and human rights at all levels of society. As we will discuss in detail, these are some reasons why grassroots dispute resolution processes have continued to exist in Lao culture and play an important role in addressing conflicts in the family, workplace, and community. Traditional conflict resolution processes are familiar, accessible, well respected by the local population, and contribute to overall social harmony. They take into account the cultural, religious, social, economic, and political context of the country.

Bibliography

Amnesty International. (2007a). Destitute Hmong Still Running from Military in Laotian Jungle, New Amnesty International Report Reveals. March 23, 2007. Retrieved January 23, 2010, from www.amnestyusa.org/document.php?id=ENGUSA20070323001&lang=e.

Amnesty International. (2007b). Lao People's Democratic Republic – Hiding in the Jungle: Hmong Under Threat. March 23, 2007. Retrieved January 20, 2010, from www.amnesty.org/en/library/info/ASA26/003/2007.

Amnesty International. (2007c). Laos: Destitute Jungle-Dwellers Living on Run from Military. March 23, 2007. Retrieved April 15, 2010, from http://asiapacific.amnesty.org/library/Index/ENGASA260042007?open&of=ENG-LAO.

Amnesty International. (2008). Refugees Held by Thailand Must Be Freed. Retrieved May 6, 2010, from www.amnesty.org/en/news-and-updates/news/refugees-held-thailand-must-freed-20081117.

Amnesty International. (2009a). Document – Thailand: Fear of Forcible Return/Torture/Ill-Treatment/Fear for Safety. Retrieved March 28, 2010, from www.amnesty.org/en/library/asset/ASA39/004/2009/en/75451ced-0c52–4658–9255–3077106da1d7/asa390042009en.html.

Amnesty International. (2009b). Thailand: Thai Government Must Not Fail Lao Hmong Refugees and Asylum Seekers. January 20, 2009. Retrieved February 18, 2010, from www.amnestyusa.org/document.php?lang=e&id=ENGASA390022009.

Amnesty International. (2010). Amnesty International Report 2010 – Laos. May 28, 2010. Retrieved March 9, 2010, from www.unhcr.org/refworld/country,,,,LAO,4562d8cf2,4c03a81b46,0.html.

Askew, Marc, Long, Colin, & Logan, William. (2007). *Vientiane: Transformations of a Lao Landscape*. New York: Routledge.

Ballard, Brett. (2002). Reintegration Programmes for Refugees in South-East Asia: Lessons Learned from UNHCR's Experience *Evaluation Reports* (pp. 88). Geneva: UNHCR.

BBC News. (2012). Profile: Thailand's Reds and Yellows. Retrieved June 14, 2013, from www.bbc.com/news/world-asia-pacific-13294268.

BBC News. (2014). Laos Profile. Retrieved June 25, 2014, from www.bbc.com/news/world-asia-pacific-15355605.

Bertelsmann. (2006). Laos. Retrieved March 10, 2008, from www.bertelsmann-transformation-index.de/fileadmin/pdf/en/2006/AsiaAndOceania/Laos.pdf.

CIA. (2008). Laos. Retrieved June 15, 2008, from https://www.cia.gov/library/publications/the-world-factbook/geos/la.html.

CIA. (2009). Laos. Retrieved March 10, 2009, from https://www.cia.gov/library/publications/the-world-factbook/geos/la.html.

Coe, Michael D. (2005). *Angkor and Khmer Civilization* (2nd ed.). London: Thames & Hudson.

Conboy, Kenneth, & Morrison, James. (1995). *Shadow War: The CIA's Secret War in Laos*. Boulder: Paladin Press.

Cummings, Joe. (1992). *Thailand* (5th ed.). Hawthorn: Lonely Planet Publications.

Cummings, Joe. (1994). *Laos*. Hawthorn: Lonely Planet Publications.

Cummings, Joe, & Burke, Andrew. (2005). *Laos*. Victoria: Lonely Planet.

Demeter, Fabrice, Shackelford, Laura L., Bacon, Anne-Marie, et al. (2012). Anatomically Modern Human in Southeast Asia (Laos) by 46 ka. *Proceedings of the National Academy of Sciences of the United States of America*, 109(36), 14375–14380.

Dommen, Arthur J. (2001). *The Indochinese Experience of the French and the Americans: Nationalism and Communism in Cambodia, Laos, and Vietnam*. Bloomington: Indiana University Press.

Eberle, Marc. *The Most Secret Place on Earth – CIA's Covert War in Laos*. Directed by Marc Eberle. Germany: Gebrueder Beetz Filmproduktion, 2008.

Economist, The. (2000). Old War, New Campaign. Retrieved March 25, 2010, from www.economist.com/node/303803.

Evans, Grant. (1999). *Laos: Culture and Society*. Chiangmai: Silkworm Books.

Geertz, Clifford. (1963). *Agricultural Involution: The Processes of Ecological Change in Indonesia*. Berkeley: University of California Press.

Government of Lao PDR. (2003). Constitution of the Lao People's Democratic Republic. Retrieved October 15, 2010, from www.wipo.int/wipolex/en/text.jsp?file_id=180175.

Hamilton-Merritt, Jane. (1995). The Betrayal of the Hmong. *Freedom Review*, 26(4), 1–7.

Hockings, Paul. (1993). Lao. In Paul Hockings (ed.), *Encyclopedia of World Culture: Vol 1. East and Southeast Asia*. Boston: GK Hall & Co.

Huso, Ravic R. (2008). Laos. Retrieved February 6, 2009, from www.state.gov/r/pa/ei/bgn/2770.htm.

Ivarsson, Soren. (2008). *Creating Laos: The Making of a Lao Space Between Indochina and Siam, 1860–1945*. Kobenhavn: Nordic Institute of Asian Studies Press.

Ladouce, Laurent. (2007). The Pakxe Project: A Contribution of the Lao People to the Unity of South-East Asia and to World Peace. *Culture Mandala: The Bulletin of the Centre for East-West Cultural and Economic Studies*, 7(2), 1–22.

Leibo, Steven A. (2003). *East, Southeast Asia, and the Western Pacific 2003*. Harpers Ferry: Stryker-Post Publications.

Lewis, M. Paul. (2009). Languages of Laos. *Ethnologue: Languages of the World*. Retrieved March 3, 2011, from www.ethnologue.com/show_country.asp?name=LA.

Lonely Planet. (2014). *Laos.* Retrieved August 20, 2014, from www.lonelyplanet.com/laos/history.

Magocsi, Paul R. (1999). *Encyclopedia of Canada's People.* Toronto: University of Toronto Press.

McConnell, John A. (1997). *Buddhism and Peacemaking: Western Conflict Resolution and Buddhist Wisdom.* Victoria: UVic Institute for Dispute Resolution.

McConnell, John A. (2001). *Mindful Mediation: A Handbook for Buddhist Peacemakers.* Nedimala: Buddhist Cultural Centre.

Medecins Sans Frontieres. (2007). *The Situation of the Lao Hmong Refugees in Petchabun, Thailand* (p. 7). Paris: Medecins Sans Frontieres.

Ministry for Foreign Affairs. (2004). Country Strategy: Laos 2004–2008. Retrieved May 26, 2010, from www.sweden.gov.se/sb/d/574/a/39639.

Ministry for Foreign Affairs. (2010). Human Rights Dialogues with Laos and Cambodia. Retrieved May 20, 2010, from www.sweden.gov.se/sb/d/6671/a/140466.

Nanuam, Wassana. (2006). Ties With Laos/Returning Refugees. Retrieved April 4, 2010, from www.google.com/search?ie=UTF-8&oe=UTF-8&sourceid=navclient&gfns=1&q=nanuam+w.+ties+with+Lao%2FReturning+refugees+2006.

National Identity Board. (1993). *Buddhistic Questions and Answers Book 1.* Bangkok: Rung Slip Printing Co.

National Statistical Office. (2004). Statistical Table Population Northeastern Region. Retrieved May 25, 2014, from web.nso.go.th/en/survey/pop_character/pop_character.htm.

OSAC. (2012). Laos 2012 Crime and Safety Report. Retrieved September 10, 2013, from https://www.osac.gov/pages/ContentReportDetails.aspx?cid=11983.

Peltier, Anatole-Roger. (2000). *The White Nightjar.* Chiangmai: Mingmuang Nawarat Printing.

Pholsena, Vatthana. (2006). *Post-War Laos: The Politics of Culture, History, and Identity.* Ithaca: Cornell University Press.

Robbins, Christopher. (2005). *The Ravens: Pilots of the Secret War of Laos* (3rd ed.). Bangkok: Asia Books Co. Ltd.

Savada, Andrea Matles. (1995). *Laos: A Country Study.* Washington, D.C.: Federal Research Division, Library of Congress.

Senghaas, D. (2002). *The Clash Within Civilizations: Coming to Terms with Cultural Conflicts.* London: Routledge.

Sodarak, Houmchitsavath. (2005). Shifting Cultivation Practices in the Nam Nan Watershed. *Improving Livelihoods in the Uplands of the Lao PDR*, 1, 59–70.

Stobbe, Stephanie Phetsamay. (2006). *Cross-Cultural Conflict Resolution Spectrum: Traditional Laotian Conflict Resolution Processes.* Winnipeg: Menno Simons College/University of Winnipeg.

Stobbe, Stephanie Phetsamay. (2008). *Role of Traditional Conflict Resolution Processes in Peacebuilding in Laos.* Winnipeg: Menno Simons College/University of Winnipeg.

Stuart-Fox, Martin. (1997). *A History of Laos.* Cambridge: Cambridge University Press.

Stuart-Fox, Martin. (2006). The Political Culture of Corruption in Lao PDR. *Asian Studies Review*, 30, 59–75.

Stuart-Fox, Martin. (2007). *Laos.* Washington, D.C.: Freedom House, Inc.

Stuart-Fox, Martin. (2008). *Historical Dictionary of Laos* (3rd ed.). Lanham: The Scarecrow Press, Inc.

Stuart-Fox, Martin, & Kooyman, Mary. (1992). *Historical Dictionary of Laos.* Metuchen: The Scarecrow Press, Inc.

The World Bank. (2013). Country Gender Assessment for Lao PDR: Key Findings. Retrieved August 8, 2014, from www.worldbank.org/en/news/feature/2013/03/01/key-findings-country-gender-assessment-for-lao-pdr.

Thongmanivong, Sithong, & Vongvisouk, Thoumthone. (2006). *Impacts of Cash Crops on Rural Livelihoods: A Case Study from Muang Sing, Luang Namtha Province, Northern Lao PDR*. Honolulu: East-West Center.

UN Committee on the Elimination of Racial Discrimination. (2006). Comments by the Government of the Lao People's Democratic Republic on the Concluding Observations of the Committee on the Elimination of Racial Discrimination. *International Convention on the Elimination of All Forms of Racial Discrimination.* Retrieved April 10, 2010, from www.unhcr.org/refworld/type,CONCOBSCOMMENTS,,LAO,4537798a0,0.html.

UN Women. (n.d.). Lao People's Democratic Republic. Retrieved September 12, 2014, from www.unwomen-eseasia.org/docs/factsheets/04 Lao PDR factsheet.pdf.

UNDP. (2009). Lao PDR. Retrieved March 2, 2009, www.undplao.org/.

UNESCO World Heritage. (2014). The Plain of Jars, Lao PDR. *World Heritage.* Retrieved September 10, 2014, from www.unescobkk.org/culture/wh/ap-sites/plain-of-jars/.

UNODC. (2005). Lao Opium Survey 2005. Retrieved March 18, 2008, from www.unodc.org/pdf/laopdr/lao_opium_survey_2005.pdf.

UNODC. (2014a). Criminal Justice. Retrieved August 20, 2014, from www.unodc.org/laopdr/en/Overview/Rule-of-law/Criminal-Justice.html.

UNODC. (2014b). UNODC Lao PDR Country Office. Retrieved May 20, 2014, from www.unodc.org/laopdr/.

Unrepresented Nations and Peoples Organization. (2012). Alternative Report – Laos CERB/C/LAO/16–18. In UNPO (ed.), *UN Committee on the Elimination of Racial Discrimination*. The Hague: UNPO International Secretariat.

US Department of State. (2008). Background Note: Laos. Retrieved March 15, 2008, from www.state.gov/r/pa/ei/bgn/2770.htm.

Vientiane Times News. (2012). Foreign Experts Help Strengthen Lao Criminal Justice System. Retrieved August 20, 2013, from https://www.unodc.org/laopdr/en/stories/foreign-experts-help-strengthen-lao-criminal-justice-system.html.

Viravong, Sila. (1964). *History of Laos*. New York: Paragon Book Gallery.

Wyatt, David. (2003). *Thailand: A Short History*. New Haven: Yale University Press.

2 Face and eyes: understanding conflict through metaphors

Don't pull down your pants and let others see your bum (*bor thong derng soung loung hei pern hin goan*).

(Lao proverb)

Conflicts are a normal and natural part of the human experience as we strive for balance in our world. There is diversity in conflict just as there is diversity in conflict resolution. We must be creative in looking for innovative resolutions to different problems, as it is our response to conflict that makes it positive or negative. Statistics tell us that the amount of human displacement, corruption, war, and other symptoms of violence has been fairly stable in human history, including up to the present day. What has changed recently is our understanding of the toll that unhealthy conflict has on our world. For possibly the first time in history, our world is at a stage where it has the tools, be that through interpersonal or international efforts, to change our negative responses to conflict. Learning from the ways other cultures understand and resolve conflicts is an important part of maintaining healthy relationships in our increasingly interactive world. Only with a substantial understanding of cultural dimensions in conflict resolution will it be possible to navigate through the muddy waters of conflict and communication strategies.

Conflicts are commonly defined in the West as "an expressed struggle between at least two interdependent parties who perceive incompatible goals, scarce resources, and interference from others in achieving their goals" (Wilmot & Hocker, 2001, p. 41). Although that definition holds true in the Lao culture as well, it is too narrow to be a thorough translation of the most common Lao word for conflict: *bunha*.

Bunha is much more comprehensive and encompasses a variety of conflicts, ranging from intrapersonal to interpersonal to intergroup to international. The term would include alcoholism, drug trafficking, stealing, spousal abuse, poverty, injuries, property issues, ethnic prejudices, marital issues, and even children fighting. These conflicts involve intrapersonal struggles, such as injuries, depression, or other issues that affect the family and larger community. Poverty and ethnic discrimination are systemic kinds of conflicts. *Bunha*, therefore, incorporates a wide range of personal, interpersonal, and structural conflicts.

In Laos, conflict is viewed as a complex and unhealthy problem that contributes to social ills and general loss of face. In dealing with those views of conflict, the Lao people have developed multiple, creative aspects to conflict resolution aimed at maintaining and restoring the social balance that is so important to their communal structures. The following is a beautiful story about a very simple conflict that goes a long way to helping understand the Lao attitudes to conflict and conflict resolution. It is taken from a lovely collection of Lao folktales in *Mother's Beloved: Stories from Laos* (Bounyavong, 1999).

Folktale: *Wrapped-Ash Delight*

When Nang Piew finished washing, the sun had not yet set behind the mountain. Its yellow rays shone over the treetops beside the river, glittering on the rippled water flowing softly down below. She draped the well-wrung cloth over her forearm and prepared to climb back up the riverbank. Then a shiny object on the ground caught her eye. She picked it up to look at it more closely. It was heavy . . . valuable – it was a silver belt!

She looked around. A few steps away, down by the river, two or three people were bathing. They weren't paying any attention to her, so she hid her find under the wet cloth and continued her walk up the slope toward home, her heart thumping unsteadily. She hadn't decided yet whether she should go looking for the rightful owner of the belt or keep it for herself. However, her first reaction was to get away from that area by the river as quickly as possible before anybody saw her there.

As soon as she was over the bank, she bumped into Nang Oie, who was half running and half walking to the river with a worried look.

"Have you seen my silver belt?" asked Nang Oie.

"Oh no!" Nang Piew answered automatically, trying to keep her voice as calm as possible.

Nang Oie continued on her way to the river without any more questions, for she was in a hurry to find her lost possession.

When she arrived home, Nang Piew caressed the belt with shaky hands. She was not used to stealing or finding lost valuables. After wrapping the belt around her waist, she turned left and right in front of the mirror. She looked at her reflection in the mirror and saw an unhappy face full of worries, suspicion . . . full of questions.

"Maybe people will find out I have it," she thought first.

"There's no way they can know, because a lot of people use that place by the river for bathing. In fact, almost everybody in the village uses that spot," she assured herself, trying to regain control of her thoughts.

"Should I tell Father and Mother about it?" she wondered.

"Well, if I do, they'll probably make me return it. But I've already told Nang Oie I haven't seen it. It's not a good idea to turn my words around now."

Nang Piew racked her brain but could not come up with the right answer. On the one hand, she wanted to return the silver belt, but on the other, she wanted very much to keep it for herself. She was the daughter of a peasant couple whose life lacked a good many luxuries. If she kept the belt, she would have to wait a long time before she could wear it, as she lived in a small rural village where everybody knew everybody else. When a person borrowed something from another person, everyone in the village knew about it right away. It would take a while for everyone in the village to forget about this missing object. And when that time came, how would she explain the belt to her parents? "Where did you get that belt?" they would ask. The problem seemed to get bigger and bigger. What lies would she have to tell her parents in order to convince them?

She thought about Nang Oie who lived farther up the street at the other end of the village. She was a young teenager and began wearing her silver belt little more than a year ago. Before that, she'd worn an ordinary belt. She had not been allowed to use the silver one for fear that she might lose it. Nang Oie's mother died when she was only 10 years old. Four years later, her father remarried. It was now two years since the new wife had moved in. Nang Piew remembered well the passing of Pa Soi, Nang Oie's mother. She died after hemorrhaging in childbirth, leaving six small children as orphans. It had been a sad time for the whole community.

As she remembered this period of sorrow, Nang Piew wanted to return the belt. But another thought prevented her from doing so: nobody knew. Nobody had seen her with the belt, so it didn't matter if she decided to keep it. If there was a problem later, she could always sell the belt at the jewelry store in town. However, her conscience kept reminding her that failing to return other people's belongings isn't right. It is a sin. She hid the belt in a secure place and left the room. She looked left and right with the worried thought that Nang Oie might have followed her home.

On that same evening, the kuan bahn [or nei ban, village leader] called for a meeting at his house. Those who had gone bathing before sunset at that particular area by the river were asked to attend. Loong Pong's family, whose house was located by the riverbank, had witnessed a number of people bathing at the time. Among them were Nang Piew and four or five elders of the village. The kuan bahn and the senior members explained the situation, then admonished whoever had found the belt to return it to its rightful owner. There was a heated discussion. When it was over, nobody had admitted to the crime.

The kuan bahn was compelled to come up with another strategy. He told everyone involved to wrap ashes in a package of banana leaves. Everyone should bring his or her package the following evening to the kuan bahn's house. This would give the culprit time to reconsider his or her mistake.

On the way home, Nang Piew tried to keep her behaviour as normal as possible, but the harder she tried, the more abnormal she became. It seemed to her that many eyes followed her wherever she went. If she coughed, the cough sounded unusual. When she smiled, the expression seemed dry and empty. When she spoke, her speech seemed insincere.

Her heart was heavy. She was not very happy. She was constantly afraid that people were going to come and search her house for the belt. The following day, while she was sitting inside, deep in thought about the silver belt and wondering what to do with it, she heard Nang Oie's voice at the gate.

"Hello! Anybody home?" Nang Oie called.

Nang Piew was startled. She moved closer to the wall and, peeping through a hole, saw Nang Oie enter the yard. Suddenly, Nang Piew's mother, who was busy dyeing cloth in the back, called out to Nang Oie, "I'm over here!"

"Oh, I thought nobody was home because it was so quiet. My stepmother asked me to come and borrow a ladder from you, Auntie, to collect betel leaves. She plans to visit relatives and would like to take some betel as a gift."

"Go right ahead. The ladder is stored on the side of the barn. By the way, Oie, has your belt been found yet?"

"No, Auntie. I'm afraid it's lost forever. Stepmother is very cross with me. She thinks that I'm irresponsible."

Up in the house, Nang Piew listened quietly. When she was sure that Nang Oie was not there to inquire about the belt, she felt a little relieved and went down to meet her in the yard.

"Where's your stepmother going, Oie?" asked Nang Piew, trying to keep her voice as calm and friendly as possible.

"She said she was going to Bahn Lak Sao to ask a relative for some help in finding a soothsayer who can tell us the whereabouts of my belt. She may leave tomorrow or the day after."

Upon hearing this, Nang Piew felt more worried and, in quite a hurry, guided Nang Oie to the barn where the ladder was kept. She helped Nang Oie by carrying the other end of the ladder and walking behind her.

"So you haven't found the belt yet?" asked Nang Piew.

"No, Piew. I've looked everywhere. Oh, I miss it so much."

"Maybe it fell in the river." Nang Piew tried to deflect Nang Oie's belief that someone had really taken it.

"No, I don't think so. I searched through the water all over that area and I haven't found it."

The two arrived at the front gate. Nang Piew released her end of the ladder and let Nang Oie carry it home by herself, as it was not very heavy.

After dinner that evening, there was another gathering at the kuan bahn's house. The crowd that gathered this time was bigger than usual. People came to watch, to witness the event. The people who were supposed to bring ashes each walked to an empty room with his or her package inside a covered basket. This way, nobody knew which package belonged to whom. Each person left his or her package in the room and then came out to sit and wait with the rest of the crowd. Nang Piew put her ash package among the others. Each package, wrapped in banana leaves, contained ashes and chili, symbols of fiery pain for those who steal. After the last package had been carried in, the kuan bahn brought them all outside and placed them in front of the crowd. This was the very moment everyone had been waiting for: the opening of the packages.

An elder had the honor of opening the packages. He unwrapped each one carefully and calmly. First he pulled out the stick that held the package together, then he opened the banana wrapper, and at last he stirred the ash slowly with a stick. The crowd held its breath in mingled anxiety and anticipation. The first package contained only ash and chili, and the second was exactly the same. Starting with the third one, the elder stirred the ashes only two or three times. He didn't need to poke through it too much because the belt was a big object. As soon as the package was opened, one could easily see whether or not it was there, unlike a ring or an earring, which would require a thorough search.

The unwrapping of the packages captured the interest of the crowd. Everybody watched attentively. No one spoke, or even blinked an eye. It was like uncovering a pot of gold that had just been dug out of the earth. The opening of packages continued steadily through fifteen packages, but the object in question did not appear. Many people thought this all might indeed prove to be a waste of time. The sixteenth, seventeenth, and eighteenth packages were the same. The elder felt a little discouraged, but he was obliged to go on with the job. When he pulled out the stick that held the nineteenth package and opened the leaves, a big pile of ash came tumbling down to reveal a shiny object. Everyone cheered with delight. There were screams of happiness from those who had come to witness the event, as well as from those who had brought the ash, including the one who had returned the belt, whom no one could name. The loudest scream of all was from Nang Oie, the owner of the belt, who was choked with happiness. The noisy commotion symbolized the love, solidarity, sincerity, and brotherhood that had been shared by all in this village from many generations.

The opening of the packages ended with the nineteenth. Although five remained, no one felt it was necessary to continue. (Bounyavong, 1999, pp. 93–103)

Conflict and the concept of face in Laos

The importance of face is clearly illustrated in the "Wrapped-Ash Delight" conflict. The *kuan ban* or *nei ban* (village leader) proposed a creative response to resolve the situation. The *nei ban* called for a village meeting where everyone who was bathing in the location where the belt was lost was to bring a package full of ashes wrapped in banana leaves inside a covered basket. The people placed their baskets in the empty room and returned outside with all the others to ensure that nobody knew which package belonged to whom. This allowed the elder to open each wrapped package in front of the crowd without identifying anyone, thus allowing the wrongdoer to save face by returning the item anonymously within the wrapped package. This also helped to maintain the face of the victim by absolving her of the responsibility for losing the belt. She was no longer seen as someone who was careless and negligent in losing such an important item. In this situation, the goal was not to inflict blame and punishment on the perpetrator, but to repair the harm done to Nang Oie and her family. Overall, the whole community was able to save face in this situation.

The concept of "face" is one that is common to many cultures. Face is defined as "the public self-image, that every member of a society wants to claim for him/herself" (Brown & Levinson, 1978 as cited in Lee & Hwee Hwee, 2009, p. 159). This definition highlights face as a social image that needs to be preserved. In essence, "face" is a term that is used to define the relationship between respect and social status. For example, when individual actions are viewed negatively, a person can lose respect, thereby negatively affecting their social status. This is considered a "loss of face."

The Lao people have a particularly unique way of referring to face. They refer to conflict as a loss of face, or *sear na sear tda*, which translates to "loss of face and eyes." Many cultures in the world have an expression or belief about the eyes being "the window to the soul." In Canada, in conflict situations we often use the expressions, "Look me in the eye and say that," or "Look me in the eye and say sorry." In this instance, an inability to look someone in the eye can be interpreted as a feeling of shame or guilt. In referring to "face and eyes," the Lao people are bringing two concepts together in a very simple, yet powerful, way. "Face" is the outer appearance of one's respect and status in a communal relationship, and "eyes" are the inner aspect of one's own shame and guilt.

The word "embarrassing" is often used by the Lao in discussing a conflict situation. The Lao word for embarrassment is *ai na* or literally, "embarrassment to face." This is another example of how the Lao language uses the word "face" in describing the symptoms of conflict. Embarrassment leads to a loss of "face and eyes," and is therefore viewed as working against social harmony. Furthermore, as demonstrated by the symbol of ash and chilies, and as will be shown throughout the following chapters, embarrassment seems to be quite "contagious" in Laos, as support networks, mediators, and others involved in conflict can all be susceptible to being embarrassed, regardless of their involvement in the initial conflict situation. Just like blowing ash coats everything around a fire, even the face of a bystander can be affected by a fight.

We can understand this better by looking at the symbolism in the Wrapped-Ash Delight folktale, as well as other common metaphors that the Lao have to describe conflict. Metaphors are poetic ways of describing experiences that bring focus to emotions that can be difficult to communicate. They are used to "create a kind of compact, vivid shorthand description of a complicated process" (Ortony, 1975 as cited in Wilmot & Hocker, 2007, p. 44). The previous Lao folktale illustrates important metaphors for conflict in the description of each package as "wrapped in banana leaves, contained ashes and chili, symbols of fiery pain for those who steal." Here conflict is symbolized by ashes and chilies, which can burn and create a mess if blown around. Lao chilies are tiny in size but can be potent in their scale of "hotness." This metaphor explains how small conflicts can hurt people and, if they escalate, blow fiery, painful residue on everything and everyone surrounding them.

The Lao people have a particular gift for using metaphors in a way that is often humorous but still enlightening. The following expressions and metaphors are uniquely Lao, and are useful in describing attitudes about conflict. They are included here to provide background into the Lao psyche regarding conflict, specifically, their cultural interpretation of what conflict means in society.

1. "Your face is crooked like a scorpion ready to bite" (*na jou keur mang gcot*).
2. "Your eyes are crooked like a green caterpillar" (*tda jou keur mang bong*).

3. "Your face is sour like you've eaten pig feces" (*jou na boot keur kee moo*).
4. "Conflict is like the clanging of dishes and spoons" (*teoy gup bwung fut gun*).
5. "Conflict is like the tongue and teeth biting one another" (*lean gup fun bung kung*).

Evidently, there is a relationship between conflict and face in a way that is negative, uncomfortable, and dangerous. Conflict makes one's face and eyes "crooked and sour," makes harmony sound "clangy and awkward," and impedes communication by making the "tongue and teeth" work against each other. It works against individual and collective face by causing difficulties in seeing, hearing, and speaking or, in other words, conflict causes people to be blind, deaf, and dumb. In the Lao culture, conflict is perceived to create negative transformation in people physically, psychologically, and spiritually.

It is interesting to note that every one of the metaphors mentioned involves either the whole face or specific features of the face. Clearly, in Laos there is a very literal understanding of the social concept of "face" and how that translates into a reflection of one's actual face. Nang Piew is clearly struggling with her conscience, which kept "reminding her that failing to return other people's belongings isn't right. It is a sin." After Nang Piew kept the silver belt that she had found on the path along the river, she returned home and "looked at her reflection in the mirror and saw an unhappy face full of worries, suspicion . . . full of questions." This conflict has affected her conscience and is reflected directly in her face.

The folktale further illustrates how the conflict caused Nang Piew's heart to feel heavy, sad, and full of anxiety, as she was "constantly afraid that people were going to come and search her house for the belt." Nang Piew had difficulty trying to keep her voice calm and friendly whenever she had conversations with Nang Oie. She felt "many eyes followed her wherever she went. If she coughed, the cough sounded unusual. When she smiled, the expression seemed dry and empty. When she spoke, her speech seemed insincere." More than just the extraverted, community aspect of conflict, *bunha* also refers to conflict within oneself and the negative effect that a guilty conscience can have on one's own feelings of self-worth. Clearly, conflict is viewed as something negative and destructive on more than just a community level, but also to the individual, and the importance of maintaining and restoring "face and eyes" is extremely valuable in his or her social world.

If these metaphors are useful to the Lao people in describing the capacity of conflict to cause a loss of face and eyes, the following expressions identify the most important approaches they would take when encountering a conflict situation:

1. "No one will know your roof is leaking if you don't tell them" (*fon bor huar hern pei ga bor hu*).
2. "If you don't turn on the lights, no one will see inside your home" (*fi bor tdi hern pei gor bor hoong*).
3. "Don't fight in front of the face of others" (*bor thong pit gun thone na peur ern*).

4.   "It's not good to bring a poisonous snake into the house" (*ow gnu how ma hern bor dee*).
5.   "Don't bring other people's conflict onto your shoulders" (*ya ow bunha poo ern ma hap*).

These metaphors demonstrate the Lao cultural view that conflict, as a problem, is something that should be guarded quietly and efforts should be taken to ensure that it stays private or removed from oneself. I find the third expression particularly interesting: "don't fight in front of the face of others." This is another play on "face," specifically in the literal sense of not fighting in front of someone's physical face or in front of someone's metaphoric "face." This expression illustrates the importance of maintaining one's own face, as well as preventing damage to the faces of bystanders.

This is particularly true of their most important support network: the families of those directly involved in disputes. Maintaining family status in the social sphere is an important part of survival and success in Lao life. Because of this, there is significant cultural pressure on disputants to resolve conflicts in order to save themselves and their families from embarrassment. Taken one step further, there is obviously pressure on families to play a significant role in all aspects of conflict resolution, whether that be in finding solutions, supporting agreements, or educating their members.

> "Whenever we have conflict, we make our family lose face and respect . . . We don't want to lose face so we only go to someone outside the home to help resolve our conflict if absolutely necessary. It is embarrassing to have a conflict and we can lose face so we have to resolve it in the family."
>
> (seventy-six-year-old male Ethnic Lao teacher)

> "I teach my children to . . . be a good person and respect older people and parents. Brothers and sisters must help each other; be friendly, do similar things as our traditions and religions where our parents are from. Our parents have taught us like this to keep this message and teach our children in the future."
>
> (forty-five-year-old male Ethnic Lao)

It is no surprise that parents are expected to play a big role in transmitting these cultural values to their children and that they, along with elders, are considered the caretakers of tradition and peace. Therefore, in conflict situations, there is not only significant pressure on cultivating and maintaining individual "face," but also on the collective family "face" as the front line of social conflict education and of conflict resolution. My mother tells me that she never saw her parents fight or raise their voices in front of their children or in public. Families who display such strong emotions to their neighbours and in the community are often frowned upon and lose respect.

Open conflict is discouraged and avoided in Lao culture. These expressions, stories, and quotations are evidence of people's desire to avoid conflict and keep it as private as possible. The folktales, traditions, and metaphors of Lao culture and language demonstrate that maintaining discretion in one's personal conflicts and distance from other's conflicts is prudent. These conflict resolution etiquettes are vital to preserving social harmony and are absorbed by children at a young age as they continue the traditions imparted by previous generations.

The story of "Wrapped-Ash Delight" is not just a folktale of Lao culture. I have heard many similar stories of conflict avoidance and face saving in which people seek creative ways to resolve conflicts. On a smaller scale, returning items anonymously is a popular way to avoid conflict and save face. Some stories involve finding missing or stolen items and simply returning the item on the steps of the home from where they were taken. Returning objects anonymously ensures that no suspicion will be cast on the returner, even if he or she is not the thief. Alternatively, items can be wrapped up as a present and given to the owner in a situation where he or she is receiving many other presents, such as a wedding or celebration. As a Lao friend told me, "Some people still use this method because the item is being returned anonymously and the owner can't tell who it is from. And if the owner does figure out who it is, they can pretend that they don't know in order to save face."

The Lao concept of face is remarkably holistic. In Laos, face is applied to three different levels: the individual, the family, and the community. Conflict resolution requires being able to save one's own face, the face of the families involved in the situation, and the whole community in which the conflict takes place. The story of the stolen belt illustrates these different levels of maintaining and saving face in conflict. Nang Piew and Nang Oie both need to save their individual face by avoiding the conflict and open confrontation. Nang Piew wanted to save the face of her mother and her family by not discussing the situation with them, thereby saving them from the personal guilt they would assume as part of Nang Piew's misdeed. Nang Oie wanted to spare her family the embarrassment that their daughter had lost something precious. The *nei ban* wanted to help the whole community maintain face by devising a plan to address the conflict in a way that ensured social harmony.

At this point, enough information has been presented to develop an appropriate definition for Lao conflict, or *bunha*. As mentioned, *bunha* refers to a situation in which one or more people are in an incident or perceive a set of actions that contribute to a "loss of face" or an "embarrassment of face" for themselves and/or others that disrupts their inner psyche, relationships, and/or social harmony. Related to the Lao concept of *bunha*, an appropriate Lao definition of conflict resolution could be a situation in which one or more people are in a circumstance or engaged in actions that help to "maintain face," prevent "loss of face," or "rebuild face" for themselves and/or others in order to restore personal, interpersonal, or intergroup harmony. This is obviously a very broad definition, but it reflects the large scope of *bunha* in that it applies to intrapersonal, interpersonal, intergroup, and structural conflict. As will be discussed, this definition influences *ot* (avoidance), as well as the multi-dimensional use of *op-lom* (discussion) in conflict resolution.

Avoidance of conflict

The conflict and conflict resolution metaphors identified earlier in this chapter suggest there is a relationship between cultural views of conflict and strategies of conflict resolution. Because open conflict is perceived as working against social harmony and face, it is shunned and evaded. Avoidance of conflict is an underlying theme in Lao conflict resolution and is key to understanding the reasons behind their conflict resolution processes. The negative perceptions of conflict and the importance of maintaining privacy give birth to avoidance strategies.

The Lao language is indicative of this strategy. The term *ot* refers to refraining and abstaining from conflict. It is the root word in phrases that talk about how to stay away from conflict. For example, *ot ow* signifies acceptance or resignation, and would be used in the phrase, "sometimes I just have to take it." *Ot tone* indicates patience and endurance, as in the phrase, "sometimes I have to take it and be patient – walk away." *Ot gun bai* suggests tolerance and remaining calm together: "sometimes I have to stay calm, accept and tolerate things." All these phrases convey the importance of accepting the situation in order to avoid conflict.

Avoidance is a powerful force in Lao conflict resolution, as it is consistently compelling disputants not only to avoid conflict entirely, but also to avoid any potential escalation in conflict, thereby avoiding further loss of face and eyes and maintaining social harmony. One woman I know espoused this principle in her personal life:

> My husband was a well-known philanderer among the people in the community. However, I never once confronted my husband about his affairs, nor did I talk about the situation with my family and friends. I tolerated the situation and remained patient throughout my marriage until the day my husband passed away.

We should not be fooled into thinking that their need to avoid conflict is done out of weakness or laziness. Clearly, patience and tolerance are among the most positive of human traits, requiring tremendous energy, strength, and courage to maintain. Through hope that time will heal conflicts, or through fear of escalation, avoidance strategies have driven creativity in conflict resolution.

For example, we understand that Lao culture deeply avoids the escalation of conflict into open confrontation where loss of face is imminent for everyone involved. In order to make that possible, opportunities to relieve stress and tension, or "pressure valves," must be created to keep conflict from building. Some of the earlier stories, including the "Wrapped-Ash Delight" folktale, demonstrate that the Lao social structure is very adept at looking for quiet, anonymous, face-saving avenues of escape, in contrast to a threat-and-punishment system designed to squash conflict situations by citing consequences. Although "shaming" is a powerful tool in ensuring social cohesion, providing opportunities for conflicts to be resolved without the threat of reprisal and without a threat to social hierarchy and standing is an equally important measure in keeping both private and public peace.

The combination of avoiding loss of face due to conflict, together with providing avenues to maintain face through resolution, is the motor that makes the Lao conflict resolution process run.

In that sense, avoidance is a trait that runs through the entire conflict resolution process by encouraging people to avoid further escalation of conflict. Conflict escalation is seen as destructive to relationships and communities. When avoidance is not possible, conflict resolution becomes increasingly public, and maintaining social status becomes tenuous. Just as conflict is avoided in an effort to maintain "face and eyes," the conflict resolution process begins in the private sphere, in hopes of a resolution without expanding the conflict into the public sphere. After all, it is easier to restore face in private settings than to have to restore it to many people in a public environment.

This presents an interesting problem, namely, if conflict resolution seeks to provide anonymity as a way to maintain social standing, how are values, traditions, and codes of conduct imparted to the public social sphere? Again, "Wrapped-Ash Delight" provides an elegant answer: the *nei ban* and elders explain the missing belt situation and "admonished whoever had found the belt to return it to its rightful owner." It is not uncommon for either the *nei ban* or elders to reprimand or encourage people in non-identifying ways as part of a conflict resolution scenario. However, when these actions still did not resolve the conflict, the elders encouraged the whole village to become involved in finding the solution through the exercise of wrapping ash in banana leaf packages and placing them in unmarked baskets. In doing this, the *nei ban* and elders were able to condemn the socially destructive behavior while at the same time ensuring that any confrontation and loss of face are avoided. It allowed the offender to do the right thing and save face at the same time.

The story of Nang Piew is certainly not one of serious criminal activity where public protection is required, or even one where a simple act of stealing a belt is likely to propel Nang Piew into a life of crime. Nevertheless, its resolution is clever, creative, and effective. It gives an avenue for both the victim and the perpetrator to regain their community status and transmits social values to the larger community. As we will see, dealing effectively with simple crimes is the first step in a healthy conflict resolution system.

Conclusion

Avoiding conflict is an important part of Lao culture. Conflict is seen as something very negative, working against social harmony. As a normal and natural part of social experience, conflict is not necessarily something that we should be afraid of, but we should also be careful to react to it in appropriate ways, to prevent escalation into more serious and damaging events.

I do not believe that avoidance strategies are a negative response to conflict, nor do I think that they promote an unhealthy fear of conflict. In understanding that avoiding loss of "face and eyes" and providing avenues to maintain "face and eyes" are two pieces of the same puzzle, we can understand that the positive consequence of conflict avoidance is an inherent willingness to resolve conflict. This relationship is of paramount importance in conflict resolution. World history has repeatedly shown us that conflict does not get resolved until there is a willingness to do so, and that willingness does not always come easily. The importance of societal pressures in respecting traditions and demonstrating cultural values creates a strong foundation for a cultural willingness to resolve conflict. In the folktale, the village leader and elders did not give up after the first attempt at resolution failed. Rather, they organized another gathering, larger than the first, to address the conflict anonymously through the wrapping of ash in banana leaves and were successful in resolving the conflict. Laos shows us that a willingness to resolve conflict flows from a desire to avoid conflict, save face, and prevent the escalation of conflict.

Of course, being naturally inclined to resolve conflict is not the same as actually resolving it. An underlying theme of this chapter has been to look at the different structural positions that conflict operates in. In order to prevent a loss of face or embarrassment for themselves and others, people must resolve conflicts according to cultural traditions. These traditions have been established, maintained, and taught by parents and elders, and clarified and enforced by village leaders and authorities. Essentially, the concepts of both *bunha* and "face" exist on an individual level, a family level, and a larger community level. It is in that structure that we find the beginnings of a conflict resolution process, or as I define in the next chapter, a Conflict Resolution Spectrum.

Bibliography

Bounyavong, Outline. (1999). *Mother's Beloved Stories from Laos*. Seattle: University of Washington Press.

Brown, Penelope, & Levinson, Stephen C. (1978). Universals in Language Usage: Politeness Phenomenon. In Esther N. Goody (ed.), *Questions and Politeness: Strategies in Social Interaction* (pp. 56–289). Cambridge: Cambridge University Press.

Lee, Joel, & Hwee Hwee, Teh. (2009). *An Asian Perspective on Mediation*. Singapore: Academy Publishing.

Ortony, Andrew. (1975). Why Metaphors Are Necessary and Not Just Nice. *Educational Theory*, 25(1), 45–53.

Wilmot, William W., & Hocker, Joyce L. (2001). *Interpersonal Conflict* (6th ed.). Boston: McGraw-Hill.

Wilmot, William W., & Hocker, Joyce L. (2007). *Interpersonal Conflict* (8th ed.). Boston: McGraw-Hill.

3   *Op-lom*: the language of conflict resolution

Discuss, teach, and advise one another (*op-lom du num gun*).

(Lao proverb)

Conflicts are normal and natural in human relationships, and the conflicts in Laos are not unique, but experienced by many around the world. Family conflicts involving children misbehaving, spousal affairs, financial concerns, gambling addictions, and substance abuse are common. Workplace conflicts exist for many people, whether they are farmers, teachers, village leaders, merchants, university students, or government workers. These conflicts may include students fighting, transportation issues, droughts that prevent the planting of crops, tardy or absent employees, and insufficient funds to pay labourers. This diversity of conflicts reflects the kind of work people are involved in. Community conflicts also exist in Laos, whether one lives in small rural villages or in bigger cities. Neighbourhood children fighting, youths addicted to drugs, impoverished children unable to attend school, home robberies and theft, property line conflicts, and other community conflicts are all part of the lives of many in Laos and elsewhere.

Obviously, conflicts rarely fit into the neat categories of family, workplace, or community, but the conflict resolution field often tries to categorize conflicts for ease of understanding and interpretation. In fact, many of the conflicts described in this chapter would fit quite well into all three categories. This is especially true in cultures like Laos that view conflict holistically, affecting all in a community. Regardless of what category a conflict fits into, it causes a loss of face on an individual, family, and community scale, and must be dealt with effectively.

The Lao Conflict Resolution Spectrum

People in Laos have a well-understood and consistently identified set of processes to deal with conflicts in their communities (Stobbe, 2006, 2008). These processes could be described in terms of a spectrum ranging from interpersonal discussion to structured mediation to the court system (see Table 3.1).

Table 3.1 The Lao Conflict Resolution Spectrum

Discussion/Problem Solving	Op-lom
Parents Mediation	*Paw Mer*
Relatives Mediation	*Pah Loong/Pee Nong*
Elders Mediation	*Tow Gua*
Village Leaders Mediation	*Nei Ban*
Village Mediation Committee	*Neoy Gai Geer*
Village Court	*San Ban*
District Court	*San Muang*
Provincial Court	*San Kwang*
Supreme Court	*San Sung*

Note: The term "village" refers to both a small rural community and a neighbourhood or subdivision within a city.

Lao people describe their Conflict Resolution Spectrum and its various processes as follows:

> We always talk to our parents first about our problems. If they can't help us, then we will talk to our relatives, usually our brothers and sisters, aunts and uncles, our blood relatives. After that, we go to the *nei ban* for help in resolving our conflict. The courts are only for bigger problems. The village courts may deal with divorce cases. The provincial courts deal with cases involving deaths and murders. The Supreme Court, there are no divorce cases here.
>
> (forty-two-year-old female Ethnic Lao business woman)

> The husband and wife must discuss with each other (*op-lom*). Sometimes, they will go and discuss their problems with their relatives and elders . . . the parents will talk with them. Then they might go to the village leader's (*nei ban*) house to talk with him. Usually, the couple is given three chances to try and work things out before a final decision to remain together or to separate. First, we talk to our parents, then our relatives, then the village leader (*nei ban*), and finally we go to court.
>
> (eighty-nine-year-old female Ethnic Lao farmer)

> The parents will come and discuss (*op-lom*) the problem . . . Next, they can go to talk to their relatives, the village mediation committee (*Neoy Gai Geer*), and the courts.
>
> (sixty-one-year-old male Katdu tax collector/accountant)

These quotes demonstrate people's personal knowledge of the specific conflict resolution processes that are available to disputants, as well as the different third parties – parents, relatives, elders, village leaders, the village mediation committee (*Neoy Gai Geer*) – who can assist them in resolving conflict. Clearly, when avoidance of conflict is not possible, the Lao people use discussion, various forms of mediation, and, in rare circumstances, the court system to address their conflicts.

Op-lom *discussion*

> *An upper-class couple bought a motorcycle for their son on his sixteenth birthday, believing it would give him the freedom and mobility he needs to learn and grow into a strong person who would make their family proud. However, they have now come to think that their son is inappropriately testing and exercising his independence, creating a loss of collective face for the family. He has been spending many hours partying and going out with friends and neglecting his schoolwork. Around the neighbourhood there is talk about a new drug that the youths are becoming addicted to – ya ba (madness drug), which contains a mix of methamphetamine and caffeine. The son's parents are very concerned that his current behavior will lead him into a dangerous world that will have permanent negative consequences for him, his family, and his community. They decide to sit down and "op-lom" with him about their concerns.*

The process of *op-lom* is a way of listening, discussing, teaching, reminding, and advising parties to resolve their disputes in constructive ways (see Figure 3.1). *Op-lom* is a term that is used only in reference to conflict and conflict resolution. It means much more than just talking (*wao*, or *lom*) or speaking (*bpak*, or *son ta naa*), and signifies a process of active and intense counseling and advising for the purposes of helping people understand each other in conflict situations. The process of *op-lom* goes beyond the facilitation of discussion between parties and,

Figure 3.1 The *op-lom* process in problem solving and mediation

depending on the situation, can function as therapy, teaching, or legal advice. There is a certain richness of exchange in *op-lom* as it seeks to establish context through in-depth discussion.

When conflict is unavoidable, the first step towards resolution is for parties to talk and negotiate with one another directly:

> Before we can solve problems, both sides need to *op-lom* (discuss) and try to understand each other, however different their personalities, they have to come to talk together, sometimes they don't like to talk together because it takes a long time to solve the problem, but if they understand each other, it's easy to work out.
>
> (twenty-four-year-old male Ethnic Lao, staff at private company)

In interpersonal *op-lom*, the parties in conflict are directly involved in discussions without the assistance of third parties. This is similar to the process of negotiation, where parties agree to talk about their issues face to face, come to a common understanding of the problem, and find solutions that are mutually satisfying. Interpersonal *op-lom* is the preferred way to resolve disputes.

When a conflict cannot be resolved at the interpersonal level, the Lao people will ask third parties to assist them in resolving their dispute. Parents, older siblings, or family elders are often the third party in this form of *op-lom*. These people are expected to find the root of the problem and provide advice and suggestions for its resolution. They can then educate and encourage the parties in conflict to go through a resolution process, sometimes including a trip to the temple to calm down and find quiet space to reflect on the situation and make necessary changes.

It is clear that the *op-lom* process is central to resolving conflicts throughout the Lao Conflict Resolution Spectrum. The Lao culture highlights this communication process by helping to define right and wrong and giving a third party the decision-making authority to resolve conflicts. Like the English term "counsel," *op-lom* can mean something akin to a therapist or counselor attentively listening, or a lawyer giving counsel in a legal situation. The discussion of various third-party mediations, discussed later, will add to the definition of *op-lom*.

Op-lom is a valued concept and skill that forms a basic communication strategy for individuals and third parties within the Lao conflict resolution process. It is an important communication skill that, by its definition, brings people together through developing a shared understanding of the relevant issues, and is an activity that mediators are expected to engage in while helping people address their conflict. In that sense, *op-lom* is a communication tool that is characteristic of all types of mediation and conflict resolution processes in Laos.

In the conflict situation with the sixteen-year-old son, the parents did *op-lom* with their son and discussed the consequences of his actions. They were able to provide him with some advice and agreed to continue to trust him. The son also realized that his actions and behaviour extend beyond himself and have a significant effect on his family and others in his community. The purchase of the motorcycle had exactly the effect the parents had hoped for, namely, an opportunity for their son to learn that he is part of a larger world, and that his growing freedom and independence also come with responsibilities and obligations.

Not all conflicts are resolved as easily as this one was. When further intervention is required, the Lao people will continue down their Conflict Resolution Spectrum in order to find a solution. Conflicts that are resolved quickly are more likely to be kept private, thereby preventing loss of face. This strategy will become increasingly evident as we examine further aspects of Lao conflict resolution.

Mediation by parents and relatives

An Ethnic Lao woman married a Khammu man and, like any other young person, had dreams of having a family of her own. After being married for twenty years and having three children, her husband decided to take a second wife even though this was not legally permitted. He secretly married a much younger woman at her parents' home, with elders and the village leader in attendance. The new couple had a son. The husband kept them in a separate dwelling, visiting them a few days at a time. When his first wife found out, she became very upset and demanded an explanation. His rationale for marrying this younger woman was that she is also Khammu and he has always wanted his children to be fully Khammu. [Polygyny in Laos is rare, but somewhat socially accepted among the Khammu cultural group.] The first wife demanded that he stop seeing this woman, as it was an embarrassment to her, but the husband refused. The husband continued to lavish his second wife with gifts. One day the first wife caught him stealing her jewelry to give to his second wife. The situation escalated into domestic violence: she threw things at him, wanting to injure him. He physically attacked her and broke her arm.

The first wife is a strong woman who wants to remove herself from this abusive situation and move on with her life in a safe and healthy environment. However, she still wants to maintain face and keep things as private as possible, so she decides to ask her parents and relatives for help.

A community elder explained the connectedness of conflict, family, and face by saying:

> Whenever we have conflict, we make our family lose face and respect . . . We don't want to lose face so we only go to someone outside the home to help resolve our conflict if absolutely necessary. It is embarrassing to have a conflict and we can lose face, so we have to resolve it in the family.

Maintaining face for oneself and one's family is of utmost importance, and keeping a conflict situation within the families is of significant cultural value. As informal third parties, parents and relatives are crucial in helping people resolve their disputes.

Cultural norms and expectations dictate that people first go to their parents and relatives for assistance in resolving conflicts, as they are the ones who have significant vested interest in resolving the dispute. The intimate relationship that parties have with family intermediaries is helpful in forming strong support networks during the mediation process and the implementation of a resolution, as well as giving the disputing parties extra incentive to maintain agreements. Additionally, informal discussions with parents and relatives ensure that conflicts remain as private as possible. Cultural norms encourage people to avoid situations that could lead to "gossip" or other negative community involvement.

During these informal mediation processes, it is not unusual for the parents of the disputing parties to meet with each other in an attempt to resolve the conflict between their children. Lao parents and grandparents clearly see this as being part of their lifetime parental responsibilities, as caretakers of their family status in society. Similar to the English expression "The apples don't fall far from the tree," there is a Lao expression saying, "When you look at an elephant, you must look at the tail too." This expression refers to knowing something fully, from the beginning to the end. In understanding an individual, one must also understand his or her family, as parents are reflected in their children, and vice versa. Understanding this cultural belief gives significant insight as to why parents and relatives are very motivated to help their children, no matter what their age, resolve their conflicts. Conflicts in Laos are not limited to the individuals in conflict, but extend as a reflection on their families and communities.

Along with the incentive to see conflicts resolved before a loss of face occurs, parents and relatives are motivated to make sure that conflicts stay resolved. They have the ability to provide strong support networks for maintaining peace, to be powerful advocates that lead to socially acceptable actions and behaviours. The nature of being parents gives them a certain amount of power, deference, and authority over their children throughout their lives. As a sixty-year-old Ethnic Lao teacher shared, "It is important even when they have passed away, especially their teaching, it stays with us forever." The teachings from parents can and should have an impact over generations in a family. Parents are teachers and role models, passing on proper moral values to their children. Parents use *op-lom* as a teaching tool, where they teach their children "to have good friends," "not fight with others," or "stay on the good road according to Buddhist teachings." These are all important aspects of Lao social structure and conflict resolution.

In the story of the Ethnic Lao woman and her Khammu husband, the situation was resolved to the extent that they came to an agreement they could both live with. Her parents and relatives reprimanded her husband for hurting his wife and children and for creating a loss of face in the community. They supported her by accompanying her in communications with her husband, providing finances for her to make changes to her situation, and giving advice and encouragement when needed. The husband has still refused to agree to a divorce, and although she could legally obtain one, she has decided not to go through this more public process. The husband is providing regular financial support, including sole possession of the house, and he lives elsewhere with his second wife. She feels that she is in a safe environment, and with the support of her family, she has been able to move forward in a healthy way. Ironically, the husband and his first wife have some contact, and they continue to care for each other and help each other in times of need, but they do so from a distance now.

Mediation by elders

> *Upon the death of their father, four children from a well-to-do family encountered a difficult situation over their inheritance. Although their mother was still living, the terms of the will clearly stated how the assets were to be divided among the children. The eldest daughter in the family had found favour in her father's eyes ever since she was a young child. Although the siblings had learned to accept the apparent favoritism, the two brothers and younger sister were shocked that their sister was given the ancestral house and all the property, while they were given a little bit of money. They felt that this was unfair and that they, too, deserved a share of the house and lands. The eldest daughter felt that she deserved what was given to her, as she would be the person taking care of their mother and two younger siblings.*
>
> *Their mother was deeply troubled, and turned to her relatives for advice on how to address the situation. The relatives were unable to help so she asked some of the community elders to provide op-lom.*

When family and relatives are unable to help bring a conflict to a mutually satisfying resolution, the next step is to ask non-family elders in the community. Parties in conflict often solicit respected elders to mediate various disputes. Similar to the *panchayats* in Karimpur, India, these elders are aware that conflicts are embedded in complicated social relationships, and they will attempt to discuss a compromise that is acceptable to all involved in the conflict (Wadley, 1994).

In Lao culture, elders traditionally command great respect and possess an enormous amount of decision-making power. Status accrues with age, wealth, skill in specific tasks, and religious knowledge (Leibo, 2003; Savada, 1995; Stuart-Fox, 1997). The elders bring a tremendous amount of experience, knowledge, and memory in dealing with conflict. Through oral traditions, they are able to pass down important teachings about life, relationships, and conflict resolution skills to the younger generations.

Members of the religious community hold a special role as community elders in the Conflict Resolution Spectrum. Most Lao homes have shrines containing a Buddha, sacred relics, and offerings to various spirits placed on shelves above head level. Buddhist teachers and leaders play a vital role in working towards peace, and senior monks are revered as elders in the community. Traditionally, monks have played the role of mediators in interpersonal, family, and community disputes. Their traditions teach people that conflict is to be expected and that it has potential for benefits and growth.

When people are anxious, distressed, and in conflict, they will often *op-lom* with the monks at the temples. Monks often described their *op-lom* as calm, non-confrontational, and encouraging, with a focus on rebuilding the relationship. These are important values in any good conflict resolution process.

Due to the status and respect given to elders in the community, third parties involved in facilitating mediation processes in Laos are customarily older than the disputing parties due to their higher status. As a Lao person once said, "Of course we listen to our elders. They are older and wiser than us. If we don't listen, we will embarrass our family and cause bad omen." It is extremely uncommon to go against the advice of elders, for this causes everyone involved to lose face.

The Lao language itself is further evidence of the respect that elders in the community command. Lao people designate different titles to individuals based on their sex, age, and family relationship. Both verbal and non-verbal honorifics are used when addressing people who are older. In speaking with elders, people will use terms such as *achaan* (teacher), *paw tdu* (father), or *mer tdu* (mother). Non-verbal communication that shows respect for elders includes bowing and holding the palms of one's hands together in front of one's body in greeting (*nop*). It is also important to ensure that one is not standing or sitting above an elder in a room. It is common to see children and younger people sitting on the floor while the elders are sitting in chairs.

It is already apparent that, unlike the impartiality of Western mediators, Lao mediators are people who often have personal connections and relationships to the disputants. Lao mediators tend to have a vested interest in resolving disputes, as they understand the conflict dynamics, relationships, and personalities of those involved. It is this personal knowledge of the parties that helps Lao mediators successfully interpret conflict dynamics. The elders have lived in the community for a long time and therefore know the families and/or parties in conflict. They have developed relationships in many settings such as the markets, temples, and neighbourhoods, and can use their experience and connections in encouraging people to resolve their conflicts.

This is obviously very valuable in the open-ended process of *op-lom*. Sometimes, individuals in conflict need a listening, non-judgmental ear. It is not uncommon for mediators to be supportive by listening and keeping judgments to a minimum, while maintaining absolute confidentiality. Some parties need non-confrontational and educated advice in helping them learn the steps that should be taken to restore face and eyes. This is an example of *op-lom* functioning like a therapist who gives counsel based on his or her knowledge and experience of human relationships.

However, it is also not uncommon for Lao mediators to reprimand the parties for poor behavior, give advice as to how the conflict can be resolved, and persuasively encourage forgiveness and reconciliation. In these situations, mediators provide a "reality check" regarding the consequences of unhealthy actions and provide specific remedies to address them. These are occasions when individuals need more solid direction, similar to legal counsel and arbitration, where the third parties lecture, advise, and discuss consequences of unresolved conflicts.

These are the different aspects of *op-lom* as a therapist, a teacher, or even an arbitrator. It is the mediators' personal knowledge of the disputants and conflict situations that help them to choose which strategy to use and when. The mediators want conflicts to be resolved successfully so that there is peace and harmony in their community. Their "face and eyes" are related to their ability to deal with conflicts constructively. The disputants also want to positively end their conflicts. Their "face and eyes" are already threatened, and continuing conflict situations only augment that threat. Being unable to follow the terms of an agreement presided over by elders would only contribute to a loss of face for all parties. The parties, out of respect and concern about "face and eyes," will do their best to abide by the agreement set out by elders.

In the inheritance dispute story, the elders helped to mediate a solution to the conflict. They did so by providing advice and options on how to move forward and reminding the family members that what is fair for one member of the family is not necessarily fair to another. The siblings were in different stages of life, some more established and some less so, and each sibling had different needs. Eventually the eldest daughter agreed that since she was given the ancestral house and lands, she would be willing to build a house for her younger brother and his family on a piece of that property. The ancestral home was to be turned into a restaurant business for her mother and younger sister to operate, with the top floor of the house as their private lodging. Her elder brother, having already married a wealthy business woman and running a successful business, agreed to the provisions for the rest of the family and removed any further claim to the family estate. The eldest sister continued to live in the home she and her husband had already built on the family property.

Mediation by village leaders

> *The impoverished parents of a teenage boy were very distraught over the actions of their son. Over the past year the son had been hanging out with friends who they felt were a bad influence on him. The son had been disrespectful and verbally abusive towards his parents, particularly his mother, who is smaller than him. He fears his father, who is physically bigger and stronger. The son has been stealing money and valuables from his parents, who are already struggling to purchase food and other necessities for the family. One day his mother caught him stealing her gold necklace, a family heirloom, and demanded that he return it to her. He refused and instead took the necklace, sold it, and used the money to buy drinks and drugs for him and his friends.*
>
> *The parents had tried to op-lom with him and had gone to their relatives and elders for assistance. Still the son continued his destructive path. In desperation, the father physically forced the son to go to the village leader's home for op-lom to see what advice he might have to help resolve the situation.*

Kings, village leaders, and elders have played the role of third-party mediators in Laos since the fourteenth century (Stuart-Fox, 2008). As mentioned earlier, village chiefs or leaders (*paw ban*, or *nei ban*) are traditionally called upon to assist in resolving disputes in the communities. Since 1975, village presidents (*pathan ban*), as head of the administrative committees, have played the role of mediators (Savada, 1995), and this practice continues to exist today.

According to tradition, the *nei ban* can take up to three days to think about the conflict situation, investigate the conflict, ask the parties to come together to talk about the issues, and make decisions. Village leaders hold significant authority in the hierarchy of village life because of their power to conduct investigations and to assign and enforce compensation and punishment. Although their decisions may be appealed, the consequences of ignoring the authority of the *nei ban* can be severe.

The story of the disrespectful teenage boy is particularly vivid to me because the father brought the son to the *nei ban*'s house at a time when I happened to be there. As politely as possible, the *nei ban* excused himself and accompanied them back to their house to see how he could help the family. I found out later that one of the resolutions to the conflict was to have the boy come live with the village leader and his family for a while in hopes that the young man might learn to understand the larger issues that the community was facing, including those caused by the poverty and drugs that were driving some families to exhaustion and dysfunction. Later on that same day, around nine o'clock in the evening, there was a commotion in the house next to where I was staying. As we were sitting around a table outside in the front yard, we were able to observe what was happening. Once again, the same village leader was called to come mediate a conflict, this time between a husband and wife.

The amount of care, dedication, and immediate assistance that the village leader was willing to provide was commendable. One of the most important duties of a *nei ban* is to do as much as possible to bring social harmony to the family and community, whether that be during working hours or at two o'clock in the morning. This *nei ban* clearly took this part of his job very seriously and, in conversations with others in that village, it became evident that he was considered an excellent community leader. The parents who were having problems with their son described him as a "very good man who cares very much about the people in his village." Another villager said he was "someone who is good at explaining and discussing problems (*op-lom*) in a calm way."

This example serves to demonstrate just how important the Conflict Resolution Spectrum is in Laos and why it is understood in such a homogenous way. As noted earlier, Laos is still a very undeveloped country, particularly in its economic and educational infrastructure. Professional and social services are unavailable to the large majority of Lao citizens; therefore, the *op-lom* that is so valued in the Lao mediation system takes on those roles. There are no family therapists or marriage counsellors available to couples or families going through conflict; land surveyors are not available to neighbours disputing property lines; and financial planners and bankruptcy experts are not available to give advice to farmers affected by drought, whose poverty prevents them from paying their employees or buying seeds for planting. Insurance is a luxury that is hardly available in a country where 77 percent of the population earns less than US$2 a day (Bertelsmann, 2006). Through the process of *op-lom*, it is parents, elders, and community leaders who assume these roles and provide assistance to people in need.

Neoy Gai Geer *mediation*

> *Terraced paddy rice farming is common in the hills and mountainous terrain of Laos. From a distance these terraces look like steps going up a mountain,*

but seeing them closer up reveals they are small dams built of earth and clay, specifically designed to hold water in which to plant rice. In the countryside, these stunning terraces filled with young, bright lime-green rice shoots capture one's eyes. Water is irrigated into the top terrace, and upon reaching a certain depth, flows into the next terrace. This continues until all terraces are filled to a sufficient level for rice planting. Although the rice farmers are extremely advanced at cultivating this irrigation system, in heavy rains the terraces can overflow and burst, causing flash floods farther down.

Two farmers whose lands are on the same mountain, one right above the other, experienced such a catastrophe one year when the walls of the terraces of the farmer above collapsed and a river of water gushed down the hill and washed away the crops of the farmer at the bottom. They tried to op-lom with one another on how to resolve this problem, but could not come to an agreement. The farmer above said that it was not his fault, as the rain was particularly heavy that year. The farmer below argued that he should have built stronger terraces that would have prevented such a disaster. They followed the customary conflict resolution guidelines and sought the help of various mediators, including their relatives, elders, and village leader – but with no success. Finally, as resolving this dispute was integral to their livelihood, they went to see the Neoy Gai Geer to help them find a solution that would be mutually satisfying.

Mediation through the *Neoy Gai Geer* is a significant process for conflict resolution in Laos, yet very little has been written about it. In 1985, the government adapted several traditional mediation processes to create the *Neoy Gai Geer*, or Village Mediation Committee, in order to address more efficiently various conflicts in the family, workplace, and community. Each *ban*, or "village" (a community or neighborhood within a village, town, or city), has a *Neoy Gai Geer* whose mandate is to deal with conflicts in the community. Not surprisingly, conflicts that go to the *Neoy Gai Geer* level are those that have proven too complex and stubborn to resolve at preceding levels, as well as those that are somewhat more serious in nature: physical fighting causing serious injury or death, significant property damage, and other conflicts where large compensation may be required. The *Neoy Gai Geer* often uses precedents and traditional law (*got mai*) to help make decisions that are effective and satisfying, complementing similar decisions traditionally made by others.

The process used by the *Neoy Gai Geer* is not based on a single mediator or a co-mediator model. Instead, the committee consists of seven individuals who represent various groups within the village (see Figure 3.2). The composition of the committee reflects traditional third parties (village leaders, village elders, and informal mediators), as well as contemporary third parties (a young people's representative and representatives from the Lao Women's Union, the police, and the military). This assures that the *Neoy Gai Geer* is represented by both genders. In addition to the Lao Women's Union representative, women are sometimes on the committee as village leaders, elders, and young people. The police and military

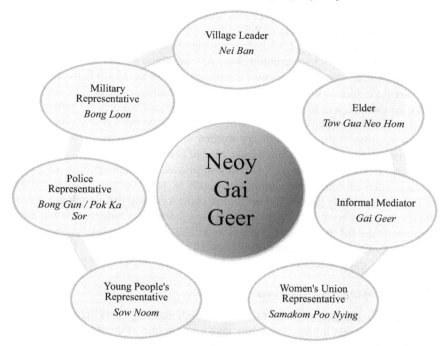

Figure 3.2 Composition of the *Neoy Gai Geer* (Village Mediation Committee)

representatives are generally men. Members of the *Neoy Gai Geer* are paid a small stipend by the government and consider it a privilege to serve on the committee, which often increases their status in society. Clearly, the composition of the *Neoy Gai Geer* is intended to reflect many of the different voices in the Lao community, including both those who have held traditional roles in conflict resolution as well as some more modern ones.

As Lao society changes, new people are incorporated into traditional systems of conflict resolution, creating new processes of mediation. An example of a contemporary third party that plays an important role in dispute resolution is the Association of Patriotic Lao Women, created in 1955 and renamed the Lao Women's Union (LWU) (*Sahaphan Maenying Lao*) in 1975. The union is the official state-supported women's organization in Laos, organizing workshops, conferences, and other activities for women across Laos. It publishes its own magazine and promotes the government's National Strategy for the Advancement of Women (2005–2010) (Stuart-Fox, 2008). The members are elected every three years.

The Women's Union plays an important role in Lao society. It offers assistance and education in the daily activities that women participate in, such as food preparation and cooking, sewing, and laundry services, but also teaches topics on women's health, maternal care, and infant care. It also provides micro-financing to women to help pay for hospital expenses or to start a business. The significance of this organization is a testament to the importance and respect accorded to women in Lao society in general and, with that, a recognition of the special status women have in contributing to their communities. All the ethnic groups of Laos are relatively egalitarian, and many of the minority groups in the uplands have a social structure that gives women a higher status than groups in the valleys do (Scott, 2009). Women often hold positions outside the home, particularly in running small businesses that earn family income. Walking around the marketplace one notices that the majority of the merchants are women. It is also customary for women to be the household accountant and to take care of the family finances.

Members of the Lao Women's Union also play an important role in mediation and resolution of family and community conflicts. It is common knowledge that the union is available for conflict resolution consulting and that people are free to discuss whatever conflict they are experiencing. Like other elder mediation, after three unsuccessful discussions, the union will refer the disputing parties to the *Neoy Gai Geer*. As already noted, a representative from the Women's Union serves on the most formal mediation processes in Laos, the *Neoy Gai Geer*.

Procedures of the Neoy Gai Geer

A mediation session of the *Neoy Gai Geer*, which normally lasts between one and three hours, is often informal and may take place at one of the disputants' homes or at the village leader's home. Often the participants sit on a bamboo mat on the floor in a circle. On account of their status and age, the village leaders and elders may be given chairs to sit on. As is customary for all gatherings in Laos, the hosts serve drinks and light snacks (e.g., fruit and dessert); a full meal may be served if the session is long. The mediation is facilitated by the village leader, who, as the official overseer of the village, is responsible for social harmony in the community. Parents, family members, elders, and other individuals from previous mediation processes (as identified in the Conflict Resolution Spectrum) are encouraged to be present at the *Neoy Gai Geer* discussion to provide information and to support the parties in conflict.

The *Neoy Gai Geer* process consists of the following stages. First, the committee meets individually with parties involved in the dispute to hear their perspectives on the conflict and to gather relevant information. Second, they speak with the parties and their respective support networks together, asking each of them to discuss the conflict and what happened. Third, the committee discusses with the whole group how best to resolve the conflict. Each person has an opportunity to provide some suggestions for a resolution and give advice to the disputing parties. Fourth, the *Neoy Gai Geer* meets privately to consider all that they have heard. Using a consensus decision-making process, the committee meets in a closed session to come to a unanimous decision about the outcome of the conflict. Finally, the *Neoy Gai Geer* returns to the whole group to communicate their decision based on their knowledge, experience, and discussions in the mediation session.

Op-lom *in the* Neoy Gai Geer

Of all the levels of mediation used in Laos, the *Neoy Gai Geer* is the most formal process. In describing the role of the village mediation committee, *op-lom* is used in the sense of "giving counsel" rather than being the "counselor." Conflicts that go through the *Neoy Gai Geer* have already become quite a public affair, and the *Neoy Gai Geer* is more concerned with protecting the public community face rather than that of individuals. They will tell the parties what they think of the conflict and may express some strong reprimands if they feel they are warranted. Through various consultations with all involved in the conflict, the *Neoy Gai Geer* provides a recommendation.

The *Neoy Gai Geer* plays an active role in the mediation process and exercises a significant level of power over the process and in decision making. Beyond giving public reprimands, they will also discuss issues of restitution regarding how the parties can repair harm and rebuild relationships, and empower appropriate support groups and authorities to enforce their findings. The *Neoy Gai Geer* makes decisions that are not always easy for the disputants to accept and, if they do not think that current support networks are adequate to help the disputants move forward, they will commission different people to assist the parties in restoring the relationship. In that commissioning, they make both the disputing parties and the support networks accountable for reconciliation.

By the time conflicts have reached the *Neoy Gai Geer* level, the responsibility for their resolution is shared by a number of people in the community. Similar to the proverb that says, "It takes a whole village to raise a child," it sometimes takes a whole community to resolve conflict. Once the *Neoy Gai Geer* has made a decision, there is tremendous social pressure on the disputing parties relative to the significant number of people involved in trying to bring about resolution. The number of people responsible for ensuring an end to the conflict, combined with the extent of "face and eyes" that are potentially at risk, is almost always strong enough to restore peace and bring about reconciliation. When everyone has accepted the terms of the resolution, the *Neoy Gai Geer* writes up an official letter that is signed by the parties and the *Neoy Gai Geer* members. The decision becomes a written agreement that is endorsed by the committee. Often, these agreements can refer to customary laws (*got mai*), legislated laws, and other written documents upon which any decisions and agreements have been based. A copy of the agreement is kept by the *Neoy Gai Geer*, and other copies are distributed to the parties.

In the situation involving the two farmers dealing with flash flooding along their rice terraces, the *Neoy Gai Geer* was able to help the parties see their interconnectedness, just as their lands were intertwined. The committee reminded the farmers that cultivating good relationships meant helping one another in times of droughts and floods, and further reminded them that the relationship between the two families had been strong for many years, so restoring harmony was important. The agreement considered that the flooding had essentially ruined both of their harvests, and as neither had any money to compensate the other, the farmers agreed to spend the usual planting season jointly fortifying each other's terraces to make them stronger and jointly replanting and harvesting crops as soon as completed areas were ready. Both farmers brought in extra family members to assist with the work.

Possible concerns with the Neoy Gai Geer

As with any dispute resolution process, the practice of *Neoy Gai Geer* raises some potential concerns. For instance, I wondered whether or not the conflicting parties felt obligated or compelled to go along with a resolution that was authored by a group of very important community people. In discussions with some of the village leaders in charge of facilitating the *Neoy Gai Geer*, they emphasized that the committee is responsible for listening and giving advice based on the full consultation and representation of all stakeholders in a conflict, while still recognizing that decisions and agreements made by the disputants themselves are much more likely to be successful. In situations where the *Neoy Gai Geer* imposes resolutions, the committee hopes that the disputants feel their voices have been heard, that they feel the committee has ensured sufficient support resources for maintaining the decision, and that the disputants feel the weight of authority wielded by the committee in holding up the resolution. The community's respect for the *Neoy Gai Geer*, as well as the committee's emphasis on broad-based consultation, are compelling reasons for people to abide by its resolutions.

In a Western conflict resolution culture, some people may feel uncomfortable with this reality. It is important to remember that in Lao culture, it is anticipated that mediators will provide specific conflict resolution advice to the disputants. This is expected of mediators because they hold some authority and expertise over the conflicting parties. In reality, I am not aware of any systemic complaints about mediators abusing their power, and many Lao people will confirm that parties are always asked to give their input before committing to a resolution.

By the time disputants have reached the *Neoy Gai Geer* level, they have already been through several other mediation processes. Obviously, they are having significant difficulty in reaching an agreement and restoring their relationship. Just as in a formal court system, one or both parties may view the judgments at previous stages as unfair, and the *Neoy Gai Geer* serves as a process for making difficult decisions. It is in these situations where respect and authority are required to maintain social harmony and where support networks become vitally important in helping the disputants obtain and maintain the terms of the agreement.

Another potential concern with the *Neoy Gai Geer* has to do with its perceived connection to the government structure. After all, the government has mandated which institutions the committee members must be selected from and provides a small honorarium for those serving on the committees. As in many parts of the world, corruption can be an issue in Laos, and from an outsider's perspective, the connections between government and the *Neoy Gai Geer* can be viewed as hindering fairness and impartiality. However, there is no evidence of dissatisfaction with the *Neoy Gai Geer* process or its members. In fact, many Lao would argue that the support of the government adds some legitimacy and allows for procedural consistency across all the villages in Laos.

The *Neoy Gai Geer* is clearly a well-respected group, committed to resolving conflicts and maintaining peace by representing different voices in the community. In my conversations with Lao people, the vast majority responded positively to questions about the *Neoy Gai Geer*. They believe the process to be effective in resolving conflicts in a cost-effective and timely manner. This is further evidenced by the incredibly small number of cases that go beyond the *Neoy Gai Geer* and into adjudication through the courts. However, if mediation with the *Neoy Gai Geer* is still unsuccessful after three attempts, the disputants are encouraged to use the next level and go to court to address their issues. In some cases, especially in complex divorce situations, the lower courts serve as the "rubber stamp" for agreements already worked out by the *Neoy Gai Geer*. In these situations the *Neoy Gai Geer* has already made a recommendation for divorce, including child custody and other arrangements. These are situations where many attempts at reconciliation have already failed or where there is physical danger to family members.

Adjudication through the courts

During conversations with many people in Laos, I heard about only one case where an individual was directly involved in a court case. The conflict was between two brothers who owned a shared business. As the younger brother did not have much money to invest in the business venture, he asked his elder brother for a loan that he promised to repay once the business started to make some profit. However, the business did not perform at the level they had expected and eventually fell apart. At this point, the elder brother asked the younger one to repay the loan, but the younger brother refused because the business did not make any money. They brought in their parents, relatives, elders, village leaders, and even the Neoy Gai Geer, but nothing was resolved. The brothers became polarized, damaging relationships between them and the other family members who were constantly pressured to take sides.

At this point the brothers and their families had already lost face in the eyes of the community. The older brother who was owed money decided to take the matter to court.

The negative consequences of continuing through the progression of methods for conflict mediation become evident when reflecting on which systems the Lao people do not want to use in resolving conflicts. This reflects the importance of social harmony in Lao culture and affirms that the purpose of conflict resolution systems is to establish reconciliation and maintain healthy relationships. Going to court is not considered conducive to rebuilding positive relationships. In the words of a Lao merchant: "If we go to the court, we will become enemies." This is by far the most common perception of what happens when a conflict is allowed to escalate to this level. Lao people believe that going to court will cause permanent relationship failures between the disputants and embarrassment for the families and relatives of those involved. Further, the expense of going to court can be debilitating to all disputants, often causing long-term debt and financial difficulty.

This is not to say that the court does not have a place in Lao society. As discussed earlier, the courts often serve as a rubber stamp for agreements and documents that have been endorsed by the *nei ban* or the *Neoy Gai Geer*. In this respect, the courts serve as a way of documenting crime and other complex conflicts where the government needs to keep records and statistics. However, as an actual conflict resolution system, the courts are not really accessible to the average Lao citizen and are in reality reserved for large business conflicts, transnational corporations, and organized criminal activity such as murders and large-scale drug trafficking. More recently, a new type of case has started to become more common in the courts, involving land disputes where one of the claimants is an expatriate. It will be interesting to see how the courts deal with this new issue in Laos.

In the conflict between the two brothers in business, matters were already at a point where relationships were permanently broken and face had been significantly damaged. Surely they felt they had little left to lose in going to court. Unfortunately, after the case had gone through several court levels, the legal costs absorbed all their finances. Their relationship is permanently damaged and they have severed all ties with each other. The other family members continue to experience anxiety around them.

Unresolved conflicts within the system

Although the processes within the Lao Conflict Resolution Spectrum have proven effective in resolving many different kinds of conflicts, there are conflicts that do not seem to have an appropriate outlet for resolution. Some of these are common throughout the world (drug use, prostitution, land expropriation, etc.). Other chronic conflicts are more unique to the culture and economic system of Laos, arising from changing regulations in farming crops, ownership of land for farming, and use of land for business use.

There are several reasons why these types of conflicts are difficult to manage – some that have solutions, and some that are more complex. The movement to a market economy in the 1980s saw state-owned enterprises (SOEs) move to privatization through share sales or leasing agreements for a specified period of time. Many were bought by family and friends of the Lao People's Revolutionary Party officials (Stuart-Fox, 2008). As occupants of a Communist state, Lao citizens do not have permanent ownership of land, but can purchase (or be given) land for a certain period of time. Pholsena and Banomyong (2006) confirm that land is the property of the government, which authorizes its use by farmers based on the hours of full-time work the family does in the fields. The government has discretion regarding when they want the land returned. There certainly are stories of hardships endured by some who have had land expropriated. Obviously, the government has a responsibility to provide services to its citizens, and those services require buildings and land. For example, a farmer told me this brief story:

> I used to be able to get to my garden in thirty minutes, now it takes me one to two hours to get to the new garden site. This is because a school was going to

be built on my garden and I had to sell my land for the school. I can't discuss with them because they won't listen so I had to sell. I only have temporary use of this new garden site. It's not my land permanently. The government lets me use this land. I'm worried about animals eating my crops and I don't know when I will have to move again. I begged the government to help but they don't care.

Nobody would argue that building a school is a poor use of land. However, some people believe that the government does not do a very good job of compensating those who are victims of expropriation. It seems the village authorities are not able to assist in mediating such conflicts. Patron–client relationships are characteristic in Lao political culture, where the power of patrons is found in relationships and client obligations (Stuart-Fox, 2008). Patrons such as village leaders are also clients of more powerful patrons through family and marriage networks, economic interests, and political loyalty. Connections to patrons may assist in the resolution of property conflicts, but those who lack such connections are left with no advocates.

A common story in the city of Luang Prabang centers on how the government prohibits people from building businesses or other ventures on riverfront property. However, the business owners across the street from the river often claim the riverfront piece of land in front of their property and build restaurants overlooking the river. Periodically, the Lao government tears down these buildings only to have the locals rebuild them in order to maintain their livelihood. The village authorities have not been able to adequately address these conflicts, as they have no authority to change the laws.

Other economic and business conflicts pertain to the growing of crops. The prohibition of swidden rice farming has had a particularly detrimental effect on some of the minority groups in Laos. Farmers who traditionally relied on swidden rice farming to feed their families have had a difficult time adjusting to paddy rice and other cash-crop farming in accordance with the 1986 New Economic Mechanism. They cannot be self-sustaining with the new kinds of farming, and since there is no organization or association to advocate for them, the farmers feel that they cannot voice their concerns.

Another crop-related source of conflict centers on drugs, which the Lao people have used medicinally for centuries. Traditionally, marijuana and opium were readily available and used to treat upset stomach and provide general pain relief (particularly for the elderly), and for flavouring foods. During the French period, the government had a monopoly over the sale of opium, and in the Second Indochina War (1965–1975), the Central Intelligence Agency (CIA) was involved in transporting opium and may even have assisted in marketing it (Stuart-Fox, 2008). In 1975, the Pathet Lao government introduced a tough policy on drugs, branding their use as a social ill introduced by the West, sending young addicts to rehabilitation camps. This drove the industry into the black market, causing a price surge in the product. For many poor and isolated farmers, opium poppies became a valuable cash crop and a means for supporting their families.

The addition and acceptance of more powerful illicit drugs by Lao youth has had its own consequences. By 2000, methamphetamines (*ya ba*) were widely available and had spread to young people as a cheap drug (Stuart-Fox, 2008). Many Lao people describe drug use and prostitution as current systemic problems leading to conflicts in Lao communities. As in many countries, drug and sex work issues continue to be a complex problem, and solutions seem difficult to grasp.

Progressive aspects of the Lao Conflict Resolution Spectrum

There are five different levels of mediation within the spectrum of conflict resolution options, ranging from informal mediation processes to the formal court system (see Figure 3.3). The conflict resolution processes move gradually from private to more public forums, and from direct involvement of the parties to informal third parties, formal third parties, and finally to formal processes. More specifically, mediation starts with parents and then involves relatives, elders, village leaders, and finally Village Mediation Committees. In many cases, mediators from previous levels will be included in subsequent mediation.

At each successive resolution stage, there is strong impetus for individuals and communities to maintain face by demonstrating their commitment to resolving the conflict. Since the third parties become progressively removed from the immediate family unit with each stage of conflict resolution, progression through the spectrum means the processes become increasingly public. The probability of damaging relationships and experiencing psychological costs through loss of reputation, face, and self-esteem becomes increasingly acute.

This progression is encouraged by the Lao cultural value of avoidance as a driving force in dispute resolution. Each level includes more people and becomes more damaging to face and social harmony. Therefore, each new level represents further loss of face and eyes and should be avoided as much as possible. It is this tendency for avoidance that causes reluctance to move further along the Conflict Resolution Spectrum. In this sense, the Lao Conflict Resolution Spectrum is very reflective of Lao culture, where open conflict is discouraged and avoided.

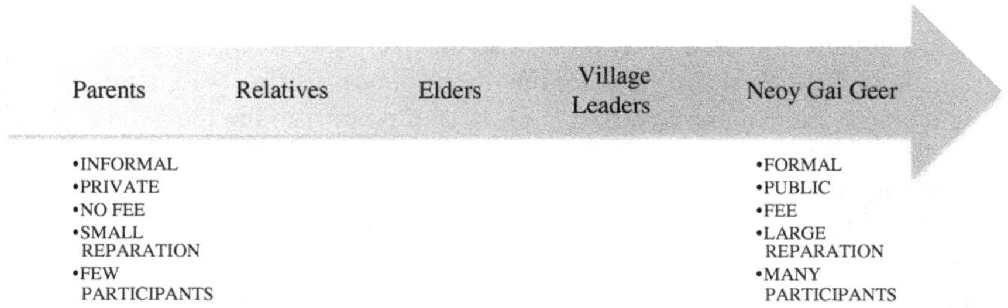

Parents	Relatives	Elders	Village Leaders	Neoy Gai Geer
•INFORMAL •PRIVATE •NO FEE •SMALL REPARATION •FEW PARTICIPANTS				•FORMAL •PUBLIC •FEE •LARGE REPARATION •MANY PARTICIPANTS

Figure 3.3 Progression through five mediation levels

Inclusion of other mediators in subsequent processes

Another progressive aspect of the Conflict Resolution Spectrum is that at each new level, mediators from previous levels are invited to participate in the process. This is a very important aspect of the entire Conflict Resolution Spectrum in Laos. It serves as a built-in consultation feature, in which information can be consistently and reliably shared through the different mediation processes. Previous mediators are present and provide background information, insights, clarity, and perspective on the issue. The accounts of the stories are given directly by the people involved in the mediation, thus reducing any miscommunication.

Previous mediators also help to provide the disputing parties with support networks and ensure compliance as they discuss the issues, brainstorm solutions, and develop the terms of the agreement. Working with the parties in conflict as parents, relatives, elders, or village leaders, a network is established that can help disputants regain lost community status. Furthermore, including previous mediators also has the benefit of ensuring consistency, scrutiny, and transparency between the different levels of mediation, as well as providing a level of accountability to previous mediators. This is especially important because mediators often lack impartiality due to their role, cultural expectations, and connections to the community. Each set of mediators knows that the next set of community members and mediators will scrutinize their work should the conflicting parties continue to advance through the different levels.

Opportunities for resolution

A willingness to resolve conflict also requires opportunities to resolve conflict. These opportunities must be accessible and desirable. In each mediation stage, from those involving the parents to the *Neoy Gai Geer*, the parties are given three chances to implement the terms of the agreement. The possibility of going back to the mediator after the first agreement allows the parties to fine-tune the resolution and gives them second and third chances to find a resolution that better meets their needs.

Having three attempts at a resolution and an opportunity to return to mediation ensures that people are working on their relationship and assumes that the mediators support their efforts. These feedback loops are vital to effective conflict resolution, for they allow the parties to return ("loop back") to further negotiations that will meet their needs more effectively (Ury, Brett, & Goldberg, 1988). If parties come before the *Neoy Gai Geer* but still cannot meet the terms of the agreement after three separate meetings, a letter from the *Neoy Gai Geer* outlining the impasse can be taken to the district court (*san muang*), where the case will be assessed by a judge. Obviously, it is not desirable to have conflict situations that are drawn out indefinitely, providing no opportunity for resolution.

Setting specific time limits for the resolution process is important because it allows the disputants to feel they can move forward in a timely manner. The amount of time allowed to pass between mediation sessions depends on the type of conflict. Sometimes those time periods are agreed to as part of a mediation agreement, whereas in other situations those times limits are based on tradition. For instance, a married couple going through separation and divorce is traditionally expected to wait at least fifteen days between mediation sessions. However, after a separation period of three months has passed, the couple can have the *nei ban* provide official documents for a divorce. As already noted, few divorce cases go through the court system, allowing mediation to be the main process of dispute resolution for marital conflict.

The price of conflict escalation

Interview participants made it clear that the fees attached to different levels of conflict resolution can encourage coming to a solution at the lower levels of mediation. The willingness to resolve conflicts early is enhanced by the fact that until one reaches the *Neoy Gai Geer* mediation, none of the traditional levels of mediation have a service fee. As an elder, farmer, and former soldier observed, "Traditional methods can help make compromises and you don't have to pay, and don't lose a lot of time."

In 2009, the fee for using the *Neoy Gai Geer* process was 50,000 kip (US$5). For many people in Laos, this is approximately one week's salary. The fee is often split between the two parties in conflict at the beginning and later paid in full if either person is found to be 100 percent liable. Sometimes, the person who requested assistance from the *Neoy Gai Geer* is required to pay up front. If the parties cannot afford the fee, family members often step in to help cover the cost of mediation. According to a number of participants, fees for each subsequent mediation session by the *Neoy Gai Geer* increase by 30,000 kip (US$3). If the first mediation costs 50,000 kip, the second will cost 80,000 kip, and the third 110,000 kip.

To put this in perspective, Laos's gross domestic product (GDP) per capita in 2010 was estimated to be US$2,400 (CIA, 2010); therefore, the fee for going through three mediation sessions with the *Neoy Gai Geer* would be approximately 1 percent of an average annual salary. Adjusted for average income, this is still a fraction of what an average North American would pay to go through a court case. However, considering that this fee would buy enough rice to feed a family of six for several months, it is still a considerable amount of money. Due to cost, there is strong incentive for resolving conflicts at levels where there are no fees attached, making informal mediation the key process in resolving disputes.

Satisfaction with traditional conflict resolution processes

Clearly, one reason that other conflict resolution systems have not taken a stronger hold in Laos is because people there are satisfied with the current one and believe that it works. The Lao system is not perfect, and as already discussed, there are structural and systemic conflicts that cause some difficulties. Yet many of those difficulties would be the same ones found in much more formal and expensive legal systems. Lao conflict resolution is an excellent example of how centuries-old traditional processes can give people a voice; save time and money; and balance the needs of efficiency, accessibility, and satisfaction in conflict resolution. Traditional methods allow for *op-lom* and in-depth discussions that can lead to better understanding of the conflict situation and provide a more satisfying resolution. This is a significant reason for people's willingness to use these methods to resolve conflict, thereby ensuring their continued acceptability and use. All these mechanisms are in place to encourage people to resolve their disputes quickly, efficiently, and as amicably as possible, making it possible to uphold the high cultural value they place on maintaining relationships.

Conclusion

Understanding culture and cultural conflict resolution processes is key to building relationships and reconciliation in any conflict, whether it is an interpersonal, intergroup, or international conflict situation. Local, community-oriented processes can be instrumental in addressing conflicts, but their potential is often misunderstood and underestimated. Resolving conflicts in culturally appropriate ways increases positive awareness, understanding, and relationships.

There is a great deal of evidence for the effectiveness of conflict resolution patterns as one observes Lao people, listens to their narratives, and reads the limited literature on their culture. Traditional Lao conflict resolution approaches can be placed along a continuum from the most simple and least costly to the most complex and expensive legalistic forms of dispute resolution. As mentioned, this continuum can be described as the "Lao Conflict Resolution Spectrum," comprising five levels of mediation that become progressively more formal and public. This spectrum allows for resolutions that are specific to the customary laws and traditions of different cultural groups involved in conflict. The *Neoy Gai Geer* (Village Mediation Committee) is the most formal of the mediation processes and involves a committee composed of various representatives from the community who use a consensus decision-making model to resolve conflicts.

Morton Deutsch (2000), a pioneer in the field of conflict resolution, defines procedural justice as fair treatment in terms of respect and dignity, and in making and implementing the decisions that determine the outcome of the conflict situation. In the mediation processes in the Lao Conflict Resolution Spectrum, procedural justice is achieved because fairness, consistency, and transparency are built into the processes. Parties in conflict feel they have been treated fairly and consistently in terms of the process and resolutions based on traditional knowledge and experience.

Successful conflict resolution and restoration of relationships do not end here, but are reinforced by celebration and ceremonies to mark the end of conflict and help people move forward. The following chapter will examine the conflict resolution rituals that are instrumental in keeping social harmony in Laos.

Bibliography

Bertelsmann. (2006). Laos. Retrieved March 10, 2008, from www.bertelsmann-transformation-index.de/fileadmin/pdf/en/2006/AsiaAndOceania/Laos.pdf.

CIA. (2010). Laos. *Central Intelligence Agency: The World Factobook.* Retrieved January 10, 2011, from www.cia.gov/library/publications/the-world-factbook/geos/la.html.

Deutsch, Morton. (2000). Justice and Conflict. In Morton Deutsch & Peter T. Coleman (eds.), *The Handbok of Conflict Resolution* (pp. 41–64). San Francisco: Jossey-Bass.

Leibo, Steven A. (2003). *East, Southeast Asia, and the Western Pacific 2003.* Harpers Ferry: Stryker-Post Publications.

Pholsena, Vatthana, & Banomyong, Ruth. (2006). *Laos: From Buffer State to Crossroads?* Chiang Mai: Mekong Press.

Savada, Andrea Matles. (1995). *Laos: A Country Study.* Washington, DC: Federal Research Division, Library of Congress.

Scott, James C. (2009). *The Art of Not Being Governed: An Anarchist History of Upland Southeast Asia.* New Haven: Yale University Press.

Stobbe, Stephanie Phetsamay. (2006). *Cross-Cultural Conflict Resolution Spectrum: Traditional Laotian Conflict Resolution Processes.* Winnipeg: Menno Simons College/University of Winnipeg.

Stobbe, Stephanie Phetsamay. (2008). *Role of Traditional Conflict Resolution Processes in Peacebuilding in Laos.* Winnipeg: Menno Simons College/University of Winnipeg.

Stuart-Fox, Martin. (1997). *A History of Laos.* Cambridge: Cambridge University Press.

Stuart-Fox, Martin. (2008). *Historical Dictionary of Laos* (3rd ed.). Lanham: The Scarecrow Press, Inc.

Ury, William L., Brett, Jeanne M., & Goldberg, Stephen B. (1988). *Getting Disputes Resolved: Designing Systems to Cut the Costs of Conflict.* San Francisco: Jossey-Bass.

Wadley, Susan S. (1994). *Struggling with Destiny in Karimpur, 1925–1984.* Berkeley: University of California Press.

4   Rebuilding through rituals

> Rituals serve to restructure the social experience and the social identity of the actors and participants and thus to frame social memory.
>
> (Evans, 1999, pp. 192–193)

As a child, my interest was captured by the *soukhouan* celebration that took place in various homes to mark special events in the community. I particularly remember the more elaborate events, where people dressed in their finest clothing. The women were especially beautiful in their traditional, brightly colored Lao silk skirts and scarves, their hair put up in buns and pinned with jewels. There was always plenty of laughter, socializing, and food. The tables were filled and refilled with amazing Lao dishes. The celebrations often continued late into the night, and the children would inevitably fall asleep before the revelry ended. I never questioned the ceremonies that were hosted in our home or in the homes of others in our community, simply accepting them as part of our Lao cultural tradition. What did stand out in my mind was the feeling of acceptance, community, and friendship at these celebrations.

Celebrations like the *soukhouan* ceremony continue to define both Lao culture and religion. Only when I began to study the traditional conflict resolution processes of different groups around the world and to conduct research on the Lao diaspora in Canada did I begin to develop a keen interest in exploring my own roots, and specifically the conflict resolution rituals of Laos. When I traveled to Laos to continue my research, the people I interviewed talked about the importance of these ceremonies for conflict resolution and relationship building. Through these discussions, I was able to explore the meanings and significance of the conflict resolution and reconciliation rituals of the Lao people.

The most well-known and frequently practiced ritual in Laos is the *soukhouan* ceremony (sometimes known by its Hmong name, a *baci* ceremony). It has many purposes, one of which is as a mechanism for conflict resolution. A second type of event, the *soumma* ceremony, is a more intimate celebration that functions as a process of forgiveness and reconciliation.

The *soukhouan* ceremony

The Lao people have a culturally unique way of memorializing agreements through specific rituals. The *soukhouan* ceremony is so deeply ingrained in the collective Lao culture that it deserves special attention as a ritual that has become a cultural and cross-cultural conflict resolution structure in itself. Whether you are a Lao Loum, Lao Theung, or Lao Soung, the *soukhouan* is among the most common and celebrated activities in Laos. For this reason, it provides an excellent opportunity to see community building and cultural interaction at work. Most formal processes of dispute resolution, such as the court system, do not have ceremonies designed specifically for celebrating the end of a conflict. In Laos, once a conflict is resolved, a traditional *soukhouan* ceremony is usually organized. Although the scope and scale of this event depend on many variables, the ceremony itself is vital to the well-being of people in the community.

> We perform a *soukhouan* when relatives visit to show love and respect for each other; when someone is sick, in order to make them better; when there's a wedding, to bless the couple; after a death/funeral, to ensure the spirits are happy; and when there's a big conflict in the family or injuries to another person, to repair the harm that's been done.
>
> (sixty-seven-year-old female Ethnic Lao baker)

> A *soukhouan* is performed when there is injury to someone in a car accident, physical fight, other accidents, and deaths; at New Year's for our parents and elders; when we are wrong in a conflict situation, we must do a *soukhouan* for the other family; when our children are leaving for study in another city or country; and when guests come to visit.
>
> (sixty-year-old female Ethnic Lao merchant)

One of the most important purposes for holding a *soukhouan* is to publicly demonstrate a commitment to resolving a conflict. A relatively large and elaborate *soukhouan* that I attended in Houayxay in 2009 involved approximately 100 people and included family members, friends, elders, monks, and other community members. The *soukhouan* was organized by an elder aunt, her adult children and their families, and close friends to celebrate the return of one of the aunt's siblings after many years of separation. This family had experienced a long-simmering conflict between these two members, but with typical Lao avoidance style, no one had really acknowledged or discussed the conflict. Because the sibling had already moved away from the village, the family felt it was best to leave things alone. But when the sibling returned, all the old emotions surfaced and the atmosphere became uncomfortable within the extended family. The elder aunt finally took the initiative to *op-lom* and encouraged the family members in conflict to discuss their issues with one another, especially as they were all getting older and needed closure to their conflict. The parties in conflict were able to have a discussion among themselves and to understand the other's perspective on various issues under contention. The family decided to have a larger celebration that included other family members, elders, friends, and community people to show that all was well in the family and to welcome the younger sibling back into the family.

Days before the ceremony took place, the hosting family and friends were already busy making preparations for the special event. A large, beautiful flower arrangement (*makbeng*) in the shape of a cone was set in the middle of a silver vase placed on a round bamboo serving table about 36 inches wide and 18 inches high (see Figure 4.1). Within the flower arrangement were tall, thin, wooden sticks around which were tied numerous 10- to 12-inch white, homespun cotton threads

Figure 4.1 A *pa khouan* or *makbeng*. Note the white threads (*fei pouk khene*) that will be used to tie around the wrists of honored guests, symbolizing restoration

© Stephanie Phetsamay Stobbe, 2013

arranged in neat rows, with a few coloured threads taken from the Buddhist temples. Small, special floral bouquets wrapped in fresh banana leaves containing rolled-up money in various denominations were also tucked within the cone-like bouquet. During the preparation of this special arrangement, the elder aunt told me stories of how Buddhism is akin to the lotus flower: out of a muddy pond a beautiful, fragrant flower emerges to bask on top of the water in the warm sun. She explained that the flower arrangements are more than just beautiful to look at, but also represent beauty in life, beauty in reconciliation, and beauty in growth together.

Also in the flower arrangement were five pairs of tall candles. Some of the participants at this *soukhouan* explained that the candles represented "respect, wisdom, knowledge, and enlightenment"; "new ideas"; and "light to show us the way"; or "the beautifulness of the bouquet." The meanings attached to these candles are important in the overall ceremony as the purpose is to bring respect, wisdom, and new ideas that help create a more beautiful relationship between the parties and the families involved. The candles are a symbol of a positive future and new possibilities.

Preparation for the floral arrangement can take up to three days, depending on how elaborate it is. As a guest in the host's home, I was able to directly observe and participate in the preparation for the *soukhouan*. It was wonderful to watch as the women, usually older (although younger women can assist), sat on the floor chatting, telling stories, and laughing about various things in their lives. One older woman had traveled from her small village in order to attend this special celebration. Although some had not seen each other in a long time, their conversations revealed the closeness they still felt with one another. The older women chewed on betel leaves and betel nuts while working on the floral arrangement. The laughter, reminiscing, and renewing of old friendships was occasionally interrupted by the harsh sounds of the blood-red betel nut juice being spat into little buckets, just like chewing tobacco. (It is believed that these leaves and nuts have medicinal properties such as curing bad breath, relieving pain, as an aphrodisiac, and as a mild stimulant.)

Early in the morning on the day of the *soukhouan*, family and friends were preparing for the event. Older children helped clean and tidy up the house, wash dishes, and prepare the meal. The meal was to consist of a common dish called *kao poon*, a noodle dish served with fresh vegetables and herbs in a spicy, red curry and coconut chicken broth. The chicken for the broth was freshly prepared early that morning so the large cauldron of soup could cook all day. The fresh fragrance of the lemongrass, mint, coconut milk, and red curry permeated the air of the streets around the house. The noodles were freshly made for the day of the event. A lot of talking, laughing, and joking took place as the food was being prepared. Just before the *soukhouan*, bowls of fruit, sweets, and eggs were placed around the flower arrangement on the serving table (*pa khouan*).

At this *soukhouan*, people were well dressed. The women wore traditional Lao silk skirts (*sin*) and scarves (*pa biang*), and the men wore Lao scarves over the left shoulder. The degree of formality of the dress code depends on the purpose of the celebration. A *soukhouan* as part of a marriage ceremony is the most formal of occasions and tends to be the most elaborate in terms of dress, food, and celebration. The attire for a welcoming *soukhouan* depends on who the guests of honor are. Celebrations involving whole communities tend to be more formal, whereas those intended only for family and close friends tend to be more informal.

Once people had arrived at the *soukhouan* in the late afternoon, the honoured guests were seated around the main table with the *pa khouan* on the floor mat in the living room area. A senior monk in attendance gave a prayer and blessing for the honoured guests and ceremony. Our monk for the evening was particularly eloquent, and his prayerful chant went on for at least twenty minutes. During this time, the people in attendance held up their hands, palms together in front of their chests, in a prayer. At the end of the prayer, I turned to some elders in the room to ask what the monk was saying, and they responded, "We don't know exactly. It's an ancient Buddhist chant from the Pali script, from a long time ago. Even the monks don't know what they're chanting. It's just part of our tradition." With a little research, I found out that these prayer recitations are part of paying respect to the Buddha, his *dhamma* (truth) and his *sangha* (clergy), and vowing to abide by the five precepts (teachings) (Stuart-Fox & Mixay, 2010). The monks were praying for tolerance and acceptance of others according to Buddhist teachings. At the same time, they were blessing the house, people, and the community where the *soukhouan* took place.

Once the monk's prayers were done, the elders were given an opportunity to offer further blessings for the event while the honoured guests and those around them placed one hand on the bamboo table holding the flower arrangement and the other hand raised with the palm open by the side of their heads. Those who were not close enough to the table held onto the arm or elbow of those in front of them, representing a connection between all present at the ceremony. This was explained to me as a way of strengthening the blessings by supporting them with the power of the community.

Once the blessings were complete, each person took two pieces of thread (*fei pouk khene*) from the flower arrangement and tied one on each wrist of the honored guests. During this process, the honoured guests kept one palm face up while having the thread tied and put the other hand up in a prayer-like gesture while receiving blessings and well wishes. The wishes could be things like, "Oh, sister, I wish you health and happiness. May you bring your family joy and make them proud. May you succeed in life. May you have many, wonderful children." (My husband once had a woman say to him, "May you have many wives.") Due to their many years of experience, the elders in attendance were usually able to recite their blessings like a musical chant. While this was taking place, others continued to hold onto the arm or elbow of the person being blessed. This is seen as creating a spiritual force that reinforces the wishes of the person tying the thread (Stuart-Fox & Mixay, 2010).

Once the blessing was finished, the blesser placed a few food items from the table into the hands of the blessed. It is customary to eat some of the food to show respect and acceptance. As this part of the ceremony continued, the people gradually broke into smaller groups, tying the sacred threads around the wrists of those around them, giving blessings and receiving well wishes. The honoured guests had the most threads tied to their wrists, but everyone present had the opportunity to get their wrists tied and to receive good wishes and blessings.

At the end of the *soukhouan* ceremony, everyone was invited to partake in the meal prepared and visit with each other. Again, the honoured guests were served first, but there was (as always) an abundant amount of food for everyone. In this *soukhouan*, several people who just happened to be walking by in the neighbour-hood were immediately invited to join in the welcoming festivity. The atmosphere was one of celebration where families, friends, and the community came together to celebrate an important event.

Religion and symbolism in the soukhouan *ceremony*

Although Theravada Buddhism is the dominant religion in Laos, there is also an intermingling of animist beliefs within the Lao people's spiritual system, especially among minority ethnic groups. Even the Buddhist clergy (*sangha*) have incorporated a belief in animist spirits (*phi*) into their religious teachings and duties. For example, some monks are respected for having the ability to exorcise malevolent spirits from the sick or to keep them out of a house. As part of appeasing any stray spirits that might disturb the proceedings in a *soukhouan*, a monk will perform Buddhist meditation chants (*soot mon*) and bless the home (*soot hern*) where the event is taking place. Most Lao people believe there are supernatural forces such as house, ancestor, and forest spirits.

This belief originates in the animist view of spirituality that is still very influential in Lao religious life. As described by a Khammu man, "According to Khammu traditions, we celebrate various festivals throughout the year – *Boon Ka Ler* (fifth month) and *Boon Dern Jim* (first month). We are now Buddhists, but we still believe in spirits." The *soukhouan* is steeped in this blend of Buddhist and animist traditions that is so prevalent in Lao culture.

A number of articles are required to conduct the *soukhouan* ceremony. These are symbolic gifts that are given as part of the Buddhist tradition of earning merit, as well as the animist belief of returning any stray *khouan* to one's soul (see Table 4.1). *Khouan* can be thought of as the unique components that are part of one's soul or morale. Occasionally, *khouan* are believed to wander, and a *soukhouan* is performed to bring them back together. The name *soukhouan* literally means "the meeting or coming together of *khouan*."

Following Buddhist tradition, many of the items necessary for the *soukhouan* ritual must come in sets of five (*kun ha*) (five pairs of candles, five pairs of flowers, and so forth). The central floral arrangement (*makbeng*) also contains five arms holding the cotton threads. A village leader explained the significance of the number five as being related to the Buddhist *dhamma*, or truths, which teach five precepts (*sin ha*) for people to follow. First, do not kill (*sin pa na*), but love and respect all life. Second, do not steal (*sin bor luck/sin a tit na*), but take care of all things. Third, do not lie (*sin moo cha*), but talk to one another to ensure there is no misunderstanding. Fourth, do not have affairs or behave in sexually inappropriate

Table 4.1 Soukhouan articles and their significance

Item	Significance
Large flower arrangement (*makbeng*)	Represents gifts for the *khouans*; represents beauty; represents Buddhism
Small floral bouquets with money tucked within (*dok mai took tien*)	Flowers represent the highest level of respect; represent Buddhism; *soukhouans* have flowers; represent love and beauty
Money (*gern*)	Money represents *boon koon* or gratefulness; giving back; obtaining merit
Thread (*fei mut khene*)	Represents restoration of *khouan*; connection; strength in spirit
Incense and candles (*tien*)	Represents respect; wisdom; symbolic for knowledge and enlightenment; represents light and new ideas; represents light to show the way
Clothing gifts, shirts, traditional Lao skirt (*sin*) or scarf (*pa biang*)	Represents *boon koon* or gratefulness; giving back; obtaining merit *Note*: Shirts and scarves should be white to present purity, wholesomeness, and clarity
Chicken (*gai*), pig (*moo*), cow (*ngoor*), or buffalo (*kwai*)	Is dependent on culture; size of the *soukhouan*; seriousness of the conflict; compensation
Food (*pa kao samakee*)	Represents new beginning; all is well; commitment and care for well-being; offering of sustenance

ways (*sin ga may*), but respect oneself and others. Fifth, do not use drugs or intoxicants (*sin su la*), but keep a clear mind and healthy body.

The Ethnic Lao people describe the importance of showing *boon koon* to parents, elders, and monks for their assistance in teaching people about proper conduct and taking care of the family. The term *boon koon* means to show respect and gratitude. By showing *boon koon* a person acquires merit – the Buddhist means of advancing one's status in the afterlife or future reincarnation. This merit making can be achieved through various generous acts to others, good conduct, showing respect to elders, and giving to monks.

The concept of *boon koon* is clearly illustrated in what an older Ethnic Lao woman with adult children told me:

> In Lao traditional past, I used to hear that if you have long hair and cut it off to sell in order to obtain some money to buy clothing for your mother, then you will reduce *bap* (sin) and *vein* (bad luck) . . . they've [parents] looked after us and sacrificed much . . . and if we give a *sin* (Lao skirt) to our mothers, then it represents *boon koon* (respect or gratitude).

The daughter's act of giving up her own hair in order to purchase her mother a Lao skirt demonstrates love and respect for her mother, recognizes the sacrifices that her mother has made on her behalf, and is a generous act that is deserving of merit. That mixture of respect, gratitude, and merit is what defines *boon koon*.

Boon is also a word the Lao people use in referring to festivals. Opportunities for gift giving, generous acts, and showing respect and gratitude are part of many Lao festivals and celebrations, including the *soukhouan*. During the *soukhouan*, the money placed in the flower arrangements and the gifts that are distributed between guests are part of *boon koon*. Like the word *boon*, the *soukhouan* can be both part of a festive celebration and a means for gaining merit.

According to animist tradition, the tying of sacred threads around a person's wrists symbolizes the reuniting of the thirty-two components of an individual's spirit essence (*khouan*) into the body (Leibo, 2003; Savada, 1995; Stuart-Fox, 1997). It is believed that the "absence of any *khouan* weakens the vital spiritual force of a person, who may as a result become indecisive, depressed, or ill. The *soukhouan* therefore restores a person's spiritual force and enables them to face life reinvigorated" (Stuart-Fox & Mixay, 2010, p. 19). These cotton threads are to be worn for at least three days before they are removed by untying them. It is important to untie the threads and not cut them off, as the act of cutting would disperse the spirits again.

The metaphor of tying of threads to reunite *khouan* is a very important aspect of the *soukhouan* ritual. In doing this, people are essentially restoring souls to individuals, thereby giving them strength to reconnect with their communities and bringing people back to healthy relationships. Many Lao believe that when conflicts and fights occur, it is because the spirits are wandering and unhappy (*phi khouan keert*), disrupting people's lives. The cotton threads (*fei pouk khene*) on the floral arrangement (*makbeng*) contain a knot in the middle to represent the containment of blessings. When people tie double knots in the thread (*yun*) around the wrists, it symbolizes strength, unity, and support, both in restoring *khouan* and in maintaining positive relationships. Tying the threads restores harmony in the body, spirit, and social relationships, and this theme of restoration is what gives the *soukhouan* its relevance in conflict resolution.

The soukhouan *ceremony in conflict resolution*

The purpose of this ritual in conflict resolution is to repair any harm that has been done, rebuild relationships, and create healing in the communities. This corresponds to the restorative justice paradigm that emphasizes the importance of relationship and restitution in repairing, restoring, and nurturing such connections. Domestic violence, physical fights causing injury, car accidents involving injury and death, and dogs attacking people are examples of conflicts that require the wrongdoer to conduct a *soukhouan*. It is hoped that this will help reduce the anger of the victims and encourage them to remain calm.

The size of the *soukhouan* reflects the gravity of the conflict situation. Family conflicts that require a *soukhouan* normally involve just the family members and close friends. This is consistent with the values of avoidance and maintaining privacy when in conflict. But sometimes it is important to increase the size of the *soukhouan* to involve the whole community, especially when a larger support network is required to provide restitution, maintain relationships, and establish reconciliation.

Situations involving fights, physical injuries, and deaths require a *soukhouan* in order to provide compensation, repair damage, and prevent further escalation of conflict. A *soukhouan* helps to address violent situations when the perpetrator, with support from his or her family, must apologize and ask forgiveness of the victim and his or her family. In doing so, the perpetrator promises in front of both families not to commit such violent acts again. Because the perpetrator apologizes, takes responsibility for his actions, and makes restitution to the injured party, a *soukhouan* helps to reduce anger and revenge. As noted by Just (1998), "praise is far more meaningful and useful when it contributes to a person's public moral standing" (p. 115). It is a way of asking those who have been wronged for forgiveness, and a way of restoring the spirits of those in conflict by moving them towards restoring healthy relationships.

The *soumma* ceremony

The *soumma* ceremony is another important celebration marking the end of conflict. It represents an intimate acknowledgment of conflict and reconciliation, and is usually held in a small, private setting within families. *Soummas* reflect the Lao culture and tradition that show respect for parents and elders in a way that allows reconciliation to take place. This honoured tradition is instrumental in maintaining good relationships in a family, especially after a conflict where parents and relatives have assisted in a mediation process.

A family is an important system in human life. It provides existential purpose in our lives, interconnectedness and support, behavioural boundaries and rules in relationships, self-motivating mechanisms to maintain and repair itself in different situations, information processing between members, and collective force and synergy that are greater than the sum of its parts (Miller, Wackman, Nunnally, & Miller, 1992). Healthy families require a balance in adaptability and cohesion. When in conflict, the family becomes unbalanced and needs to find ways to become productive again. Through the assistance of other family members who can play the role of mediators, the family can resolve their conflict and become a collective force in supporting one another. The *soumma* is an important conflict resolution mechanism that exists to maintain and repair family relationships.

I have had a number of opportunities to observe and participate in *soummas* during my time in Laos. One particular *soumma* illustrates the significance of this ceremony in bridging relationships and positively impacting the lives of all those affected. The conflict involved a mother and daughter in a painful relationship where there was deep hurt, anger, bitterness, and resentment from both parties. This estrangement lasted over a forty-year span, through various wars in Laos, the deaths of family members, and numerous other life situations. When the daughter was still just a little girl, her father, a village leader, was tragically killed. The mother was left with nine children to raise on her own. The mother had a sister and brother-in-law who were unable to have children. The sister begged to raise this daughter as her own and, eventually, the mother agreed. The daughter's new parents were poor farmers. When they went to work on the farm, the daughter would spend the day with her biological mother and siblings. However, at the end of the day, the daughter would always have to leave and return to the farm where she now lived. As the daughter grew up, she began to question this and developed feelings of animosity and anger towards her biological mother. The daughter could share the companionship of her siblings and friends during the day, but always felt the stress of knowing she could not stay with them and would have to return to the loneliness of the farm.

The bitterness grew as the daughter came to believe that her biological mother had enough financial means and support to care for all her children. Although the daughter kept in touch with her biological mother throughout her adult life, their relationship was never close and was often strained. They had talked over the years about the situation, and the daughter eventually understood and forgave her mother. However, closure remained elusive for them as they struggled to regain some form of closeness and normalcy that would define a typical mother–daughter relationship. Finally, after forty years the daughter decided to perform a *soumma* for her mother in order to fully address the situation and help restore the relationship.

With the assistance of her older sister, the daughter prepared floral bouquets (*dok mai took tien*) to present to her mother, along with candles and gifts. The daughter and her own children went to visit the mother and presented this peace offering. The mother sat in a chair and the daughter and grandchildren sat on the floor, talking about the conflict situation and how important it was to bring some sort of closure and move forward after so many years of tension. The bouquets were offered to the mother, and a mini *soukhouan* was performed, where threads were tied on all participants' wrists and blessings were given. The mother gave blessings to the whole family, and all the participants offered each other wishes for health, happiness, and success. After the hugs and well wishes, the family shared a meal together and visited throughout the evening and into the night, even after the electric generators were turned off. They talked, told stories, and laughed as the candles burned in the background.

The *soumma* allowed each person to discuss her or his thoughts and feelings about the situation and relationship and see the situation from the other person's perspective. In a process akin to North's (1998) reframing, the daughter used the *soumma* to show her mother that she understood the context in which the conflict situation originated and could now more fully appreciate the circumstances that contributed to her decisions. By looking at her mother's actions in context, she was able to empathize and view the situation in a way that made the actions more understandable.

Furthermore, the respect and status associated with age in Lao culture can sometimes be prohibitive to parents and elders in admitting wrong and apologizing. In this case, the daughter provided a culturally appropriate avenue for reconciliation. The painful experiences were acknowledged, both parties took responsibility for their part in the conflict, and apologies were given. The mother and daughter were able to accept the sincere apologies and forgive one another. The *soumma* finally brought closure to the family after so many years of unspoken tensions.

The *soumma* ritual symbolizes more than just forgiveness – it is a complete commitment to reconciliation and represents the act of involving one's whole spirit, body, and mind in establishing a healthy relationship. It is important for families to invent "mechanisms of forgiveness" because "love is an act of endless forgiveness" (Ustivov as cited in Phipher, 1997, p. 140). In addition to offering forgiveness, these ceremonies are akin to taking a solemn oath to personally work towards reconciliation. Stories, history, and traditions are important in promoting in-group identities (Senehi, 2000), and this was evident in the *soumma* event that reconciled the mother and daughter.

Religion and symbolism in the soumma *ceremony*

In performing these rituals, the Lao people are well aware of the significance behind these ceremonies and their impact on them as individuals and as a collective. The religious teachings connected to the ceremonies remind people to love, apologize, and be more patient. These rituals have symbolic importance for interpersonal interactions, helping people to commit to and re-establish healthy relationships.

The ceremonial symbols of the *soumma* are essentially the same as those of the *soukhouan*, except that they are somewhat smaller in scale. For example, a *soumma* does not necessarily require the use of monks and elders to lead in prayers, there is no large floral arrangement (*makbeng*), there is less food to prepare, and there is less compensation to be made. The difference between these two events is akin to that between a full-scale symphony and a string quartet. One is more elaborate, complex, and ornate, and the other is about closeness and intimacy.

In addition to marking forgiveness and reconciliation, *soummas* may be conducted to honour parents, grandparents, elders, and senior monks in the community. The children, young people, and families perform these ceremonies to show respect for these people. Typically, younger children will conduct *soummas* for their parents, older siblings, and elders. I have heard the *soumma* described as a "festival to show respect and to give thanks to our parents" (*boon tan koon paw mer*). The term *boon koon* is used to describe this act of showing love, respect, and thankfulness to the elder generation.

Traditionally, a person conducts a *soumma* at least once a year, during the Lao New Year (*Pi Mai*). The significance of holding a *soumma* during the New Year celebration allows people to ask forgiveness for all the wrong that they have done during the year and to begin the new year with a fresh start. However, the *soumma* can be conducted at any time, just like other informal rituals that deliberately encourage opportunities to share, communicate, and connect with each other to increase awareness of gaps in our assumptions and to fill them with facts, context, and history (Kolb & Putnam, 1997).

According to the Lao people, *soummas* are conducted to obtain blessings, show respect for elders, restore face after conflict, apologize and ask for forgiveness, and honour parents and elders for their love and care. The ritual is part of recommitting to healthy relationships, contributing to the well-being of everyone. When children ask their parents for forgiveness, offering them flowers, candles, and other gifts, the parents accept the apology and in return give them blessings. Through both words and actions, the family members show their readiness to leave past hurts behind and to focus on the present and future with a clear conscience.

In performing a *soumma*, the younger generation is apologizing for wrongs they have done that have affected their parents and elders. They are honouring their parents for the sacrifices that they have made in caring and providing for them. Apart from New Year's celebrations, the *soumma* ritual is performed when people need to ask for forgiveness from their family in order to restore relationships. The *soumma* is especially relevant as reparation for embarrassment, to "repair their face and eyes" (*bpeng na bpeng tda*) or to "bring back their face and eyes" (*ow na tda kern*). This reference to restoring "face and eyes" during a *soumma* is a common theme identified by Lao people. Conflicts create embarrassment for parents and elders that must be remedied by a *soumma*. The ritual helps to restore not only the face and eyes of parents, but also the community's perception of the parents as good role models for their children. Such metaphors and references to repairing the face and eyes are of utmost importance in the Lao community.

Since the *soumma* ritual is a private ceremony and normally only involves the family that has been affected by conflict, it allows the family to address the conflict internally and to maintain face in the situation. The ceremony still includes support from the rest of the family for the parties involved in the conflict. The *soumma* provides an opportunity for the family to become closer by restoring harmonic relationships.

The Lao *soukhouan* and *soumma* exemplify Schirch's (2005) definition of ritual as symbolic acts that take place in unique spaces that form and transform people's worldviews, identities, and relationships. The symbolic sacred threads, bouquets of flowers, centerpiece floral arrangements, food, and various other items reflect people's values and beliefs in conflict resolution traditions. The ritual process transforms relationships from brokenness to wholeness. After a *soukhouan* or *soumma*, the parties in conflict, families, and communities are reunited in spirit, mind, and action. Supporting the principles of restorative justice (see Umbreit, 2001; Zehr, 1990, 2001), these ceremonies allow for (1) acknowledgment of the wrong-doing, (2) accepting responsibility for one's actions, (3) restitution according to cultural customs, (4) reparation of the harm done, (5) acceptance of apology and reparation, and (6) support and accountability in repairing the relationship. Emotions such as anger, hurt, and pain have been lifted and are replaced by forgiveness, acceptance, and healing. Celebrations of reconciliation between former disputants are happy occasions shared by the whole community. Giddens (1991) states that

> [w]ithout ordered ritual and collective involvement, individuals are left without structured ways of coping with tensions and anxieties . . . Communal rites provide a focus for group solidarity at major transitions . . . connected individual action to moral frameworks and to elemental questions about human existence. The loss of ritual is also the loss of such frameworks.
>
> (as cited in Irani & Funk, 2000, p. 18)

The *soukhouan* and *soumma* ceremonies are part of the maintenance, reparation, and restoration of relationships that contribute to overall social harmony in the community.

Ceremonial connections to the heart (*chai*)

Thich Nhat Hanh, a renowned Buddhist monk, once stated, "Forgiveness will not be possible . . . until compassion is born in your heart. Even if you want to forgive, you cannot forgive" (as cited in Briggs, 2008, p. 25). This metaphoric connection to the heart comes up frequently in conversations about the *soukhouan* and *soumma* ceremonies. A woman once explained,

> "There are many methods for doing a *soumma* . . . in terms of what to wear, other decorations, and items such as gold and money. Some materials don't cost anything, but it's okay because it comes from the heart for the older people."

The reparation can be creative and does not necessarily cost a lot of money or material expenses. Giving gifts from one's heart is the most important requirement of *soummas* and *soukhouans*.

A successful *soukhouan* or *soumma* should meet the needs of the heart, or *por chai*. The expression *Koi dee chai lai* (My heart feels very good, or I am very happy) is used to describe a successful resolution to conflict and the participants' contentment with *soukhouan* and *soumma* rituals. Conflict resolution and rituals that satisfy the heart are essential for the transformation of conflict and the establishment of reconciliation between the parties, families, and communities.

The analogy of effective resolutions as coming from one's heart is reflective of Lao culture and language. The term *hua chai* (head of the heart) refers to the heart, the mind, or the spirit. When there is a conflict, people are described as having *chai hi* (a strong heart or fighting heart, in the sense of being angry or mad) and *hawn chai* (a hot heart, in the sense of having a hot temper). These expressions of anger and bad temperament are associated with conflicts and the parties' inability to resolve them constructively. These are negative traits that are not valued in Lao culture. Third-party mediators are respected for their *chai yen* (a cool heart, in the sense of having a calm temper), an important characteristic that enables mediators to calmly assist others in the resolution of conflict. Being calm, clear headed, and patient are attributes of a respected mediator. As an elder woman once said to me, "We always go see my eldest brother when we have a conflict because he is good at listening and not making judgments. And he is good at giving advice and keeping the situation confidential."

When people are making decisions about important conflicts, they are said to *tdat sin chai* (make a decision according to the heart). Again, this expression stresses the significance of a resolution that meets "the hearts" of those affected by the conflict. The process of decision making is taken seriously, with deep contemplation and insight. The satisfaction in a given resolution is described as *por chai* (the heart is satisfied, or enough), *dee chai* (a good heart, or happy), or *kow chai gun* (understand our hearts, or understand each other). An effective resolution must meet the needs of the heart, mind, and spirit. This holistic approach to creating a resolution makes the conflict resolution agreement more gratifying and durable. It also allows for the rebuilding of relationships, as the resolution is heart-felt and sincere. All these components of decision making make it possible to move towards full reconciliation.

Rituals and the Conflict Resolution Spectrum

As already discussed, the most common responses to conflict situations in Laos are avoidance and *op-lom*. These two approaches allow the parties to either ignore the conflict or to have private discussions among themselves. Obviously, the level of privacy decreases as third parties become involved and make their way through the Conflict Resolution Spectrum. Larger, more complex, and stubborn conflicts that require the *Neoy Gai Geer* for resolution are already public conflicts. At this point, a great deal of face has been lost with the decrease in privacy, but at the same time, a great many people are involved in helping to restore that face. In these circumstances, the entire village may become involved in the celebration of the resolution of the conflict.

The *soukhouan* and *soumma* ceremonies are mechanisms for restoring face, relationships, and social harmony after a conflict. The choice of which ceremony to use, as well as the size of these ceremonies, is contingent on the size of the conflict and the number of people who have become involved in its resolution. In this way, the level of privacy in conflict resolution rituals corresponds to the progressive nature of the Conflict Resolution Spectrum. The more people involved in the conflict, the larger the ceremony becomes. The more public celebrations are those that involve larger conflicts, such as conflicts between ethnic groups and conflicts causing injury and death. In this sense, conflict resolution, as demonstrated by the use of mediation and rituals, is owned by the grassroots, specifically those people who are directly affected by the conflict.

Once, while riding in a *tuk-tuk* (a *tuk-tuk* is a truck with bench seats in the box, operating as a taxi), the driver told me, "Suppose a husband and wife make their parents sad, then we have to do a *soumma* for them with candles, flowers, towels for them, and so forth." The use of a *soumma* in conflict resolution is almost always reserved for parents and family. A *soukhouan*, on the other hand, can include extended family members and the larger community. A conflict that is more public and involves more people was described in a conversation with an elder *nei ban*: "If you hit someone with a motorcycle and that person is hurt, then you must do a *soukhouan* according to the injured's traditions." In this case, more people are affected by the conflict, including anyone who is affected by the injured person's recovery, whether in having to provide care for that person or to accommodate any responsibilities that the person is no longer able to perform. The *soukhouan* ritual would include all of those people, including extended family members and possibly other community members.

The motorcycle accident scenario is a reminder of the large scope of the Lao word for conflict: *bunha*. Here, the injured person may no longer be able to maintain his or her status, position, and responsibilities in the community, and conducting a *soukhouan* is thought to give the individual renewed strength with which to face new challenges. The described scenario gives further evidence that regardless of who is at fault in the accident, both parties are in *bunha*. The driver is involved in an injurious accident and has lost face, whether he or she is at fault or not. Therefore, both parties need help from others to regain face.

By conducting a *soukhouan*, the motorcycle driver is not necessarily admitting guilt and trying to make amends for the conflict, but is rather demonstrating *boon koon* and good will for the injured person. This is also evident in the example of the *soumma* described earlier, involving the estranged mother and daughter. The daughter was not admitting responsibility for the dispute, but was giving *boon koon*, saying that fault or guilt was not important. Rather, she was committed to reframing the conflict, providing an avenue for apologies and forgiveness, and reconciling the relationship.

In this way, conducting a *soukhouan* or a *soumma* can be described as drawing attention to oneself. The host is publically either admitting wrong and trying to make amends for the conflict, or demonstrating *boon koon* by sending good wishes and good will, thereby demonstrating that he or she is a good person. In this sense, both parties are in a "win-win" scenario. This is acted out in front of the people involved in a particular conflict situation and serves as affirmation of the action taken. The act of giving flowers, money, clothes, and food in a *soukhouan* represents *boon koon*. It is an act of validation and empowerment for both the giver and receiver, recognizing that they have something valuable to offer each other (Hardy & Laszloffy, 2005).

Relationship in conflict resolution

The previous discussion of rituals confirms an important theme in Lao conflict resolution – that of relationship. The use of *op-lom*, parents, other mediation facilitators, and the *soukhouan* and *soumma* as tools in building relationships all point to the high value given to healthy relationships, be they in the family or with other community members.

Expanding one's social network is obviously an important cultural value that helps to establish diverse support systems in times of conflict, economic adversity, and other events where friends can make a big difference in one's ability to survive and succeed. The weight of this reality is not lost on the young in Laos. As beautifully stated by a young student, "Focus on being a good person, don't fall in the river or set fires. Goodness not many people see, but when you do bad things, many people can see." Being friendly is more than just a personality trait – it is important to one's survival and requires constant effort.

The importance of maintaining friendship, specifically in seeking forgiveness when problems arise, is especially important. Archbishop Desmond Tutu defines forgiveness as

> taking seriously the awfulness of what has happened when you are treated unfairly. It is opening the door for the other person to have a chance to begin

again. Without forgiveness, resentment builds in us, a resentment which turns into hostility and anger. Hatred eats away at our well being . . . *Ubuntu* (African word) speaks about the essence of being human: that my humanity is caught up in your humanity because we say a person is a person through other persons.

(Enright & North, 1998, p. foreword)

The *soukhouan* and *soumma* ceremonies are rooted in Lao spiritual symbolism and significance, offering ways for people to reconcile relationships through the restoration of *khouan* and *boon koon*. The public or semi-public nature of the *soukhouan* and *soumma* rituals is part of the restoration process. As described, the act of holding onto others' arms or elbows creates community connectedness and energy, helping to empower the blessings and give strength to the receiver of these blessings. Through the strength of friendship and community, these rituals heal, restore, and give strength for forgiveness and reconciliation, demonstrating that "a person is a person through other persons." These rituals are part of the community act of building relationships and helping disputants move towards forgiveness and reconciliation.

The statement "Goodness not many people see, but when you do bad things many people see" is a comment on the importance of one's own personal etiquette in maintaining relationships. In order to maintain diverse social friendships, it is necessary to nurture relationships by giving them one's personal attention. In accepting that diverse support networks are a means to survive and succeed in life, there is a real sense that "bad things many people see" indicates a cultural pressure to be good neighbours, thereby maintaining friendships and support networks. The cultural willingness to resolve conflict is closely tied to not wanting to be seen in a bad light by people.

This is why the resolution of conflict in Laos focuses on healing and restoring relationships between people involved in conflict. It goes beyond repairing the harm between parties to addressing the concerns of their families and communities. Focusing on whole communities allows for the possibility of larger reconciliation. The *soukhouan* and *soumma* rituals help bring people together to acknowledge what has happened, to forgive, and to move forward in their relationship.

The *soukhouan* and *soumma* are processes of conflict transformation – ways of moving beyond resolution of conflict to building healthy relationships and communities (Lederach, 2003). Personal relationships are at the heart of these Lao rituals. The repairing and rebuilding of relationships between disputants and their families prepares the path for reconciliation in the community. Reconciliation involves (1) focusing on relationships as components in any system, (2) providing an encounter between conflicting parties to allow acknowledgment of experiences and emotions and to enhance interdependence, and (3) looking outside mainstream conflict resolution traditions for innovative approaches (Lederach, 1997). The *soukhouan* and *soumma* ceremonies are creative approaches to reconciliation that focus on relationships and provide a space for interaction between the parties. Reconciliation promotes an encounter between people, provides a place for truth and mercy to meet in order to renew relationships, and recognizes that justice and peace require time and place to envision an interdependent future (Lederach, 1997).

Conclusion

The *soukhouan* and *soumma* ceremonies allow for new relationships to be developed based on a new understanding of the conflict and the parties in conflict. The *soukhouan* specifically acknowledges the wrong done and the willingness to make things right again through restitution and reparation, according to the different cultural requirements of the ethnic groups. The more intimate *soumma* ritual explicitly allows for forgiveness that often leads to reconciliation between the parties. Both of these cultural activities provide an opportunity to "restore the face and eyes" of people, their families, and communities in conflict.

It is important to study traditional and religious practices of dispute resolution in order to fully understand the roles that grassroots conflict resolution structures play in communities. Traditional conflict resolution processes and rituals have been observed for centuries and teach people valuable skills and knowledge for effective conflict resolution and transformation. The Lao rituals are performed with the assistance and guidance of families and other support networks, who are responsible for enabling and ensuring parties meet resolution agreements. As rituals and ceremonies that celebrate the end of conflict, the *soukhouan* and *soumma* provide insights into practical relationship-building activities that are culturally sensitive.

Bibliography

Briggs, Kenneth. (2008). *The Power of Forgiveness*. Minneapolis: Fortress Press.

Enright, Robert D., & North, Joanna (eds.). (1998). *Exploring Forgiveness*. Wisconsin: University of Wisconsin Press.

Evans, Grant. (1999). *Laos: Culture and Society*. Chiangmai: Silkworm Books.

Giddens, Anthony. (1991). *Modernity and Self-Identity: Self and Society in the Modern Age*. Stanford: Stanford University Press.

Hardy, Kenneth V., & Laszloffy, Tracey A. (2005). *Teens Who Hurt: Clinical Interventions to Break the Cycle of Adolescent Violence*. New York: The Guilford Press.

Irani, George E., & Funk, Nathan C. (2000). Rituals of Reconciliation: Arab-Islamic Perspectives. *Kroc Institute Occasional Paper*, 19(2), 1–34.

Just, Peter. (1998). Conflict Resolution and Moral Community Among the Don Donggo. In Kevin Avruch, Peter W. Black, & Joseph A. Scimecca (eds.), *Conflict Resolution: Cross-Cultural Perspectives* (pp. 107–144). Westport: Praeger.

Kolb, Deborah M., & Putnam, Linda L. (1997). Through the Looking Glass: Negotiation Theory Refracted Through the Lens of Gender. In Sandra E. Gleason (ed.), *Workplace Dispute Resolution: Directions for the 21st Century* (pp. 231–258). East Lansing: Michigan State University Press.

Lederach, John Paul. (1997). *Building Peace: Sustainable Reconciliation in Divided Societies*. Washington, DC: United States Institute of Peace Press.

Lederach, John Paul. (2003). *The Little Book of Conflict Transformation*. Intercourse: Good Books.

Leibo, Steven A. (2003). *East, Southeast Asia, and the Western Pacific 2003*. Harpers Ferry: Stryker-Post Publications.

Miller, Sherod, Wackman, Daniel, Nunnally, Elam, & Miller, Phyllis. (1992). *Connecting: With Self and Others*. Littleton: Interpersonal Communication Programs, Inc.

North, Joanna. (1998). The "Ideal" of Forgiveness: A Philosopher's Exploration. In Robert D. Enright & Joanna North (eds.), *Exploring Forgiveness* (pp. 15–34). Wisconsin: University of Wisconsin Press.

Phipher, Mary. (1997). *The Shelter of Each Other: Rebuilding Our Families*. New York: Ballantine Books.

Savada, Andrea Matles. (1995). *Laos: A Country Study*. Washington, DC: Federal Research Division, Library of Congress.

Schirch, Lisa. (2005). *Ritual and Symbol in Peacebuilding*. Bloomfield: Kumarian Press, Inc.

Senehi, Jessica. (2000). Constructive Storytelling in Intercommunal Conflicts: Building Community, Building Peace. In Sean Byrne & Cynthia L. Irvin (eds.), *Reconcilable Differences: Turning Points in Ethnopolitical Conflict* (pp. 96–114). West Hartford: Kumarian Press.

Stuart-Fox, Martin. (1997). *A History of Laos*. Cambridge: Cambridge University Press.

Stuart-Fox, Martin, & Mixay, Somsanouk. (2010). *Festivals of Laos*. Chiang Mai: Silkworm Books.

Umbreit, Mark. (2001). *The Handbook of Victim Offender Mediation: An Essential Guide to Practice and Research*. San Francisco: Jossey-Bass.

Zehr, Howard. (1990). *Changing Lenses*. Scottdale: Herald Press.

Zehr, Howard. (2001). Restorative Justice. In Luc Reychler & Thania Paffenholz (eds.), *Peacebuilding: A Field Guide* (pp. 330–335). Boulder: Lynne Rienner Publishers.

5   Cross-cultural conflict: from micro to macro

> Laos is a land of festivals. Every village, every temple, and every ethnic minority not only holds its own special festivals but also joins the wider Lao community in celebrating the national ones as well.
>
> (Stuart-Fox & Mixay, 2010, p. 1)

Any discussion of cross-cultural conflict resolution is bound to be fraught with problems, the most basic of which is "what is a culture?" It is necessary to devote some time to the topic of culture, as it is a complex concept with multiple definitions and approaches to research. For the purposes of understanding the different groups in Laos more completely, the following section discusses the basic characteristics of culture and how it is formed.

In identifying the basic characteristics of a culture, care must be taken to avoid oversimplification that might lead to inaccurate generalizations of different groups. My biggest issue in discussions about culture is that we often use culture as a stereotyping reference to groups of individuals who hold commonalities in their particular worldview, including language, food preferences, and sometimes even skin colour. Although stereotypes may be useful in some circumstances, as a tool for looking at a group of people, they rarely produce significant truths, but are instead based on the eccentricities of a few identifiable individuals. We must safeguard against making incorrect assumptions about individuals or groups based on generalizations. It is important to keep this in mind as we develop further discussions on culture.

Culture "is one of the two or three most complicated words in the English language" (Williams, 1983, as cited in Avruch, 2003, p. 140). The problem is multifold, partly because culture has several very distinct meanings (for example, as somebody who is cultured, or as somebody who belongs to a culture, or even a bacterial culture as a biological product). As an overriding concept linking individuals and groups of people, Avruch (1998) defines culture as multi-faceted, dynamic, and continuously evolving. Individuals are not from a monoculture, but possess a number of cultures, depending on their experiences within social institutions and structures. Because people possess multiple cultures, it is important to acknowledge that each person's identity is shaped by a culture composed of shared experiences and expectations while at the same time retaining their own unique qualities (Singelis & Pedersen, 1994). This definition highlights the concept that culture is the continuously evolving derivative of individual experience that gives a collective group a shared mechanism for interpreting information and obtaining meaning from the world around them.

Discussions of culture tend to break the large and complicated topic into smaller, more manageable variables (e.g., culture and communication, culture and conflict, culture and facework, or culture and knowledge). What is important here is recognizing the profound influence that culture has on many aspects of our lives, including communication, education, conflict resolution, gender relationships, and human rights. Therefore, culture is composed of different variables that can each be dissected and analyzed as interrelated parts. The sum of these individual parts makes up a larger cultural identity, yet the larger cultural identity continues to dynamically influence those individual components.

Even though we recognize that culture is dynamic and flowing, with a life of its own, we are often presented with a picture of a culture that incorrectly assumes a static collective of people. Cultures inherently evolve with continued interaction, as experiences and expectations influence changes in relationships. The active component of culture is influence. There is the influence from the individual on the collective, and there is the influence from the collective on the individual. Essentially, a culture is composed of individuals whose influence together defines a collective worldview, and of a collective influence that regulates individual actions. These two parts are constantly evolving and often competing. This is similar to the dialectical process described by the philosopher Hegel, suggesting that every idea has its opposite, and the amalgamation of these two thoughts combine to create a new thesis or idea. From this new thesis, the process begins again and continues to evolve. In China, Daoist and Confucianist thought philosophize on the opposite polarities of yin and yang (e.g., female/male, good/bad, and positive/negative) as interlocking and interdependent, requiring balance to create harmony.

The continual evolution of culture only becomes more complicated in multicultural places like Laos, where the influence of several different cultures can be felt at any given time. It becomes clear in these cases that a combination of individual experience and choice plays a role in governing behaviour. Recognizing that people can accept or deny different aspects of cultural influence, especially in a multi-cultural setting, leads us to another very important element of culture – identity. Identity is a core element for human beings, and countless volumes have been dedicated to the effect of identity on our individual and collective lives. Certainly, "identity-based conflict" (see Azar, 1990; Azar & Burton, 1986; Burton, 1990a, 1990b; Galtung, 1990; Kelman, 2001, 2010; Lederach, 1997; Northrup, 1989; Rothman, 1997) has become a major field of study in conflict resolution, and understanding the effect of identity in ethnic violence will be a topic for governments and international organizations for a long time to come.

Laos demonstrates how complicated the term "culture" actually is. Here influence and identity become tangled up in defining a larger culture that consists of multiple, distinct, smaller cultures. So culture is seen as both inclusive and exclusive. This point becomes a significant factor in writing about the Lao culture, especially as it relates to identity. Specifically, when referring to Lao culture, is the reference to all people who identify themselves as Lao, or is it to the conglomerate of different, distinct ethnic groups that comprise the Lao identity? The answer is both. The dynamic nature of culture is important in understanding how each ethnic group is a culture unto itself, how all the ethnic groups are part of a larger cultural identity, and how the larger cultural identity exercises influence over the individual cultural components.

Lao culture is a beautiful example of this truth. As a young child, I was always fascinated with the different Lao cultural rituals. One of the most important events revolves around the Lao New Year celebration in April where the whole community is actively involved in organizing and participating in one big celebration that lasts for three days. I still enjoy listening to my mother tell me stories of those events:

> *Merchants lined the streets selling handicrafts, food, and flowers that were given as offerings to the temples. Many different ethnic groups roamed the streets, participating in the ethnic Lao New Year celebration, just as we would celebrate in their festivals. Each group would come in their finest traditional dress and costumes, playing traditional games, bringing unique and interesting musical instruments to celebrate with. The scent of charcoal fires cooking interesting foods would be pungent when up close. The curries and coconut milk (khua kari num mak pow) of the ethnic Lao, the bitter bamboo shoot soup (kaeng nawmai) of the Khammu, the sweet pork with eggs (thom kem) of the Hmong could overpower your senses, eventually drifting together where you could smell them all at the same time. Food, songs, and celebrations would flow through houses and streets.*
>
> *As a young girl, my friends and I would run around the neighborhood pouring water over everyone in sight, including a few astonished guests. The children and adults alike were involved in the "water fights" of Lao New Year. More than just plain fun, in the heat of that season* [April is the hottest month of the year in Laos, with temperatures regularly going above 40 degrees Celsius] *it felt very refreshing and cleansing. Symbolically, water represents purification and renewal, and my parents would pour water over the Buddha images and sprinkle water over monks to make merit, and sometimes I would pour water over my older family members' hands to mark respect for my elders. Then we would bring out the rice pots used to steam sticky rice over an open fire, and smear the black soot from the bottom of the pots onto the faces of friends and bystanders for good luck. It was a great celebration, and all of the ethnic groups would come and enjoy our New Year, just as we would take part in their New Year's celebrations.*

In actuality, there are five different New Year celebrations in Laos: the Hmong in November, the Khammu in December or January, the Western in January, the

Chinese in February, and the Ethnic Lao in April (Stuart-Fox & Mixay, 2010). Each celebration is different from the others, according to the different traditions and customs of their calendars. In true Lao cross-cultural fashion, all the ethnic groups participate in each other's New Year celebrations. For them, any excuse to celebrate is a valuable addition to their cultural traditions. As late president Phom-vihane proclaimed, "Each ethnic group possesses a good and beautiful culture and belongs to the national Lao community [*vongkhananyat heng saat lao*], like all the kinds of flowers which thrive in a colorful garden and give off different scents" (Pholsena & Banomyong, 2006, p. 175).

Of course, cultural bridging in Laos is more complicated than a few New Year's parties. Although the government promotes solidarity, the diverse ethnicities in Laos have made it difficult to create a common Lao cultural identity. These groups have come from different cultures and have come at very different times to the region that is now considered Laos. As mentioned previously, the Khammu people are part of a large group that is Austroasiatic in origin and occupied northern Laos for at least 4,000 years (and likely significantly more) (Savada, 1995). The Ethnic Lao people are part of the same group as their Thai neighbours, who slowly moved into Southeast Asia about 1,200 years ago and have been the dominant group since the fourteenth century in the areas of Chao Phraya, the Mekong Rivers, and Shan highlands in Burma. The Hmong people are much more recent residents, having been co-occupants of Laos for only about 200 years, migrating from southern China to flee political unrest and find arable land (Stuart-Fox, 2008; Stuart-Fox & Kooyman, 1992).

Historically, these groups were easily distinguishable from one another because of their different languages, family hierarchies, foods, crops, music, and clothes. Furthermore, these groups have had different political leanings and have supported opposing sides in the political struggles and violence that have often been part of Lao life. Displacements during wars and government policies on relocation as part of national development and for the collective good have greatly affected the ethnic minorities (Pholsena & Banomyong, 2006). There is no question that, even within the urban centers, many of these differences continue to exist.

However, it is also quite clear that these groups share a very similar conflict resolution spectrum and similar rituals in the *soukhouan* and *soumma* ceremonies that help build relationships. The creativity, flexibility, and commonality of the conflict resolution process, with its dependence on mediation, make it possible for different ethnic groups to enter a conflict resolution dialogue with a certain level of comfort. As discussed in previous chapters, third parties such as monks, elders, and other representatives are instrumental in helping to lead discussions and create resolutions that are culturally appropriate and satisfying. Being familiar with the mediation process and having connections with the mediator increases the probability that people in the different communities will be able to successfully resolve conflicts. Common knowledge of traditional conflict resolution processes and mutual acceptance of third-party interventions are an important part of addressing the cross-cultural conflicts that occur in people's lives.

There are some differences in their systems, particularly in the resolutions (which will be discussed later in this chapter). Procedurally, the order in which the spectrum flows can be different for some groups, as village elders (*tow gua*) might hold a higher status than village leaders (*nei ban*) amongst ethnic minority groups. The important difference is that the village leaders might be perceived as having a stronger connection to political structures. Depending on the political leanings of an individual village, this might make village leaders somewhat less trusted. In these cases, conflict parties from minority groups might be more likely to ask elders to mediate higher-level conflicts. Elders and village leaders are the most likely mediators in cross-cultural situations, although, as we shall see, different *Neoy Gai Geer* groups can also get involved in particularly stubborn conflicts.

Cross-cultural conflict resolution process

The resolution process used to address conflicts involving different ethnic groups and villages can be somewhat more complex. As with many conflicts in Laos, the most typical response is avoidance, which is especially evident in conflicts between different ethnic groups. Many of the people I interviewed in Laos responded that they have no conflicts with other cultural groups. In fact, the participants sometimes had difficulty remembering conflicts between Ethnic Lao and Hmong, Khammu and Ethnic Lao, or Hmong and Khammu. Avoidance plays an even stronger role between ethnic groups, leading to an unwillingness to engage in a conflict resolution process and very careful attention paid to issues of privacy. Sometimes I wonder if people are less likely to discuss ethnic *bunha* (conflict). From observing and interacting with the people in Laos, I believe that there is a general perception that these conflicts have more potential to spiral out of control than others, leading people to act more carefully and avoid possible confrontation. Considering Lao history, there is likely an element of truth to this.

That said, the process in multi-ethnic conflict resolution is a familiar one. In cases where *bunha* is between two people or small groups of people of different ethnic groups within the same village or community, the process is almost identical to the ones already discussed. In this case, the elders or village leaders will discuss with each party the various issues and concerns that were raised related to the conflict, guiding them towards a mutually satisfying resolution. If the conflict cannot be resolved, the third parties will investigate and try to find all the facts of the case in order to obtain a more holistic picture of the situation. The next step is to engage in individual conciliation, or shuttle diplomacy, to convey important information from one party to another. (Conciliation, or shuttle diplomacy, refers to an informal process of coaching and engaging parties to discuss conflict issues through a third party and/or in joint meetings.) Up to this point, the conflict resolution process has been relatively informal. Going beyond this requires the parties to move into the mediation process, with the elders or village leaders acting as mediators to help the parties resolve their conflict. Finally, complex and persistent conflicts can use the *Neoy Gai Geer* (Village Mediation Committee) to help find a resolution. As stated in previous chapters, conflicts are normally resolved at this level, driven by the parties' need to maintain face.

Inevitably, conflicts occur between people of different villages. Cross-cultural conflicts often happen in these situations (it is still not uncommon to have villages where only Hmong, Khammu, or another ethnic minority group resides.) As usual, there is hope for a resolution at the initial level of interpersonal and informal *op-lom*, including the early levels of third-party intervention, allowing for a natural progression to the next levels. However, although connections between ethnic groups are relatively common, there is a desire to have conflict resolution be somewhat more "official" in cross-cultural conflict situations. Again, I believe that this is partly because of Laos' history of polarization amongst ethnic groups. Therefore, parties in conflict typically go to their respective elder or village leader to discuss the issue. The elders or village leaders are often the first set of mediators in attempting to restore "face and eyes" through an *op-lom* dialogue and discussion process. At this point, the third parties or mediators from each village will conduct their own investigations to gather information about the conflict. Similar to a fact-finding process, they will collect evidence, talk to witnesses, and ask about the history behind the conflict. The mediators will conduct a joint meeting with each other to discuss the situation and then convey relevant information to their respective parties, again similar to a process of conciliation, or shuttle diplomacy. If the conflict is still unresolved, the mediators will call the parties and their families to participate in a mediation session. The mediators co-facilitate the discussion and resolution of conflict. If the mediation is unsuccessful, the mediators may refer the case to the *Neoy Gai Geer*. In a case where there are two distinct villages involved in a conflict, the respective *Neoy Gai Geer* of each village will work together to resolve the conflict. This process is summarized in Table 5.1.

Table 5.1 Cross-cultural conflict resolution process

Process	Third Parties
1. Dialogue and discussion (*op-lom*)	Elders or village leaders
2. Investigation and fact finding	Elders or village leaders
3. Joint meeting of third parties (conciliation/shuttle diplomacy)	Elders or village leaders
4. Elders or village leaders mediation	Elders or village leaders
5. Village Mediation Committee(s) (*Neoy Gai Geer*)	Village Mediation Committees or representatives from each Village Mediation Committee

The following statements describe a cross-cultural mediation process in Lao communities:

"A conflict between people in different communities – must go see the *nei ban* in each village who will help to mediate the conflict. The two *nei bans* will meet to talk and will invite all the parties involved to come and talk about the situation."

(sixty-five-year-old male Ethnic Lao teacher)

"If there is a conflict between people in different communities, then the *nei ban* from each village will talk with one another."

(sixty-three-year-old male Khammu elder)

These processes are the norm in resolving cross-cultural conflicts. The parties, the families, and the communities understand what needs to be done in such conflicts, specifically, who the third parties are, their roles, and the procedures involved in conflict resolution.

Acceptable resolutions, according to different ethnic groups, is one area where differences may be found. Developing and negotiating culturally appropriate terms of an agreement is a delicate task, requiring a great deal of sensitivity and care. Different symbols have different meanings for each cultural group; therefore, their use in resolution is likely to be interpreted differently. We have already discussed the use of customary laws (*got mai*) in providing consistency in resolutions, particularly in higher levels of mediation, but it seems important to discuss this concept more fully here, as customary laws follow different traditions. Therefore, they must also be flexible enough to work in cross-cultural conflict situations.

New civil and criminal codes were established in Laos in the late 1980s (Stuart-Fox, 2006) to address different conflicts. In practice, those legislative laws often work together with customary laws as objective criteria for which to determine the resolution of conflict. As a Lao teacher said, "We do things according to traditional customs and traditions (*got mai*) . . . We resolve conflicts according to our culture (*hit kong papenee*). We must respect each other (*nup ter gun*). We must trust each other (*seur chai gun*)."

Customary laws (*got mai*) include traditional resolutions to conflict or village customs that are widely accepted by the general population. They are often based on reciprocity and exchange and evaluated in terms of mutual benefits. When conflicts occur at the community level, these are unwritten cultural guidelines which villagers and mediators understand when addressing issues of ethnic cultures, customs, reparation, and restitution.

References to customary and legislative laws may be made during the process of reaching an outcome in conflict situations, but it is important to note that these laws are not conflict resolution processes in and of themselves. They serve as accepted cultural standards for decision making and judgment in an attempt to resolve conflict. For example, in cases involving land disputes, the mediators will refer to objective criteria, such as any available legal papers that describe land divisions between properties, in assessing the situation.

Understanding that customary laws are cultural guidelines makes it possible to have greater creativity in the process and resolution of the conflict itself. The customary laws of different ethnic groups may vary, but with some innovative negotiations and resourcefulness, culturally appropriate conflict resolution is often possible. The following quotes explain how customary laws are used and adapted in a cross-cultural conflict resolution procedure:

"If there is a conflict between an Ethnic Lao and Hmong, whoever is wrong must do what the other side wants according to their tradition. If I wronged a

Hmong, then I have to do what he asks. He may ask for a pig and I have to give that to him."

(forty-two-year-old Ethnic Lao businesswoman)

"If I am wrong in a conflict situation, then I must make things right according to the other person's culture and community."

(forty-two-year-old Ethnic Lao housewife)

"If an Ethnic Lao hits a Khammu, the villagers would have to be involved in the decision-making and provide comments about the situation. The Ethnic Lao would have to negotiate and make things right according to Khammu traditions combined with the rules."

(fifty-seven-year-old male Khammu farmer and former *nei ban*)

These statements make an important point in looking at cross-cultural conflict resolution. In conflict resolution cases where parties are from different ethnic groups, the terms of any restitution will be developed in accordance with the customary laws and traditions of the wronged party. Sometimes those are simple differences and are not difficult to understand or implement. As a sixty-five-year-old Ethnic Lao teacher stated, if one wrongs a Khammu, the person may require a big barrel of alcohol, a pig, and cigarettes as restitution, but when an Ethnic Lao person is wronged, the person may require a cooked chicken, eggs, and alcohol. If the conflict involves an injury, money, payment of hospital bills, and a *soukhouan* may be required.

However, in other cases the differences can be more marked and require somewhat more cross-cultural education in appropriately addressing cultural differences. For example, the *boon sep sern* is the Katdu equivalent of a *soukhouan*. The *boon sep sern* includes giving a water buffalo, rice wine, and water to splash over all the participants to represent cleansing and purification, to remind them that they are one family. There tend to be more participants in their celebrations as part of their conflict resolution customs. An Ethnic Lao *soukhouan* does not include a buffalo as part of the proceedings, but rather a chicken (fewer people to feed), and there is no water to splash people. However, the Katdu ritual does not require the flowers and candles that are part of the Ethnic Lao Buddhist tradition. This might not seem like a big difference, but the subtle differences in what happens during these rituals can play a big role in how well a resolution agreement works. Furthermore, a water buffalo is significantly more expensive than a chicken. Depending on the scope of the conflict, these differences can often be negotiated, but it does add a level of complexity to resolution agreements and ensures that each party leaves the resolution process with a new awareness and appreciation for the cultural habits of different ethnic groups. These symbolic details play an important role in understanding and restoring relationships among groups.

If the responsibility for organizing and paying for the ceremony rests with the person at fault, how does that party educate themselves on the correct procedures and offerings to be part of the event? As one individual said, "We have to follow ours and their traditions, and both sides can get along with this. We always discuss (*op-lom*) with each other and then we have to follow what they ask." Obviously, there is significant discussion (*op-lom*) between the parties that is part of organizing, especially if the *soukhouan* is to be a large event. This can be difficult, but it is recognized as part of the community-building experience, building and rebuilding relationships, and seeing each other not as adversaries, but as "different flowers in the same garden."

In reality, there are as many cultural differences in the way the *soukhouan* ceremony is conducted as there are cultures in Laos. As we know, the *soukhouan*'s use as a tool for restitution and community building is always based on the traditions of the family that has been injured, and the symbolic differences often present practical issues that have a direct effect on the success of the event. Oftentimes those differences are found in different religious leanings. For example, Hmong groups generally require less emphasis on Buddhist tradition and more emphasis on animist traditions, whereas the Ethnic Lao focus more heavily on Buddhist teachings.

The fusion of Buddhist and animist traditions in the *soukhouan* ceremony is generally representative of the overall spirituality that is part of the Lao cultural tapestry. As already discussed, the Lao people have a complex religious foundation, which is a conglomeration of Theravada Buddhism, animism, mythologies, and rituals, to explain experiences in their lives, family, and community. Laos is often described as a land of festivals where "[e]very village, every temple, and every ethnic minority not only holds its own special festivals but also joins the wider Lao community in celebrating the national ones as well" (Stuart-Fox & Mixay, 2010, p. 1). A number of festivals celebrate significant dates in Theravada Buddhism as practiced by the Ethnic Lao, interwoven with religious practices of the earlier animist traditions often associated with minority groups. The animist beliefs can be connected to the worship of numerous deities and spirits, both friendly and unfriendly.

Clearly, the collaboration of Buddhist and animist traditions that forms the basis for the *soukhouan* and *soumma* ceremonies is significant in helping the different ethnic groups relate to each other. Each group has incorporated the different religious principles of the others into their own cultural worlds to a certain extent, giving them a good foundation for relationship. For example, an Ethnic Lao woman once warned me about the importance of not angering a Khammu person. She whispered quietly,

"I fear Khammu people because they believe in spirits. If I do something wrong to them, they will call upon their spirits to do me harm. They can put evil curses and spells on me and my family. I try to avoid them as much as possible so there's no conflict."

Obviously, this Ethnic Lao woman, even though she is Buddhist, still believes that animist spirits can have destructive powers. Similarly, a Khammu man and I were discussing cultural differences between groups, and he said, "We believe in the spirit religion. In general, we respect the Lao Loum because they observe spirits and Buddhist religion. It is similar, before we do anything we have to inform the spirits." This man clearly sees more similarities than differences between different ethnic groups and respects them for their cultural beliefs.

It would be difficult to overestimate the role that ceremonies, festivals, and rituals have played in bridging relationships between Lao's cultural groups. They serve as a mechanism to invite people to become part of the community, to bless them in the Buddhist tradition and expel any evil spirits in the animist tradition, to educate each other about cultural differences, and to create a positive relationship in a general way. It provides a "point of ritual linkage across ethnic groups in Laos . . . elevated into a 'national' custom" (Evans, 1998, pp. 77–78). Still, each *soukhouan* is unique and customized during the mediation process in a way that reflects the scope of the conflict and the cultures of the parties. In doing so, it has been a source of education, communication, resolution, restitution, empowerment, and bonding between groups.

A *soukhouan* helps to rebuild damaged relationships, to publicly acknowledge wrong, and to show the community that the parties are working to make things right again. Obviously, it has become deeply ingrained in Lao culture because it is such an effective tool, a tool that people enjoy participating in. I have attended dozens of *soukhouan* celebrations for weddings, welcome parties, and conflict resolution rituals and have enjoyed them all. In many years of trips, research, and asking people from different ethnic groups about their feelings regarding *soukhouan* and *soumma* ceremonies, I have yet to hear a negative comment. Many times I have heard quotes like, "A *soukhouan* helps people to feel good, loved, honoured, and respected, and leads to overall harmony and peace in communities"; "A *soukhouan* helps to make things right"; "A *soumma* is an old Lao tradition, it has good results"; or "A *soumma* is part of building our relationship and is a good thing for our family." The fact that these rituals have common characteristics and are fun and meaningful within and between different ethnic groups contributes to the acceptance and support of such traditions in cross-cultural conflict resolution.

Development of shared Conflict Resolution Spectrum and rituals

The importance of common systems that are known and respected by different ethnic groups is vital to resolving conflict, building relationships, and achieving reconciliation in society. From the previous discussions, it is evident that mediation and rituals in Laos have characteristics that cut across cultures. Each ethnic group has similar mediation and ritual practices that are valued by the community. When there are cross-cultural encounters, the process and ritual of dispute resolution are respected and familiar, and any differences in expectations are generally understood by each other. Therefore, people find these approaches legitimate in meeting their needs.

The early part of this chapter was devoted to a discussion of culture, noting that culture is continually evolving because of the influential role played by changing relationships and environments. It seems reasonable to assume that the different Lao ethnic groups developed this similarity in conflict resolution together, rather than by a stroke of luck or fate that they shared these mechanisms upon first contact. For example, we know that the Hmong groups are relatively recent co-occupants of Laos, and they share the use of the *soukhouan* ritual (called the *baci* in their language). We also know that their Miao ancestors who still live in China do not use this ritual. How these common processes of conflict resolution and rituals have developed is an important part of comprehensively understanding culture, as well as providing insights into how other groups can build relationships.

Over many years of contact, the different Lao groups have developed cultural commonalities, including conflict resolution mechanisms and rituals, to help them work towards a peaceful co-existence. In understanding how these processes have led to the development of a shared cultural identity, it is important to explore Kimmel's (2000) concept of microculture where people of diverse cultural backgrounds develop "commonalities in meaning, norms of communication, and behavior; shared perception and expectation; roles" (p. 453) through interactions over time.

The early interactions in a cross-cultural relationship represent the development of a microculture. These dynamic interactions between individuals create a pattern and expectation in communication that is a vital part of a growing and healthy relationship. Stability in these associations would have provided a basis to begin an exchange of goods, services, and ideas. Cultural groups would have developed these microcultures further as economic relationships between groups became more and more entrenched. The different agro-ecological zones of the uplands and lowlands made the different Lao communities natural trading partners, where they "provided essential goods and services to each other. Together they represented a robust and mutually beneficial system of exchange" (Scott, 2009, p. 105).

Microcultures continue to be influenced by each respective culture. However, through negotiations, people in cross-cultural relationships learn new rules for behaviour and develop a shared understanding of the cultural components required to make their relationship work. In doing so, they define their microculture in a way that is particular to their interaction. I would suggest that the earliest contact between autonomous ethnic groups in Laos would have been indicative of this, and the natural progression of this process is the reason that the different ethnic groups in Laos have developed similar cross-cultural conflict resolution strategies and rituals.

Specifically, as contact became more frequent between these groups and microcultures continued to grow, conflict resolution structures developed to foster effective communication in progressively varied settings. The third-party mediation processes and *soukhouan* rituals are examples of conflict resolution structures that have fostered these relationships. As a Khammu member of the *Neoy Gai Geer* stated,

"When we have conflict in the family, we talk with families from both sides, one, two, and three times. After that we have to go to the *Neoy Gai Geer*. This process is the same for both the Lao Loum and the Khammu."

This, as well as many other quotes already mentioned, illustrate that the different ethnic groups have similar structures of conflict resolution and use them to maintain and build stronger relationships within and across ethnic groups. They have created a common system of understanding conflict, developed ways of addressing restitution, and constructed mechanisms for reconciliation.

The influence of many microcultures produces clear understandings of the roles, expectations, and behaviour amongst the larger population, including conflict resolution and reconciliation structures that help maintain relationships. Over generations of increasing diversification through exposure to each other's goods and services, most people living within the boundaries of Laos now share a macroculture of common identity based on mutual relationships, even if they do not share a cultural heritage. In recognizing this, we see cultural evolution in all its glory, part influence and part identity, growing from micro to macro.

It is important to recognize that these cross-cultural shared characteristics take time to develop, and the journey toward successful cross-cultural conflict resolution mechanisms is not necessarily smooth. As mentioned in the introduction, I have always been intrigued by the complexity of Laos, particularly in the peaceful and relaxed people who I have come to know, contrasted with the brutal violence of their past. If the Lao people have common respect and identity, why is their history plagued with violence?

I would concur with many other authors who suggest Laos has often been a battleground for the ambitions and purposes of other parties and nations, who have regularly used ethnic differences to ignite tensions between groups in order to destabilize relationships and secure support for their own goals (see Evans, 1999; Robbins, 2005; Savada, 1995; Stuart-Fox, 1997). This is the propaganda of war everywhere, one that is all too familiar for the people of Laos. The Lao have an expression, "Do not bring lice onto your own head" (*Ya ha how ma ha heor*). The expression is a metaphor for conflict being akin to having "lice," feeding on the host and causing significant discomfort for yourself and others around you. Unfortunately, lice are highly contagious and, as much as the Lao people have not brought most of this conflict on themselves, other powers have often transferred their own "lice."

Dealing with multi-ethnic cultures has been the focus of nation building for as long as nations have existed, and Laos has certainly seen its share of different political strategies. The pre-war Royal Lao government ignored the problem, knowing that they had no real ability to control or incorporate the non-lowland groups into either their financial economy or human capital. On the other hand, the post-war Communist government tried to recognize ethnic differences in an effort to incorporate them into a new, tightly regulated, and controlled "Socialist" identity (Pholsena, 2006), thereby increasing its power base both in numbers and control. They were not overly successful, however, as their encouragement for citizens to embrace their respective ethnic heritages often served as a reminder of the tensions between the groups. This was particularly true for the minorities, who perceived this as a demonstration of the majority Ethnic Lao dominance in numbers, wealth, and power.

Clearly, there is a delicate balance between celebrating differences and recognizing similarities in a way that strengthens relationships. On a global and historic scale, the interference in the development from microcultures to macrocultures by those in influential positions has fueled violence for as long as humanity has existed. Across the world, groups who share historic common bonds are torn apart through an unhealthy focus on differences and a fear of losing their values or unique identity to another group, no matter how likely or unlikely that reality may be. These situations make it obvious that conflict is not necessarily a competition between two or more players, a fight for resources, or a rivalry for power, but is often a defense for perceived threats to ideals, morality, or other cultural values. These conflicts, based on ideals and identity, can be the most entrenched and inextricable.

The propaganda of war in polarizing ethnic groups illustrates a common theme in Lao history, namely, that people in high-level leadership positions, whether foreign or domestic, have made decisions that have created tension and mistrust between Lao people. As Stuart-Fox (1997) discussed:

> . . . for many believed that Lao would never have fought Lao had it not been for foreign intervention: the war had been fought not because of Lao intransigence or intractable political hatred, but because external powers had made use of Lao territory for their own needs.
>
> (p. 165)

The Cold War philosophies and ideologies that were championed by opposing foreign players were, in reality, entirely unimportant to the general Lao population, who were busy in the market and in the fields trying to make a living to feed their families. This fact has been paramount to why wounds have healed and how peace has always found its way back to the Lao cultures. The relationships built between grassroots groups as a mutually beneficial system of exchange have, on the whole, been more important than those relationships with either the foreign or domestic upper-level leadership that has occasionally divided group associations.

Conclusion

As briefly mentioned earlier, the mediation systems and rituals that underscore Lao conflict resolution are "owned and operated" by those people who are directly affected by the conflict. Considering this, combined with the historical upheaval caused by foreign interference and upper-level leadership, I believe the key to cross-cultural relationship in Laos is in the grassroots. Culture is not something that can be mandated by government or written by lawyers. The Lao culture has been forming slowly over centuries of grassroots interactions that have formed many common ways of resolving disputes. It includes distinct groups that have been inhabitants of that area for many millennium, but also groups that are much more recent immigrants to Lao society. Disruptions can and do occur, but as long as there is a solid foundation in the grassroots, these conflict resolution processes will continue to exist, facilitating peaceful relationships.

Social identity refers to a person's membership in formal or informal social groups, such as sex, race, nationality, and religion, and this membership has emotional and valuable significance (Northrup, 1989). The concept of identity, or "membership," is important to the Lao culture as a whole. As a group they have developed an interdependent relationship and common conflict resolution practices that have helped them to unite as Lao people at the grassroots level.

Since the kingdom of Lan Xang in the fourteenth century, there has been continual movement towards creating a Lao identity. The diverse ethno-linguistic groups in Laos have experienced different histories as indigenous peoples and immigrants. However, generally speaking, these communities consider themselves to be part of a larger Lao national community, which incorporates many other groups as well. As some Lao friends elegantly said to me once, "We are Lao people, we don't forget our main traditions. We don't leave it, we bring everything together. We don't separate the ethnicities, all ethnicities are the same, any ethnic group is important." The vast majority of Lao people hold these views, whether they are farmers, tax collectors, men, women, monks – essentially all the people who are part of grassroots society. These grassroots people and relationships define the larger Lao identity, and it is their cultural quality of acknowledging, incorporating, and adding to their own traditions that has helped them to develop similar conflict resolution mechanisms, which in turn has helped ethnic groups maintain their membership in the larger Lao identity.

This kind of openness, collaboration, and respect deserves to be celebrated by all the ethnic groups, each according to their own tradition, yet united in a common celebration of shared identity. Laos has already developed a great tribute to that idea that is practiced and celebrated by all groups during five different months of the year. If you happen to be in Laos in January, February, April, November, or December, please do take the time to wish everybody a happy new year!

Bibliography

Avruch, Kevin. (1998). *Culture & Conflict Resolution*. Washington, DC: United States Institute of Peace Press.

Avruch, Kevin. (2003). Culture. In Sandra Cheldelin, Daniel Druckman & Larissa Fast (eds.), *Conflict: From Analysis to Intervention* (pp. 140–153). London: Continuum.

Azar, Edward E. (1990). *The Management of Protracted Conflict*. Hampshire: Dartmouth Publishing Company Limited.

Azar, Edward E., & Burton, John W. (eds.). (1986). *International Conflict Resolution: Theory and Practice*. Sussex: Wheatsheaf Books.

Burton, John W. (1990a). *Conflict: Resolution and Prevention*. New York: St. Martin's Press.

Burton, John W. (1990b). *Human Needs Theory*. New York: St. Martin's Press.

Evans, Grant. (1998). *The Politics of Ritual and Remembrance: Laos Since 1975*. Honolulu: University of Hawaii Press.

Evans, Grant. (1999). *Laos: Culture and Society*. Chiangmai: Silkworm Books.

Galtung, Johan. (1990). *International Development in Human Perspectives*. London: Macmillan.

Kelman, Herbert C. (2001). The Role of National Identity in Conflict Resolution: Experiences from Israeli-Palestinian Problem-Solving Workshops. In Richard D. Ashmore, Lee Jussim, & David Wilder (eds.), *Social Identity, Intergroup Conflict, and Conflict Reduction* (pp. 187–212). Oxford: Oxford University Press.

Kelman, Herbert C. (2010). Conflict Resolution and Reconciliation: A Social-Psychological Perspective on Ending Violent Conflict Between Identity Groups. *Landscapes of Violence: An Interdisciplinary Journal Devoted to the Study of Violence, Conflict, and Trauma,* 1(1), 1–9.

Kimmel, Paul R. (2000). *Culture and Conflict.* San Francisco: Jossey-Bass.

Lederach, John Paul. (1997). *Building Peace: Sustainable Reconciliation in Divided Societies.* Washington, DC: United States Institute of Peace Press.

Northrup, Terrell. (1989). The Dynamics of Identity in Personal and Social Conflict. In Louis Kriesberg, Terrell Northrup, & Stuart Thorson (eds.), *Intractible Conflicts and Their Transformation.* New York: Syracuse University Press.

Pholsena, Vatthana. (2006). *Post-War Laos: The Politics of Culture, History, and Identity.* Ithaca: Cornell University Press.

Pholsena, Vatthana, & Banomyong, Ruth. (2006). *Laos: From Buffer State to Crossroads?* Chiang Mai: Mekong Press.

Robbins, Christopher. (2005). *The Ravens: Pilots of the Secret War of Laos* (3rd ed.). Bangkok: Asia Books Co. Ltd.

Rothman, Jay. (1997). *Resolving Identity-Based Conflict in Nations, Organizations, and Communities* (1st ed.). San Francisco: Jossey-Bass Publishers.

Savada, Andrea Matles. (1995). *Laos: A Country Study.* Washington, DC: Federal Research Division, Library of Congress.

Scott, James C. (2009). *The Art of Not Being Governed: An Anarchist History of Upland Southeast Asia.* New Haven: Yale University Press.

Singelis, Theodore M., & Pedersen, Paul. (1994). Conflict Mediation Across Cultures. In Kenneth Cushner & Richard W. Brislin (eds.), *Improving Intercultural Interactions: Modules for Cross-Cultural Training Programs* (vol. 2, pp. 184–204). Thousand Oaks: Sage Publications.

Stuart-Fox, Martin. (1997). *A History of Laos.* Cambridge: Cambridge University Press.

Stuart-Fox, Martin. (2006). The Political Culture of Corruption in Lao PDR. *Asian Studies Review,* 30, 59–75.

Stuart-Fox, Martin. (2008). *Historical Dictionary of Laos* (3rd ed.). Lanham: The Scarecrow Press, Inc.

Stuart-Fox, Martin, & Kooyman, M. (1992). *Historical Dictionary of Laos.* Metuchen: The Scarecrow Press, Inc.

Stuart-Fox, Martin, & Mixay, Somsanouk. (2010). *Festivals of Laos.* Chiang Mai: Silkworm Books.

Williams, Raymond. (1983). *Culture and Society: 1780–1950.* New York: Columbia University Press.

6 Grassroots conflict resolution: building from the ground up

People's techniques, processes, or practices for resolving or managing conflicts are addressed by means of "ethnopraxis" [capacity to resolve conflicts on their own].
(Avruch, Black, & Scimecca, 1998, p. 11)

The role of grassroots leadership, initiatives, and ownership in promoting positive relationships in the communities in Laos is the underlying theme of their conflict resolution system. Grassroots mechanisms include *op-lom* conflict resolution processes conducted by parents, relatives, elders, village leaders, and the *Neoy Gai Geer* and the conflict resolution ceremonies and symbols in the *soukhouan* and *soumma*. A male Khammu *nei ban* told me the following story, demonstrating how ingrained grassroots conflict resolution is in the Lao culture:

> There was a conflict in the rice fields involving a shortage of water. The rice fields closest to the water supply got water first, and those farmers would fill up their fields so they could sow the rice paddies (see Figure 6.1). Unfortunately, there was not enough water for the fields farther down the water supply, and these farmers were not able to sow their crops. After some tense situations in the village, the farmers gathered to op-lom with one another. The village authorities also attended the meeting and encouraged discussion and options, but did not force the farmers into any decisions. Early in the conversation, the farmers agreed that, should a consensus resolution not be possible, they would hold a vote on several different options. The field owners farther down the water supply asked for the water to be released to flow down to the next fields. Much of the discussion centered on "gaining together and losing together." Through the course of discussion, several options were presented that would allow all farmers to have access to a smaller amount of water and still have a reasonable chance of having a successful crop. This helped the farmers to come to an agreement, and water was released to the other fields without the need of a vote. In the end, the individual yield for each farmer was not as high as it would have been if they had a full amount of water. But the farmers agreed that the total community yield was considerably higher than it would have been if only the first farmers had a full yield and the other farmers had none.

Figure 6.1 A flooded rice field with bunched rice seedlings ready to be separated and planted in rows. The back part of the field is already complete

© Stephanie Phetsamay Stobbe 2006

This is an example of a structural conflict called the "tragedy of the commons" (Hardin, 1968). The expression refers to situations where multiple individuals act in their own self-interest in order to maximize personal gain, resulting in the destruction of a shared group's limited resource in the long term. If the resource is not managed properly, it becomes vulnerable to exploitation, depleting the sustainability of the resource (Marten, 2007). Rice farming is a difficult, time-consuming, and labour-intensive occupation. In this case, the farmers recognized their mutual dependency. The community's survival was dependent on the food provided by the farmers, who were in turn dependent on each other for access to tools, manpower, seed, and so on. If some farmers fail, the entire resource becomes more fragile. Clearly, the interdependence among the different farmers is illustrated here. As told by the *nei ban*, the farmers defined this concept of interdependence as "gaining together and losing together." The fact that their livelihood depended on the cooperation of all the villagers gave the farmers significant incentive to work together to resolve this conflict. This is an "essential web of relationships of mutual support" (Black, 1998, p. 148). It is noteworthy that they also agreed early in their discussions that if no consensus was reached, they would give themselves the option of an open vote based on majority rule.

Here, the grassroots – the people directly involved in the conflict, had face-to-face *op-lom* as to how this structural conflict could be resolved in a way that presented the best options for all farmers and the whole community. With the assistance of village authorities, they brainstormed for other options as well. The resolution of the conflict remained in the hands of the farmers themselves, as the authorities did not make any decisions for them. Based on their grassroots conflict resolution system, this community found a mechanism to create oversight and establish rules for sustainable water usage, ensuring the protection of their food resource and farming livelihood, as well as positive community relationships.

In Chapter 3, we discussed the use of *op-lom* as a term that describes communication in relation to conflict and conflict resolution. We have seen how it is used as a part of teaching, listening, active counseling, mediating, and arbitrating in conflict situations. With this in mind, *op-lom* defines an encompassing and holistic view of what conflict is and where it occurs. Because the process of *op-lom* falls under the responsibilities of parents, relatives, elders, village leaders, and community leaders, the conflict resolution process and participants are held within the grassroots organization of Lao communities.

In the West, conflict resolution tends to be placed under the jurisdiction of lawyers or formal, rule-of-law, legal systems. In reality, conflict resolution happens in a much larger circle of settings than just through the legal system. Marriage counselors, guidance counselors, therapists, child and family service providers, politicians, financial advisors, employment service providers, and other career people make up a large part of our professional workforce. These people are all part of a social services system that is dedicated to the prevention and resolution of conflict at an interpersonal to international scale.

As in much of the world, Laos has a limited structure for social services. Access to professionals in these fields for the average Lao citizen is much less common than in more economically developed countries. *Op-lom* is the mechanism by which these services are accessed, through non-professional grassroots individuals who are familiar with the communication and conflict resolution needs of a community. For them, social services, as part of a conflict resolution system, are held in the hands of the grassroots community. Many of the same people who use the system as beneficiaries also operate the system as its workforce.

To understand this fully, it is important to review the Lao Conflict Resolution System as seen through a grassroots lens. The primary individuals tasked with leading conflict resolution are identified as parents, relatives, elders, village leaders, and *Neoy Gai Geer*, who are personally connected to the parties in conflict (see Figure 6.2). This connection becomes more distant as one moves from parents to the *Neoy Gai Geer* levels. These leaders are members of the community and understand the situation surrounding the conflict.

The choice of mediators and their progression from "insiders" to "outsiders" as interveners in a conflict situation demonstrate the preference to resolve conflicts at the grassroots level. The parties in conflict recognize that "insiders" may have an inherent bias, but these "insiders" may also have advantages in reaching an agreement. Because they understand the personalities involved in the conflict,

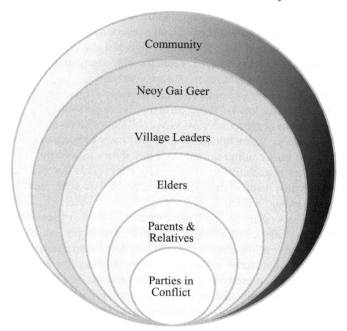

Figure 6.2 Lao grassroots leaders and support networks in conflict resolution

these mediators can identify with the parties in terms of the conditions that generate conflict (e.g., social, economic, political, and cultural factors) and understand the direct consequences of decisions made. They have a vested interest in resolving the conflict because it directly affects themselves and their community.

The *Neoy Gai Geer* would be considered to be a full representation of grassroots community leaders. As discussed in previous chapters, these representatives reflect the various groups in the community, which have specific perspectives on different issues. Although they would not be professionally trained as conflict resolution experts, they are a natural bridge to a more specialized group. In conflict cases that are legally required to have district court oversight, the courts serve as a rubber stamp for the *Neoy Gai Geer* process that has already taken place.

As already discussed, *op-lom* is the communication skill that provides what Western countries would call social services – a place for educating, advising, talking, discussing, questioning, clarifying, and reminding parties in conflict that they need to work at fully understanding the situation by looking at conflicts from different perspectives. The grassroots leaders' role is to maintain social harmony in the community by effectively advising the parties and constructively addressing the conflicts. Their success ensures that "face and eyes" are protected on all fronts – for those parties in conflict, as well as their own.

The Lao rituals and ceremonies are key features of the grassroots approaches to conflict resolution. The *soukhouan* and *soumma* rituals are local, cultural ceremonies that are essential in dispute resolution and post-conflict relationships. They are instrumental components of overall peacebuilding in their communities. These grassroots initiatives help to acknowledge and celebrate the resolution of conflict and move the parties toward reconciliation, as organized and performed by those families and communities who were involved.

Both the *soukhouan* and *soumma* rituals are grassroots initiatives used to address conflict and conflict resolution. These ceremonies are performed by families and local communities in order to acknowledge conflict, make restitution, and repair as much as possible any harm that has been done. Many cultures in our world have extremely limited post-conflict initiatives. Laos shows us that bottom-up, grassroots, post-conflict peacebuilding is culturally appropriate for their community structure and valuable in maintaining a holistic approach to adhering to agreements and preventing further conflict.

As discussed, only rarely do conflicts progress to a group of specialized professionals, which is evidence of a strong desire or need to resolve conflicts at the grassroots level. Some might comment that this is because of a lack of accessibility to those more formal structures. The more likely explanation is that the lack of development towards a more formal structure is because the community does not feel a need for it. Essentially, the success of the grassroots system is why the Lao people continue using these conflict resolution processes, inherently keeping them within their communities.

Grassroots collaboration and agency have played an important role in conflict resolution in Laos. For example, several people have brought up the following interesting story, demonstrating the integrative power of the grassroots community.

In many Lao villages, there is a daily early morning ceremony where the monks, dressed in their bright orange robes, walk through the streets in silence, carrying only their alms bowls. A few minutes before the monks arrive, local people line the streets, waiting to place rice, dried meat, or fruit in the bowls of the monks in exchange for spiritual blessings. The ceremony takes place in total silence, and the lay people are very careful to respectfully kneel as the monks approach. (The ceremony is an incredible tourist attraction now, and every morning thousands of tourists jockey for a coveted position from which to take an uncountable number of flash pictures. Unfortunately, this often becomes a distraction to the serenity of this deeply spiritual, thousand-year-old ritual.) In the early days of the Lao People's Democratic Republic (Lao PDR) government after taking power in 1975, a policy was adopted that prohibited citizens from their daily ritual of giving alms during the monks' morning procession. Without this ceremony, the clergy would have no other means of meeting their basic needs. Because the alms-giving tradition was so integral to their cultural and religious beliefs, the vast majority of citizens simply ignored the government policy and continued to give the monks their daily rations. The act of being ignored forced the Pathet Lao government to change its position. In order to maintain any credibility, the government quickly rescinded their ban, allowing traditional alms giving, and offered their own daily ration of rice to the clergy (*sangha*) (Cummings, 1994; Pholsena, 2006). For a government that at least initially had connections to Mao Tse-Tung's philosophy that "[p]olitical power grows out of the barrel of a gun" (Tse-Tung, 1960, p. 13), this must have been an enlightening experience.

This story demonstrates a powerful truth – that in the vast majority of situations, political power is given to leaders by the masses of ordinary citizens. In the Lao case, the people did not do this as a willful act of protest, but rather displayed that "power of the people" is a commitment to culture, heritage, and belief, rather than an expression of strength through civil disobedience. Here, cultural identity and influence was too strong a voice for the government leadership to change or even ignore. Collective cultural influence changed individual behavior, even that of its most powerful leaders. This is evident in many historical conflicts, and many scholars on non-violent action believe that power resides in the people whose good will, decision, and support allow leaders to rule (Sharp, 1973). After all, Gandhi did not revolutionize India on his own – he had the help of a few hundred million Indian citizens. Nelson Mandela and Martin Luther King Jr. mobilized vast numbers of people, forcing political leadership and the world to listen. Grassroots populations are powerful motivators for leaders, and if for no other reason than that, the key to peace lies with them.

Change at the personal, relational, structural, and cultural levels is what Lederach (1997) calls conflict transformation. This term refers to conflict resolution that promotes positive change through emotional and spiritual growth individually, through interdependence and interaction between parties, through fostering structures that uphold human needs and human rights, and through changing cultural patterns that encourage an inclusive and productive human environment. Knowing this, we can see that grassroots mechanisms are capable of complete conflict transformation, and that they can and do play a very important and positive role in our world.

In revisiting the cross-cultural evolution of how these conflict resolution structures begin to foster relationships between groups, we see that there is an elegant simplicity and beauty to their development, from the simple early relationships between a few people to maintaining a bond and identity between millions of people. As Lao history has clearly shown, there has been violence within and between these groups as they have played different roles for the opposing entities that have sought to divide them. But what is so interesting is that these groups have been willing and able to find harmony and peace after such brutal violence. They have maintained and celebrated their common identity in spite of having an incredibly ethnically diverse society and in spite of being used as pawns in larger global ideals and conflicts. It begs the question, how is it that other conflicts fueled by cultural difference, ethnic division, and identity-based needs are having so much trouble finding some traction towards a path to peace?

Lebanon is an interesting case study. Violence has been prevalent throughout its recent history. Although the civil war in Lebanon officially ended in 1990, just fifteen years later than in Laos, they are still under a constant threat of violence. Political and religious assassinations occur every few years, and struggles between different religious groups continue on a fairly regular basis. Is there any evidence that a grassroots conflict resolution system could be useful in developing more peaceful relationships?

In 2000, King-Irani published "Rituals of Forgiveness and Processes of Empowerment in Lebanon" (Zartman, 2000), giving consideration to a traditional conflict resolution system that could be useful in helping Lebanon deal with its violent past. Lebanon was ravaged by civil war between 1975 and 1990, resulting in not only physical damage, but also emotional, moral, and spiritual devastation. The war ended due to external political pressures, but many still have deep feelings of bitterness, fear, anger, despair, powerlessness, and frustration (King-Irani, 2000a). Psychological, social, and political aspects of communal life require acknowledgment of wrong, reparation, forgiveness, and transcendence (King-Irani, 2000a). King-Irani (2000a) suggests that the Lebanese individuals and society must call for spiritual, emotional, moral, and transformative powers in order to heal from the war.

This transformative power is found in traditional Lebanese rituals that are critical to individual and communal harmony and social integration. *Sulha* (peacemaking or reconciliation) is the indigenous Lebanese ritual that has been an important part of the communal traditions in the Arab world, yet has never been implemented at the national level. The *sulha* is a mechanism of village life used to manage, resolve, and prevent conflicts between different families, clans, and tribes. It is used to resolve conflicts involving everything from violation of rights or norms (e.g., thefts, slight injury, or honor) to manslaughter in order to prevent further escalation of destructive violence.

The *sulha* consists of three stages: (1) respected leaders in the community are chosen as *muslihs* (mediators) who will investigate, conduct fact-finding, publicly acknowledge the violation, and assign blame as necessary; (2) a pardon ritual to be held in the home of the injured party, where the *muslihs* will extol honor, generosity, and nobility to the injured party's family; and (3) a public, formalized demonstration of reconciliation between the parties through words and symbolic acts (King-Irani, 2000a). There is a rite of passage within the *sulha* that separates the offenders from the rest of society, and during mediation, with the assistance of the *muslihs*, the offenders are transformed into co-existing fellow human beings and reintegrated into society (King-Irani, 2000a). This method of conflict resolution and ritual of reconciliation could potentially help the Lebanese come to terms with the past and rebuild their future, similar to truth and justice commissions in South Africa and other places (Irani, 2004, 2006; Irani & Funk, 2000; King-Irani, 2000a, 2000b).

So why has Lebanon had so much trouble finding peace, especially when they have a grassroots conflict resolution that could be a binding, relationship-building point of linkage between groups? Why are they not successful in resolving conflicts? I admit that I am hesitant to address this question, especially considering that volumes of books have been dedicated to it and this book will only include a few paragraphs. This is not an in-depth analysis of the situation in Lebanon, nor is it a thorough comparison with Laos, but is included simply as a conversation starter. It is difficult to ignore that, just as Southeast Asia was the active focus of international military action in the 1960s and 1970s, the Middle East is now.

Are the religious differences too big? As we have seen in Southeast Asia, the difference between animism and Buddhism in Southeast Asia is very wide, yet they have found a place to exist together. Currently, a severe division exists between different religious groups in the Middle East, but in other parts of the world these groups have found some relative peace. Could these hardened positions be the result of some other factor(s)? Others might suggest that the cultural differences between their groups are too vast. Again, Laos shows us that these issues can be overcome. Still others might suggest that the political divide in the population is too large. But the civil war in Laos centered around hard differences between Communism and democracy. Peace in Laos came in spite of these issues.

Clearly, one of the significant differences between Laos and Lebanon is the timeline. Their respective civil wars ended only fifteen years apart, but in Lebanon there is still massive foreign involvement and international conflicts surrounding the country that are constantly spilling over the entire Middle East. These situations have ensured that hardened positions, entrenched attitudes, and intolerance maintain their grip in the region. Whether it comes from internal or external sources, violence begets violence, and until that cycle is broken, there is little hope of establishing lasting peace.

I am not an expert on the situation in the Middle East. I do, however, know something about grassroots conflict resolution and the power it has to promote transformation. Hopefully, given an opportunity, there might be systems buried deep in the grassroots that could help them heal. King-Irani (2000b) suggests that there might be. Those systems will have to move between conflicting parties, establishing and re-establishing relationships that will eventually force leaders to listen, talk, and propel those conflict resolution systems into a full-blown peace process. Peace will not be mandated by a few signatures of important people in top leadership, but will be founded in a process that is the culmination of a million smaller ones. Recently, I met a non-government organization (NGO) worker in Syria and Lebanon who shared a story of Muslims who invited Christians to join them in a lamb-slaughtering ritual to thank God for blessings and sustenance and to strengthen relationships in their community. Conversely, there are stories of Christians sharing food baskets with their Muslim neighbours, demonstrating their views of equality and respect before God, and inspiring joy and peace in their area. In the midst of violence and destruction, there is hope for peace in these small, grassroots examples. Given time and an appropriate environment, I believe these stories can grow into something that can change their world and ours.

Going from micro to macro, the grassroots nature of Lao culture and conflict resolution suggests that this is possible. In developing a Lao identity, there were no walls to separate one group from another. Groups developed relationships based on the advantages to their economic well-being, and established communication strategies and conflict resolution structures to foster that. In spite of violence, conflict resolution structures have remained in those groups, and their usage has nurtured education and relationships between individuals, growing to bridge an entire multi-cultural identity. As a thirty-six-year-old female person of the *Oh* ethnic group so beautifully said to me,

> "Traditional methods can be used with other cultures. According to other ethnicities, they have to follow our traditions and we have to follow them too. If we don't know how, then we can compare which is good and beautiful, and we can choose which one. If it's a good tradition we can learn and discuss with one another."

As long as those grassroots structures are maintained, and as long as they are allowed to support individual relationships between ethnic groups, there will be a mechanism for peace. However, putting a wall between group interactions and allowing conflict resolution structures to die will create a much more complex path to peace. In 1987, US President Ronald Reagan made one of the great conflict resolution challenges of the twentieth century when he stood at the Brandenburg Gate in Germany and said, "Mr. Gorbachev, tear down this wall!" The Soviet Union's General Secretary Mikhail Gorbachev, having committed to an incredible agenda of political change that would set the stage for massively improved global relations, was finally able to oblige him some two years later. We now look back at the fall of the Berlin Wall as the symbolic end of the Cold War. How fitting that one of the world's great conflicts would be ended by the tearing down of a wall and the rebuilding of grassroots relationships.

Balancing conflict resolution systems

We must be aware that as our global world becomes smaller, more and more populations are coming together and looking for ways to communicate with each other. There are often tensions, and conflict resolution systems that speak to vastly different cultures are not always easy to find. Historically, many governments have been hoping that culture clashes would eventually give way as a more dominant cultural group eventually assimilated the smaller groups. But cultural assimilation over the last few centuries has proven far more difficult than was anticipated.

Clearly, the Lao Conflict Resolution System is different from the more professional structures we have in place in the "Western or developed" world. Still, these are two systems that are both generally effective; respected by the groups engaged with them; and on the whole successful in providing peaceful avenues for conflict resolution that aim to provide protection, social justice, and maintenance of relationships. Over the years, I have spent many hours comparing the inner workings of these two systems and wondering if there is a middle ground between them. Eventually, we must recognize that these conflict resolution systems are designed to serve two very different populations with very different cultural worldviews. But as different cultures increasingly interact in an era of easy communication, access to information, and global business and travel, there is a new interest in looking at cross-cultural conflict resolution and how to bridge differences. Up to this point, we have looked at this on a grand scale in terms of cultural and conflict resolution evolution. However, there are situations that have more immediate requirements, and that need is driving the question, "Can grassroots and professional systems co-exist?"

Formal legal systems

North American culture and conflict resolution often focuses on individual rights, interests, and goals, and values horizontal relationships, achievement, competition, and autonomy (Augsburger, 1992; LeBaron Duryea, 1995; Schellenberg, 1996). In concert with that cultural norm, the preferred process for resolving disputes is a court system where the proceedings are formal, rational, and adversarial in reaching an agreement.

Briefly, the Western court system is about legal representation. Lawyers are retained to represent the different interests involved in a dispute, including the perpetrator, victim, and other private and public interests. Lawyers are strictly bound to their clients, and their job is to represent their clients' interests above all else. They enter into a confidentiality agreement with their clients and advise and act on behalf of them in formulating legal arguments that will work to their clients' best advantage. Cases that cannot be resolved through less formal discussions between lawyers and other legal experts will go to trial, where an impartial judge or a jury that is representative of the community listens to the legal arguments and finds "fault" in conflict situations. The judge is in charge of the proceedings, making sure that legal rules are followed and information and arguments are presented in a way that gives the best chance for justice. In making final decisions, judges have some latitude in assigning punishment and compensation, but still within the parameters of what has occurred in other similar cases (Schellenberg, 1996; Zehr, 1990).

Written transcripts of legal proceedings are meticulously detailed, and references to these notes and the transcripts of other similar cases are regularly referred to as part of presenting legal arguments. Decisions can be appealed to higher courts, but the possibility of an appeal is usually based on finding faults in court proceedings that unfairly affected the outcome of any earlier trials. It is important to note that issues of ethical misconduct are largely self-governed. For example, lawyers and legal experts are the ones who are reviewing the conduct of their colleagues as impartially as possible (e.g., law societies and judicial councils). Obviously, professional systems involving highly trained and specialized individuals like this one are very expensive.

Court systems are not the only avenue for conflict resolution in the Western world. Mediation in the West is a relatively new conflict resolution mechanism, and community mediation centers began to establish themselves in the 1970s. Lessons from the practice of labour relations and international diplomacy have led to a rise in Alternative Dispute Resolution (ADR) practices (Roy, Burdick, & Kriesberg, 2010). Like lawyers and judges, mediators in the West are impartial professionals from outside the communities. Their role is to facilitate the mediation process, clarify conflict issues and interests, and help the parties find their own solutions to the problem. Mediation is voluntary, private, confidential, and takes place in a neutral location. Mediation is the main ADR to a formal court process.

Other social services also play a very important role in conflict resolution. Counseling services for marriages, students, finances, mental health, and other things are performed by many different professionals (e.g., doctors, therapists, or financial advisors) and are available to anyone who can afford them. In some cases, these services are paid for by governments, but accessibility due to cost can be prohibitive. North American political institutions and community leadership consist of local officials, such as mayors and city councils; however, they do not feel a personal responsibility to assist individual citizens in resolving their disputes unless they involve the city's services or properties (Callister & Wall Jr., 2004). North American city officials often have conflict-of-interest regulations designed to ensure impartiality, which in some circumstances prevent them from participating in dispute resolution. Protestant, Catholic, and Jewish religious institutions have ministers, priests, and rabbis who assist their congregational members in resolving their disputes, but mediation is not seen as a primary responsibility (Callister & Wall Jr., 2004).

The use of written documents is a very important part of formal legal conflict resolution. Doctors, advisors, counselors, and social service workers are almost always required to take notes on meetings and decisions so that situations will be understandable to other professionals who might become involved in a case, or so information can be reviewed by others in supervisory positions. This oversight creates transparency and accountability of the professional services that are paid for by clients.

Similarly, the very detailed transcripts that are recorded in court proceedings form a body of case law and, combined with constitutional and legal laws and regulations, serve as a basis for assigning reparation. Although laws and regulations have requirements that often define penalties and reparation, different cases involve different individuals, and the contrasting histories, backgrounds, circumstances, and consequences of those involved will all be considered in forming a basis for reparation. Legal experts try to incorporate enough flexibility in the system to allow for these differences, and written documentation from previous similar cases often helps as a reference for appropriate judgment throughout legal proceedings, verdicts, penalties, and compensation.

Accessibility is not always easy in professional systems. Costs for obtaining professional, specialized services can be extremely high, demanding significant financial investment. Further, these systems can get backlogged and getting timely service can be difficult. Conflicts that go through the formal legal system can take many months to be officially resolved, and difficult cases can take years to work their way through the system. These delays often create barriers to effective resolution, exacerbating both financial costs and psychological stress.

In terms of rituals and celebrations, there are really no official communal ceremonies conducted at the end of a conflict. Shaking hands, signing documents, paying fees, and completing or paying the required restitution usually complete the conflict resolution process. Sometimes at the conclusion of mediation and community justice forum sessions, coffee and refreshments may be served to the parties as the terms of the agreement are being written up. Parties then go their separate ways, and the community does not witness a public resolution.

Because of the individualized nature of these cultures, inclusivity, support networks, and relationship building have evolved differently in these systems. These components are found in social service structures in the West, where counselling and therapy can encourage and assist in finding appropriate support networks, whether those be friends or other professional services (e.g., Alcoholics Anonymous, John Howard Society, religious groups, or anger management therapy groups). These support networks often focus on relationship building as part of a healing process and path to rehabilitation, but relationship building is not necessarily a premise on which conflict resolution is built in Western cultures. A major difference between the Lao system and more professional Western systems is that in Laos we see inclusivity, support networks, and relationship building as inherent parts of the conflict resolution system, whereas more professional Western systems have very different institutions that take responsibility for those provisions. Often, the onus is placed on the individual to find and engage in these services. In each case, the system is designed for the culture it serves and, for the most part, they are relatively successful.

There are situations where the cultures are thrust together and adaptation to the other conflict resolution system is tested. As discussed, political tensions and violence related to the Second Indochina War caused many Lao people to flee their home country and immigrate as refugees to North America in the late 1970s. Local sponsoring groups often took initial responsibility for the settlement process. Sponsors believed these obligations would include providing for the refugees' needs in terms of food and shelter, enrolling them in educational classes, finding employment opportunities, and helping in other aspects of resettlement that would enable them to adapt, become self-sufficient, and thrive in their new surroundings.

Because these Lao refugees often came without their larger, extended family and support networks, they sought to develop their conflict resolution networks with relationships developed in their new settings. In many cases, the individuals involved in their sponsoring groups were seen as their surrogate parents and elders. They would designate names for their sponsors, such as *paw* (father), *mer* (mother), *matow* (grandmother), *patow* (grandfather), *pah* (aunt), and *loong* (uncle). By using terms that suggested elder status as well as matriarchal or patriarchal positions, the Lao believed they were adding respect to their sponsors, whereas the sponsors believed that they were perceived as being old – even ancient. Seemingly, the more praise the Lao gave to them, the more offense the sponsors took. For example, one couple with a young family referred to one of their sponsors as *matow* (grandmother) as a sign of respect and honour for someone older than themselves, and the woman took grave offense (Stobbe, 2006). Neither party was comfortable in the relationship and neither fully understood the intent of the other.

In reality, the sponsors were not always prepared to take on some of these roles. Because the refugees' social structure had been destroyed as part of their displacement, they felt a strong need to re-establish their community hierarchies to help them create and access a conflict resolution system with which they were familiar, giving them the support networks that they needed to more comfortably adapt to their new surroundings. These social systems simply did not exist in their new surroundings and, unfortunately, adaptation was slow for them. Refugees often sought each other out in order to ask for assistance in addressing conflicts, but when these people were not available, especially for the first wave of refugees, the sponsors and others in the community became surrogate mediators. Full access to the professional systems of conflict resolution available in larger North American society was really only realized when their children went through the educational system and had the resources to access professionals (or became those professionals) and helped their parents become familiar with the system.

Assimilating the Lao people into the Western conflict resolution system has been slow, but working in the other direction has been equally problematic. A judicial system of criminal code and laws was adopted in Laos in 1989 (Savada, 1995). There are ongoing attempts to implement a formal legal system to support this rule-of-law structure, but success has been very modest to this point. There is a very small professional system that is mostly used in dealing with international bodies and other large businesses. Unfortunately, it is sometimes controlled by officials who have little accountability, making the system prone to a corrupt environment that unfairly supports those with means over those without. With fewer than 100 lawyers, Laos' weak legal and criminal justice system limits accessibility and accountability to the rule of law. Lack of judges and funding for basic legal training for members of the National Assembly and the legal sector contribute to the weak judicial system (UNODC, 2014). We have seen that it has a very limited ability to provide social justice to its citizens. This ineffectiveness, combined with the success of their traditional system, is why most Lao people today will never go through a "Western-style" professional legal process.

Looking at this, we begin to see why these traditional and legal systems are not easily interchangeable. They both work effectively for their corresponding cultural group, but learning to move between them is a long and complicated process. The Lao people are looking for help from those inside their circle, not from professional strangers who they do not know and who they perceive as having no real interest or stake in their conflict situation. Further, the large majority of the Lao population is far less educated and has significantly less disposable income than those who are accustomed to Western professional systems. Written documents are less available, less understandable, and less familiar to the average Lao citizen, and Lao citizens have less ability to access professional help in trying to address this gap. The legal language is difficult enough for those who are familiar with the system, but for those who are unfamiliar with the language, it is even more debilitating. Also, the legal systems do not inherently provide support networks and are not as directly involved in rebuilding community relationships, making them less effective in contributing to the Lao social world.

This reality of multi-cultural settings requires an examination of how the two systems can work together to effectively address conflicts to the satisfaction of both parties. Conflict resolution does not work in the same way for all people, but it is still important to find avenues to address conflicts between groups. One place to look for answers is found in indigenous conflict resolution systems. This style of conflict resolution represents another form of grassroots conflict resolution and has deep roots in trying to relate to more formal legal systems. The unfortunate history of imbalanced relationships between indigenous peoples and Western colonists has recently led to a fresh look at bridging these two types of conflict resolution systems.

New Zealand's traditional conflict resolution processes

New Zealand represents a turning point in conflict resolution study and application. In the mid-1980s, during a period of escalating violence in families, schools, and local communities, authorities began to focus on indigenous conflict resolution methods as a potential solution to a chronic problem. In New Zealand, the indigenous Maori people make up 12 percent of the 3.5 million population, but disproportionately represent 43 percent of the juvenile offender population (CCJC, 1996). This is an unfortunate reality in many of the world's justice systems, namely, that indigenous populations far outnumber the dominant population in incarceration facilities. In most of these circumstances, a combination of systemic injustice, racism, and corruption has left these groups with few viable options in their pursuit of social justice. In New Zealand, the need for a different approach to meet juvenile justice led to the creative use of a traditional process to address contemporary problems (McDonald, Moore, O'Connell, & Thorsborne, 1995).

In pre-colonial times, the justice system for the Maori involved restoring balance through compensation, promoting kinship responsibility, imposing corporal sanctions, giving chiefs considerable discretion, temporary or permanent exile, withdrawal and separation within the community, and instituting public punishments (Cunneen, 2004; Pratt, 1996). The teachings of the Maori Family Group Conference (1) emphasized consensus involving the whole community, (2) sought reconciliation and settlement acceptable to all involved, (3) was more concerned with reasons for wrong behaviour than with blame, and (4) was more concerned with restoration of harmony than with breach of law (Ross, 2006). As is common in many indigenous cultures, a conflict resolution process requires public condemnation of the act as well as public assertion that the offender remains a valued member of the community.

The Maori tradition of justice follows the protocols of a meeting (*hui*) of community members who help to resolve conflicts through teachings from elders (*kaumatua*), communication skills of speaking and listening, consensus decision making, and collective responsibility to uphold the *hui* decision (Wearmouth, McKinney, & Glynn, 2007). The *hui whakatika* (meeting; putting things right) conference process adheres to the following steps:

1. Prayers (*karakia*) and greeting (*mihimihi*) to acknowledge the presence and dignity of all present;

2. Written or spoken message that there is a problem but the person is not the problem;
3. Each person gets a chance to speak about what he or she hopes to gain from the *hui*;
4. Each person tells his or her own version of the problem;
5. Each person discusses the effects of the problem on those present and on others;
6. The group thinks about a time when there was no problem;
7. The group portrays new descriptions of people when there is no problem;
8. The group discusses what amends are needed to repair the harm caused by the problem;
9. The group brainstorms ideas and resources to overcome the problem;
10. The group discusses how these plans meet the needs of all people who are affected by the harm;
11. The group is given responsibility to administer the plans and to move forward, allowing for follow-up;
12. Prayer (*karakia*) and thanks, and perhaps hospitality, are offered (Restorative Practices Development Team, 2003 as cited in Wearmouth *et al.*, 2007, p. 197).

For the Maori, the resolution of conflict must respect and restore the *mama* (individual autonomy, integrity, self-esteem, and standing in the community) of all parties involved in conflict. The *whanaungatanga* represents the many inter-relationships in one's life and the support of the various relationships (extended families, relatives, or communities) (*Wearmouth et al.*, 2007). For centuries, the Maori people used this process, sometimes referred to as Family Group Conferencing (also referred to as Community Accountability Conferencing or Community Justice Forums) to resolve disputes involving young people, where extended networks of family and friends shared the responsibility for the young offender's behaviours and involved the victim in the resolution of the conflict without resorting to formal adjudication processes (*McDonald et al.*, 1995; McElrea, 1996).

Although not an entirely similar system to that in Laos, it does share some characteristics. Both systems recognize that conflict is a disruption to collective face, affecting the whole community, and that conflict resolution processes help to revitalize the collective face. The importance and accountability of extended community networks is imperative as a support mechanism for victims and perpetrators as they repair relationships and reintegrate into their communities. This inclusivity contributes to an overlying goal of relationship building and re-harmonizing social connections, and promotes healthy conflict resolution. In theory, the rather public nature of the process is one that lends itself to a certain degree of transparency, and there seems to be enough community inclusivity to provide a reasonable level of accountability between all parties in a conflict resolution scenario.

Unfortunately, the New Zealand situation demonstrates something that is common in many places that were affected by colonization, especially amongst indigenous groups. It shows us that grassroots conflict resolution systems embedded in a cultural social structure can be destroyed. Through generations of cultural oppression, the destruction of family and extended social relationships, infringement on land and environment, the general dismantling of an economic system of self-sufficiency, and the oppression of a spiritual worldview, the social infrastructure that supports their conflict resolution system has been eroded to a point where it is no longer viable as a justice system. In essence, there is no longer familiarity with the system, no accessibility to use the system, and no acceptable alternative process available to help them resolve their conflicts.

With no avenue for obtaining social justice, violence and other destructive forms of behaviour follow, leading to systemic stereotypes, biases, and other forms of racism with clearly defined cyclical patterns of violence. The various conflicts and issues involving indigenous populations around the globe show us how integrated our conflict resolution systems are with other aspects of our cultural worldview and how devastating the results of ignoring that are.

Recognizing the negative impact caused by the destruction of the Maori social system, researchers sought to find a way to draw attention to lost Maori traditions, rediscover their historic and current value to New Zealand society, and find ways of introducing these traditions into the formal legal system. In 1989, New Zealand introduced the Children, Young Persons and Their Families Act. which initiated the development of Family Group Conferencing (FGC) to address the issues of young offenders charged with criminal offences other than the most serious crimes (CCJC, 1996; Jantzi, 2004; McElrea, 1996; Pratt, 1996; Ross, 2006). This act focused on a restorative justice process that was similar to the traditional Maori conflict resolution system in hopes that it would be more effective than the criminal justice system in repairing harm and reintegrating offenders back to their communities.

Restorative justice is a different paradigm of understanding crime and justice and shares a common worldview with many indigenous conflict resolution structures. According to Zehr (1990), the restorative lens (1) defines crime as harm to people and relationships; (2) aims to identify needs and obligations to make things right; (3) encourages dialogue and mutual agreement; (4) gives victims and offenders central roles; and (5) is judged by responsibilities assumed, needs met, and healing of individuals and relationships. These characteristics are in contrast to "retributive" justice in the Western, formal criminal justice system that defines crime as harm to the state and then determines blame and administers appropriate punishment (Zehr, 1990). A restorative justice practice for someone with behavioural problems might be illustrated through schools and communities which focus on the Maori protocol of involving the whole community in seeking resolution and support for the offender. The use of traditional community conflict resolution processes might be better equipped to resolve tensions and restore harmonious relationships between individuals and communities (Wearmouth *et al.*, 2007).

Clearly, the hope was that in using a conflict resolution system that was more closely akin to the traditional Maori conflict resolution system, offenders would be better reintegrated into their communities, resulting in decreased crime and incarceration rates. In fact, the model has since been introduced in many justice systems around the world. In 1990, FGC model began expanding in Australia. In 1991 it was tried in police services in New South Wales, and in 1994, FGC was adapted by schools in Queensland and South Australia to address school bullying and other incidents. FGC was introduced to the United States in 1995 and in Canada in 1996 (McDonald *et al.*, 1995; RCMP, 2009).

A 2011 report, "Reoffending Analysis for Restorative Justice Cases 2008 and 2009," published by the New Zealand Ministry of Justice, reports that offenders going through restorative justice in New Zealand had a 20 to 23 percent lower chance of reoffending and a 33 percent reduced chance of re-imprisonment. It also demonstrates that these numbers are as effective, or even more positive, for Maori people than for non-Maori people. Clearly, the idea of restorative justice is one that has some potential in providing social justice for groups that have been resistant to other so-called "retributive" forms of criminal justice.

In looking at this system through the Lao lens, I suggest that the reasons this system holds promise are largely due to the increased weight put on community inclusiveness, support networks, and relationship building. The community involvement in this system lends credibility and trust, giving it a greater perception of transparency and accountability, while at the same time defining who the support networks of both victims and offenders will be and including them as aids to completing reparation and relationship building.

I am not suggesting that the New Zealand system is a cure-all for the very complex issues involving indigenous minority peoples within larger Western cultures. As long as the massive systemic issues and conflict indicators (e.g., poverty, education, or health) continue to negatively affect indigenous populations more than majority populations, indigenous groups will unfortunately have higher rates of representation in our criminal justice systems. That said, conflict resolution systems are the front line for dealing with the symptoms of inequality and need to find ways of addressing the root causes of such conflicts in order to give these groups the best chance to move into a healthy relationship with their communities. New Zealand is an excellent case study of how an alternative criminal justice philosophy can be legislated, resulting in restorative encounters (Masters, 2004).

Canada's restorative conflict resolution processes

Canada has a large population of Aboriginal people, with over 1.4 million people identifying as Aboriginal (Government of Canada, 2014). Similar to New Zealand, Canada is trying to deal with inequities in its justice system. Canada also suffers from significant overrepresentation of Aboriginals in its prison system and has actively looked to grassroots systems as part of a solution. Specifically, Canada has focused on the examples presented by New Zealand and South Africa, hoping that the efforts of these two nations might demonstrate the beginnings of a conflict resolution system that bridges formal and traditional justice.

In 1996, Canada developed a restorative justice initiative called the Community Justice Forum (CJF). Typical of grassroots conflict resolution, the CJF uses support networks (e.g., family, friends, teachers, other professionals or community members) in an attempt to help the victim and offender re-establish positive relationships in their community. Cases that are diverted through a CJF process are handpicked by professionals in the criminal justice system and agreed to by both parties as a voluntary process. Typically, offenders have already taken responsibility for their actions by admitting guilt.

The session(s) are conducted in a circle where the victim, the offender, and their support networks sit on either side of the facilitators. This seating is pre-arranged to allow the parties to face one another and discuss honestly the impact of the conflict on everyone in the circle. The circle format represents inclusivity, wholeness, unity, equal power among the participants, and the importance of voice and consensus decision making. In larger processes, there may be more than one circle, with the people closest to the conflict situation encompassing the inner circle, and each consecutive outer circle representing different segments of the community and professionals (e.g., lawyers, teachers, or principals).

The facilitator's role is to help guide the process to resolution, including an agreement on appropriate reparations that may include community service, compensation, and apologies. Closure is reached when the facilitator drafts written agreements which can designate responsibilities to support networks in helping to maintain the arrangements. Participants sometimes share informal time together, especially during closing proceedings. This allows for further dialogue and possibly a light snack (RCMP, 2009).

The goal of this process is to encourage offender responsibility and reintegrate him or her into the community, to give the victim a central role in problem solving, and to encourage healing within the community. It is hoped that through such processes, balance and harmony can be achieved in a way that more effectively prevents future conflicts, bringing both the victim and the offender back into a positive community relationship.

Canada also looked to South Africa for a larger-scale event that aimed at addressing some of its systemic human rights abuses against Aboriginal people who were forced into residential schools over the past century. South Africa introduced a Truth and Reconciliation Commission (TRC) in 1996 to investigate gross human rights violations during the apartheid regime in South Africa. Its success propelled many countries to promote and engage in various forms of TRC (see Argentina National Commission on the Disappearance of Persons, Brazil National Truth Commission, Colombia National Commission for Reparation and Reconciliation, Chile National Truth and Reconciliation Commission, and others).

Canada launched its own TRC in 2009, a five-year project, to address the impact of more than 150,000 First Nations, Metis, and Inuit children who were forcibly removed from their families and sent to residential schools. The Canadian TRC focused on documenting the traumatic experiences that had been passed from generation to generation in hopes of rebuilding the relationship between Aboriginal peoples and other Canadians and leading to reconciliation after more than a century of trauma and injustice (TRC of Canada, 2014). The goals of the TRC were to (1) acknowledge residential school experiences, impacts, and consequences; (2) provide holistic, culturally appropriate, and safe settings for students, families, and communities to discuss their stories; (3) witness, support, promote, and facilitate truth and reconciliation events at national and community levels; (4) promote awareness and public education of Canadians on the Indian Residential School (IRS) system and its impacts; (5) identify sources and create a complete historical record of the IRS system and its legacy and make it accessible to the public; (6) produce a report, including recommendations to the government of Canada concerning the IRS system and experience, and the ongoing legacy of residential schools; and (7) support commemoration of former IRS students and their families (TRC of Canada, 2014). The TRC of Canada's National Research Centre at the University of Manitoba houses videos, audio-recorded statements, digitalized archival documents, photographs, and works of art, among many other items pertaining to residential schools.

Like New Zealand and South Africa, Canada's foray into indigenous conflict resolution is only one way to alleviate the problems facing its most marginalized people. To its credit, Canada has recognized that there has been historical injustice to a specific segment of its population and has begun a process of involving that group in searching for solutions. In Laos, we see how its conflict resolution mechanisms serve multiple functions in healing and in education between groups. In committing to these same functions, Canadians are hopefully embarking on a road that will more fully appreciate the history of its indigenous population and give voice to those who need healing. At the same time, it will educate all its citizens on how traditional Aboriginal customs and rituals have a place in every Canadian's life. Through these kinds of processes, reconciliation becomes increasingly possible as truth, mercy, justice, and peace come together in a unique space of dialogue (Lederach, 1997).

Conclusion

Jeong (2005) states, "[O]ne of the most critical conditions for making a peace process sustainable is the inclusion of local communities" (p. 33). In countries of diverse ethnicities, cultures, and religions, it is vital that local approaches to conflict resolution be studied and utilized to resolve conflicts in the community. The international community is slowly beginning to recognize this, but the ramifications of putting this truth into practice are significant. The previous examples show that in fully committing to peacebuilding, international bodies have to change the way their internal and external relationships work. Imposing cultural ideals on other groups has proven ineffective time and time again. Forcing democratic reform and rule-of-law systems is not a magic bullet, especially when accompanied by military action. But putting systems in place that allow cultural identity to evolve together from a position of mutual benefit and respect might present a path to peace. Sustainable peace requires culturally sensitive peacemaking and peacebuilding at the "local, regional, and global, one that does not perceive insiders as the problem and outsiders as the solution" (Bercovitch & Jackson, 2009, p. 14).

The idea of conflict resolution systems design is not one that has taken a firm hold in our global consciousness. Effective and sustainable resolutions take a lot of creativity, flexibility, and above all, patience. Our first requirement is to understand the principles that underlie a successful conflict resolution process. How does conflict resolution work in real-life cases? Are there overriding principles that must be in place to ensure a positive result? In short, how do we approach conflict resolution from the ground up?

What the world needs is an example demonstrating that this works on a large scale. I suggest Laos, not because it has perfect relations between its ethnic groups, is able to manage every type of conflict effectively, or has anything close to perfect governance, but because Laos has a history of resiliency and perseverance in moving forward. Its people have a history of making peace from violence, finding ways to improve their quality of life, maintaining a rich culture, and finding ways to be inclusive in spite of their differences. Laos shows us that local, community-oriented processes can be instrumental in addressing conflicts and reconciliation. We see how peace moves from micro to macro, from one relationship to multiple relationships. The mediation processes that involve various local community representatives, as well as the *soukhouan* and *soumma* rituals, all show the importance of the role of the community in conflict resolution, the celebration of people coming together, and as support networks in post-conflict situations. Grassroots processes help build important relationships that become the foundation of peace. It is through those mechanisms that a people so violated with violence can still know peace and commit to an inclusive identity.

Bibliography

Augsburger, David W. (1992). *Conflict Mediation Across Cultures: Pathways and Patterns*. Louisville: Westminster John Knox Press.

Avruch, Kevin, Black, Peter W., & Scimecca, Joseph A. (eds.). (1998). *Conflict Resolution: Cross-Cultural Perspectives*. Westport: Praeger.

Bercovitch, Jacob, & Jackson, Richard. (2009). *Conflict Resolution in the Twenty-first Century*. Ann Arbor: University of Michigan Press.

Black, Peter W. (1998). Surprised by Common Sense: Local Understandings and the Management of Conflict in Tobi, Republic of Belau. In Kevin Avruch, Peter W. Black, & Joseph A. Scimecca (eds.), *Conflict Resolution: Cross-Cultural Perspectives* (pp. 145–164). Westport: Praeger.

Callister, Ronda Roberts, & Wall Jr., James A. (2004). Thai and U.S. Community Mediation. *The Journal of Conflict Resolution*, 48(4), 573–598.

CCJC. (1996). *Satisfying Justice: Safe Community Options That Attempt to Repair Harm From Crime and Reduce the Use or Length of Imprisonment*. Ottawa: The Church Council on Justice and Corrections.

Cummings, Joe. (1994). *Laos*. Hawthorn: Lonely Planet Publications.

Cunneen, Chris. (2004). What Are the Implications of Restorative Justice's Use of Indigenous Traditions? In Howard Zehr & Barb Toews (eds.), *Critical Issues in Restorative Justice* (pp. 345–363). Monsey: Criminal Justice Press.

Government of Canada. (2014). Aboriginal Peoples in Canada: First Nations People, Metis, and Inuit. Retrieved January 26, 2014, from www12.statcan.gc.ca/nhs-enm/2011/as-sa/99–011-x/99–011-x2011001-eng.cfm.

Hardin, Garrett. (1968). The Tragedy of the Commons. *Science*, 162(3859), 1243–1248.

Irani, George E. (2004). Islamic Mediation Techniques for Middle East Conflicts. In Fred E. Jandt (ed.), *Intercommunal Communication: A Global Reader* (pp. 360–375). Thousand Oaks: Sage Publications.

Irani, George E. (2006). Apologies and Reconciliation: Middle Eastern Rituals. In Elazar Barkan & Alexander Karn (eds.), *Taking Wrongs Seriously: Apologies and Reconciliation*. Stanford: Stanford University Press.

Irani, George E., & Funk, Nathan C. (2000). Rituals of Reconciliation: Arab-Islamic Perspectives. *Kroc Institute Occasional Paper,* 19(2), 1–34.

Jantzi, Vernon E. (2004). *What Is the Role of the State in Restorative Justice?* Monsey: Criminal Justice Press.

Jeong, Ho-Won. (2005). *Peacebuilding in Postconflict Societies.* Boulder: Lynne Rienner Publishers.

King-Irani, Laurie E. (2000a). Rituals of Forgiveness and Processes of Empowerment in Lebanon. In I. William Zartman (ed.), *Traditional Cures for Modern Conflicts: African Conflict "Medicine"* (pp. 129–140). Boulder: Lynne Rienner Publishers.

King-Irani, Laurie E. (2000b). Rituals of Forgiveness and Processes of Empowerment in Lebanon. In I. William Zartman (ed.), *Traditional Cures for Modern Conflicts: African Conflict "Medicine"* (pp. 129–140). Boulder: Lynne Rienner Publishers.

LeBaron Duryea, Michelle. (1995). *Conflict Resolution and Analysis as Education* (3rd ed.). Akron: Mennonite Conciliation Service.

Lederach, John Paul. (1997). *Building Peace: Sustainable Reconciliation in Divided Societies.* Washington, DC: United States Institute of Peace Press.

Marten, Gerald G. (2007). *Human Ecology: Basic Concepts for Sustainable Development.* Sterling: Earthscan Publications Ltd.

Masters, Guy. (2004). *What Happens When Restorative Justice Is Encouraged, Enabled and/or Guided by Legislation?* Monsey: Criminal Justice Press.

McDonald, John, Moore, David, O'Connell, Terry, & Thorsborne, Margaret. (1995). *Real Justice Training Manual: Coordinating Family Group Conferences.* Piperville: The Piper's Press.

McElrea, Frederick W. M. (1996). *The New Zealand Youth Court: A Model for Use With Adults.* Monsey: Criminal Justice Press.

Pholsena, Vatthana. (2006). *Post-War Laos: The Politics of Culture, History, and Identity.* Ithaca: Cornell University Press.

Pratt, John. (1996). *Colonization, Power and Silence: A History of Indigenous Justice in New Zealand Society.* Monsey: Criminal Justice Press.

RCMP. (2009). *Community Justice Forum Facilitator's Guide to the RCMP Learning Map.* Ottawa: Royal Canadian Mounted Police.

Ross, Rupert. (2006). *Return to the Teachings: Exploring Aboriginal Justice.* Toronto: Penguin Canada.

Roy, Beth, Burdick, John, & Kriesberg, Louis. (2010). A Conversation Between Conflict Resolution and Social Movement Scholars. *Conflict Resolution Quarterly,* 27(4), 347–368.

Savada, Andrea Matles. (1995). *Laos: A Country Study.* Washington, DC: Federal Research Division, Library of Congress.

Schellenberg, James A. (1996). *Conflict Resolution: Theory, Research, and Practice.* Albany: State University of New York Press.

Sharp, Gene. (1973). *The Politics of Nonviolent Action: Part 1 Power and Struggle.* Boston: Porter Sargent Publishers.

Stobbe, Stephanie Phetsamay. (2006). Cross-Cultural Experiences of Laotian Refugees and Mennonite Sponsors in British Columbia and Manitoba. *Journal of Mennonite Studies,* 24, 111–128.

TRC of Canada. (2014). Truth and Reconciliation Commission of Canada. Retrieved August 19, 2014, from www.trc.ca/websites/reconciliation/index.php?p=312.

Tse-Tung, Mao. (1960). *Problems of War and Strategy* (2nd ed.). Peking: Foreign Languages Press.

UNODC. (2014). UNODC Lao PDR Country Office. Retrieved May 20, 2014, from UNODC www.unodc.org/laopdr/.

Wearmouth, Janice, McKinney, Rawiri, & Glynn, Ted. (2007). Restorative Justice: Two Examples From New Zealand Schools. *British Journal of Special Education,* 34(4), 196–203.

Zartman, William I. (2000). *Traditional Cures for Modern Conflicts: African Conflict "Medicine."* Boulder: Lynne Rienner Publishers, Inc.

Zehr, Howard. (1990). *Changing Lenses.* Scottdale: Herald Press.

7   Tenets of conflict resolution

> . . . that resources for peace are sociocultural as well as socioeconomic in nature; and that the redefinition and restoration of relationships depends on creating a dynamic, conflict-responsive peacebuilding infrastructure.
>
> (Solomon, as cited in Lederach, 1997, p. x)

When I first started to commit to serious research in Laos, I asked myself three questions: (1) How can culturally specific conflict resolution processes at the grassroots level be used to promote equality, justice, and freedom in places where formal legal systems are unfamiliar, undeveloped, and are not a compelling force in promoting social justice? (2) How can traditional conflict resolution processes and rituals assist in the maintenance and reparation of relationships between parties in conflict? and (3) How can these processes be used and adapted in cross-cultural conflict resolution to establish relationships between groups? In looking through the conflict resolution processes presented, these questions have largely been answered through various examples. Like every other conflict resolution system, it has its imperfections. However, it is a system that is effective, accessible, familiar, and respected by the communities it serves.

Laos is a place that knows peace. Through grassroots conflict resolution systems entrenched in their cultural relationships, they have managed to continually re-create the social balance that has been disturbed by others with less-than-altruistic purposes. Early in this book, I wrote the following paragraph and asked a relatively simple question:

> What is so interesting about Laos is that, in spite of the political turmoil that has plagued its existence, its extremely complex social structure and diverse population have largely been peaceful and respectful. They consider themselves to be a multi-cultural society with multiple groups of different ethnic heritages, incorporated into a common national identity. Different political powers throughout Southeast Asian history have managed to wage wars for every imaginable reason, from resource expansion to ideology, but the diverse groups seem to find peace with each other relatively easily. Why here, and equally importantly, why not elsewhere?

It is important to have this conversation, to begin a journey of discussion aimed at providing a better format for bridging conflicts everywhere. But the answer is complex because conflicts are never completely alike; therefore, neither is conflict resolution. Does recognizing that no two conflicts are the same imply that every conflict resolution response needs years of study to fully understand the problem and implement a solution? Or are there ways that we can streamline and simplify our understanding of conflict and conflict resolution to speed up our ability to intervene with positive action?

Our brief look at other processes in the world has already demonstrated that such an argument is worth pursuing. To attempt a more complete response, we need to organize the Lao Conflict Resolution System into a set of characteristics or principles that will help us understand essential conflict resolution structures that are necessary for effective resolution. Hopefully this will illuminate some basic conflict resolution principles that are necessary as a kind of "universal language" for success. The twenty-first-century conflicts require new approaches to conflict resolution with a goal to end violent behaviour and establish "new forms of interactions that can reflect the basic tenets of justice, human needs, legitimacy, and equality" (Bercovitch & Jackson, 2009, p. 9).

In looking back at Lao Conflict Resolution System, certain words and concepts continually come up. Interestingly, many of these same words appeared in our brief comparison of grassroots and professional systems in the last chapter. Clearly, the dispute resolution processes are not the same, but there are seemingly some common basic requirements that are found in both of these processes. Does describing those needs or requirements provide a framework with which to view conflict resolution? Would they be useful in guiding the development of conflict resolution design? In essence, what are the basic qualities or mechanics of this process, and do they provide a useful starting point to begin looking at a way of understanding and implementing possible conflict resolution scenarios for places with broken systems?

Before delving into that question, a brief review of the Lao conflict resolution system is important. To summarize, their system requires a progression through five levels of mediation that go from private, informal mediation with close family connections to a public, formal mediation session in front of a representational mediation committee. Each level is given several opportunities for resolution, as well as opportunities to "fine-tune" any agreements that have been reached, before moving to the next level. Further, there is an expectation that mediators from previous sessions will be on hand to address mediators in subsequent levels, should they be required to answer any questions or address other issues related to the conflict. Inherently, there is a larger group of people as the conflict progresses to higher levels. We have seen that through this process there is a reliance on customary laws and that agreements made in the final levels sometimes include written documents that spell out responsibilities.

After the mediation processes are complete and settlement has been achieved, parties usually go through the rituals of conflict resolution in the *souhkhouan* and *soumma*. In relation to the progression through mediation levels, these rituals also

Table 7.1 Tenets of conflict resolution

Tenets of Conflict Resolution	Descriptor Words
1. Familiarity/understanding	Understand, known, accepted, recognized
2. Accessibility/opportunity	Opportunity, access, available, user friendly
3. Inclusivity	Encompassing, includes all affected by conflict
4. Transparency	Clear, open process, honest, frank
5. Accountability/explainability	Able to explain, responsible, answerable
6. Reparation/settlement	Settlement, rehabilitate, compensate, protect
7. Flexibility/litheness	Litheness, adapt, supple, elastic
8. Creativity/originality	Original, imaginative, innovative, resourceful
9. Relationship building	Connect, rapport, bond, link
10. Support networks	Backing, care, encouragement, reinforcement

increase in scope, as mandated by the seriousness of the conflict and the number of people involved in its resolution. These rituals are part of reintegrating both victim and offender into society with good standing, as well as defining and paying tribute to mediators and others involved in the conflict resolution agreement. Further, this allows them to stand alongside the victim and offender as supporters of the healing process. These conflict resolution rituals, with their cultural variations, are commonly used to address conflicts within and between the different ethnic groups in Laos. Ethnic differences in the resolution rituals and celebrations become part of the negotiation process, allowing for adaptations and amendments as required by the conflict situation itself and by the different cultural traditions.

In studying this process throughout the book, a number of concepts are continually referred to, and these themes deserve some attention as qualities of a conflict resolution system that play an important role in bridging relationships through conflict. I would like to highlight ten of them: familiarity (understanding), accessibility (opportunity), inclusivity, transparency, accountability (explainability), reparation (settlement), flexibility (litheness), creativity (originality), relationship building, and support networks (see Table 7.1). It is through these main principles or tenets of conflict resolution that the Lao people have repeatedly found their way back to peace over thousands of years of relationships as neighbours, business partners, and residents of this landlocked country.

The tenets of conflict resolution

These ten themes comprise some underlying principles of the Lao Conflict Resolution system, and are repeatedly referred to in the analysis of their system, as well as many other structures, including formal legal systems. They each represent a need that must be satisfactorily fulfilled for effective conflict resolution to take place, but the way that these tenets manifest themselves depends on the cultural worldview that the system is part of. Clearly, these tenets are interconnected and build on one another. For example, accountability is dependent on transparency, inclusivity is dependent on accessibility, and creativity is dependent on flexibility, and vice versa. However, there is no particular hierarchy in one over the other, and I hesitate to put them into groupings that might suggest the relationships between some of these tenets are more important than relationships between others. For the purposes of this book, it is enough to see that they exist and are important components of social justice.

Familiarity/understanding

The old expression, "practice makes perfect," is steeped in the idea of familiarity and experience. One gets more comfortable at performing certain tasks by rehearsing them over and over again. The system of conflict resolution in Laos is immersed in the traditions and experiences of the past, having been rehearsed and performed for generations. That familiarity is a significant reason for its success. Lao individuals and groups are willing to enter into a conflict resolution process because they have a clear understanding of what to expect. Children are taught at an early age to respect their elders, and if there are conflicts, to discuss them with their parents. Parents and others in the community model these values and demonstrate the use of such processes in their own conflicts. Understanding these teachings and examples helps to ingrain them in daily encounters and relationships.

Cultural communication systems serve to express the knowledge needs of the community and to educate through classrooms, myths, storytelling, rituals, and other customs. The manner in which different cultures teach knowledge is part of a complex education system, with the mandate of communicating important cultural values and developing further knowledge. These educational systems are often multi-faceted and include both formal and informal training (Bogdan & Biklen, 2007; Freire, 1990). The educational activities serve to reinforce and familiarize the cultural values of a community, while also providing a knowledge base with which to serve community members, including appropriate conflict resolution processes.

Cross-cultural conflict resolution has been successful in Laos because it is understood and familiar to individuals from different groups. Even in situations where there are cultural differences in process, many people share an understanding of what those differences mean and which method should be used in different situations. In circumstances where there is ambiguity about the process, details are negotiated through mediators and dialogue through *op-lom*. Through this process, a model can be adapted to meet the needs of the parties in conflict. We have already discussed how this becomes a type of education system between groups, providing understanding and participation for different cultural worldviews and traditions.

Because the Lao people are familiar with and understand the various mediation processes in their country, they believe that these conflict resolution procedures are fair and that their voices are represented in the different processes. Further, because they are familiar with the mediators themselves, they have a certain comfort level in the relationship, allowing them to feel at ease in discussing the conflict issues, how they have been affected, and what they need to resolve the conflict. They believe that these mediators are invested in their lives and in the conflict, providing a strong incentive to make wise choices. This familiarity in both process and participants is an important part of feeling secure and content in the resolution, understanding that decisions have been made with their cultural focus on restoring "face and eyes."

Bunha (conflict) is stressful enough, and reliving it through a conflict resolution process can be intimidating, embarrassing, and painful. Clearly, being familiar with the process enables people to have a level of control that can be empowering for those involved in conflict resolution. Conflict is often related to the breaking of social boundaries, relationships between people, connections with our environment, or struggles within ourselves. Conflict resolution is part of restoring those boundaries and relationships. Therefore, being clear on where the boundaries and relationships are in a conflict resolution process is of paramount importance. That knowledge comes through familiarity and understanding.

Accessibility/opportunity

A successful conflict resolution system is one that is accessible to all the people it serves. Whether it is having access to mediators, being able to pay for the process, or simply having enough opportunities to implement a resolution, there must always be adequate infrastructure to support parties who are looking for help in resolving conflict. Without balance between conflict and resolution, conflicts are bound to spiral out of control into violent struggle that, if unchecked, can consume generations of people and require massive international efforts to overcome.

As noted earlier, the Lao Constitution does make room for conflict resolution and does give all Lao citizens the right to a "rule of law" style of justice. We have also seen that interference and bribery continue to undermine this. Low literacy rates, low education levels in general, lack of access to qualified legal professionals (due to both expense and a shortage of expertise), lack of civil societies, and a lack of political opposition have contributed to an environment where court systems are not a compelling force in promoting social justice. Rule of law is inconsistently applied and open to significant interpretation, and has essentially become a tool to promote corruption and power inequity. Just as importantly, there already is a system that people are familiar with and that is accessible, so historically there has been very little internal pressure on the government to rectify this.

Obviously, family is one of the most accessible social structures available to humans across the world. Families act as the entry level to the Lao conflict resolution spectrum. Accessibility to each subsequent level is dependent on the contacts in the previous level. Different contacts will provide different opportunities for resolution. For example, parents would have contacts with relatives, who would then have contacts with village elders, village leaders, and so forth. Accessibility to the next mediation process and the mediators involved in that process becomes available through the extended connections inherent in the progression through the mediation levels. In the beginning stages, either of the conflicting parties or their respective mediators can pursue higher-level mediation. However, in more advanced stages, and certainly by the time a conflict case reaches the *Neoy Gai Geer* mediation, recommendation for further mediation by the village leader would be the norm.

We have seen that Lao tradition dictates that three attempts at resolution be made at each successive mediation level. This gives substantial opportunity for resolution and opportunity to revise agreements that are not being maintained. Negotiation is often part of a resolution, whether that is related to the size or cost of a *soukhouan* ritual or any other part of the agreement. Sometimes unforeseen issues present themselves. Those that cannot be resolved easily through *op-lom* between the parties can often be resolved with the help of the mediators. Often these are casual visits that serve as informal negotiation, or sometimes they are more official, representing agreements that are difficult to adhere to. In any case, continued accessibility to these individuals is of paramount importance in ironing out any problems in sustaining agreements, both in the initial stages of implementation and over time.

Inclusivity

Understanding culturally appropriate ways of being inclusive in conflict resolution is a very complicated undertaking. In Laos, maintaining privacy within an inclusive framework requires a delicate balancing act, one that we have seen successfully employed through the progression of the conflict resolution spectrum and into the rituals of conflict resolution. The growing inclusivity of this progression fuels appropriately sized support networks that encourage and support the parties in fulfilling their agreements. The support networks also experience ownership of the process and take pride in the outcome since they are actively involved from beginning to end. This is inclusivity built from grassroots initiatives – those who are directly involved in the conflict are the ones who are controlling the resolution process and how the final terms of the agreement are met.

Being inclusive in conflict resolution seems to be a fairly obvious requirement for a process to be successful. Nevertheless, it is also one of the most frequently ignored components, especially in "top-down" conflict resolution processes. These processes are difficult, as they involve resolutions that are negotiated by a leadership group of representatives on behalf of its constituency. The problems arise when the leadership is unsuccessful in obtaining a resolution that satisfies its constituency. Sometimes this is due to resolutions that are simply unfeasible or unsustainable, difficulties in educating those in conflict about mutually satisfying resolutions, and/or a lack of faith in the leadership that translates into a lack of trust in the resolutions. No matter what the reasons are, a lack of inclusivity in the process is often the cause. When people feel that they are a part of the process and their voices are heard, satisfactory resolutions are more possible.

I am not suggesting that there is no place for leadership representations in conflict resolution structures. In fact, some of the best examples of large-scale conflict resolution have been centered on leadership figures who have incredible mass support and credibility in carrying out these processes. Mahatma Gandhi and Nelson Mandela are two figures who have been the center of relatively peaceful and nonviolent conflict resolution processes, impacting hundreds of millions of lives in their respective constituencies.

South Africa is a very interesting example of successful top-down conflict resolution through a concerted, diligent effort to be inclusive. In 1995, the first black South African president, Nelson Mandela, established the incredibly large-scale Truth and Reconciliation Commission (TRC). Chaired by Archbishop Desmond Tutu, its purpose was to investigate and provide a complete report of injustices done against many people and provide a small token of restitution. It offered to listen to, document, and provide avenues for support services to anyone in South Africa who had been the victim of apartheid's systemic racial violence between 1960 and 1994. The scope of the conflict was enormous in dealing with human rights violations, reparations, and amnesty; therefore, the conflict resolution process was enormous. It needed to be inclusive enough to encompass the gravity of the injustice inflicted upon a very large number of people. The TRC was organized by a group of elders composed of independent leaders who worked for justice, human rights, and peace. It had an element of bottom-up conflict resolution because its approach was steeped in the South African culture and the idea of *ubuntu*, meaning collective solidarity, as described by the Nguni proverb "*Umuntu ngumuntu ngabantu*" (I am because we are) (Masina, 2000, p. 171). As already stated, *ubuntu* "speaks about the essence of being human: that my humanity is caught up in your humanity because we say a person is a person through other persons" (Enright & North, 1998, p. foreword).

Committing to such a grand, public process that captures international attention is not for every culture. Different cultures will need their own continuum of private and public conflict resolution processes to deal with memories of violence and past trauma (Rigby, 2012). Laos has not made use of a large, public commission to deal with its past injustices. The TRC in South Africa is a very different process than what we find in Laos, but the principle is the same. Conflict resolution must strive to include those people affected by the conflict, from the smallest conflicts to the largest. Laos has found inclusivity to deal with its very large conflicts within its grassroots approach – a million *soukhouans* for a million displaced people, not mandated by leadership, but by a cultural worldview that supports community building, one person at a time. Although the conflict resolution systems are not perfect in Laos or South Africa, and full reconciliation has not been achieved among all the ethnic groups, they have made inspiring achievements in coming to terms with their histories.

Transparency

Transparency is found through the ability to obtain information and the trust one has in the quality of that information. In formal legal systems, transparency is obtained through meticulous written documentation of proceedings, available for review by participants and others so that decisions can be logically understood, followed, referred to, and otherwise analyzed through reading transcripts. This is also true of our professional social service institutions, where note taking and written records are a fundamental part of information exchange between parties, whether that be for clients or professionals in an advising position.

Literacy in Laos, while improving, is still not at a point where written documentation would be helpful in providing transparency. This is especially true in rural communities and for some of the smaller ethnic groups. In fact, written documentation would have fostered larger inequality between ethnic groups, as the majority Ethnic Lao group has typically had a more urban lifestyle with better access to schools and education, and has spoken the only language to have a written script. But traditionally, even for them, literacy would have been reserved for only a few educated individuals. Clearly, any reliance on written documentation as a basis for conflict resolution would have been inaccessible to the majority of Lao citizens, creating an environment where the educated few would have transparency and others would not.

For an oral society like Laos, transparency is clearly wrapped up in the concept of "trust." Because conflicting parties have historically had little ability to personally review documents, having trust in mediators is paramount. Having close connections with mediators who are personally invested in restoring healthy "face and eyes" ensures that level of trust. Parents, family, and close relatives are generally people with whom we have very direct relationships and who have a level of trust in each other. As part of transparency, family members openly convey information and share personal space frequently enough to thoroughly discuss issues related to any conflict and mediation process. This allows for appropriate dissemination of information within a network of trusted advisors.

Equally important in the Lao context, it allows transparency to occur within an overwhelming cultural need for privacy. There is full disclosure to the parties within a private setting. In the event that conflict situations affect more people in the community, more community members (and "higher-ranking" ones) become involved in its resolution, thereby continuing to support this delicate balance between transparency and privacy. Laos is full of yin and yang, delicate paradoxes searching for balance between somewhat opposite but still interdependent realities.

There is value in learning to respect this balance across our world. For those of us with constant Internet access and an ability to obtain information in seconds, we must remember that transparency does not mean publicity. Transparency represents an access to information that encourages proper "checks and balances." Transparency ensures that everyone involved has been truthful and honest in their efforts to resolve conflict, thereby contributing to building trust in relationships. Publicity often results in loss of face and hardening of positions, and is rarely helpful in conflict resolution.

The Western reliance on professional, impartial mediators is a foreign concept to the majority of our world. From the Lao perspective, it does not make sense to spend time researching completely unknown mediators or other professionals in order to develop trust in them when they already have the services of individuals whom they trust and have a long-term relationship with. Personal experiences and interactions with "insider-partials," trusted third parties who are known to the disputants, allow disputants to become more transparent in their discussions of conflict. In Laos, trust and respect in relationships deliver transparency effectively and efficiently.

Accountability/explainability

There are two forms of accountability in conflict resolution. One is part of the conflict resolution agreement, and is the primary responsibility of the parties in conflict in implementing and adhering to the terms set out in the agreement. The other is part of the conflict resolution process itself, and is the primary responsibility of the mediators in acting appropriately to help the parties reach a resolution. Closely related to transparency, accountability in a conflict resolution process refers to the idea of the parties taking responsibility for their actions and how those actions have contributed to the conflict situation, as well as their willingness and commitment to work on repairing the harm. It also means making mediators answerable through expectations that they will provide explanations and justifications for their advice, decisions, and actions in trying to reach a resolution. Being accountable for a set of actions or decisions requires a mediator to be subject to oversight, review, appeal, praise, or chastisement related to their fulfillment of duties at each subsequent level of mediation.

Much like transparency, accountability requires access to information about the details of the process. Again, this takes a very different form in cultures that are based on oral tradition as opposed to written records. The progression through different levels of mediation in Lao conflict resolution is the mechanism for obtaining accountability. In cases that move through those levels, each consecutive level reviews the previous process as part of understanding the conflict and resolution processes. Like an appeals court, the decisions made in previous processes are subject to scrutiny, and agreements can be changed and/or amended in ways that will hopefully be more appropriate to fulfilling resolution requirements.

It is also important to note that this process can be initiated by any one of the disputants themselves. If one of the parties in the conflict is unhappy with the resolution or is having trouble fulfilling the terms of the agreement, they will advance the case to the next level of mediation. In many circumstances, this will require previous mediators to attend and sometimes be subject to questioning regarding their involvement in facilitating a resolution. For mediators, the possibility of being required to explain their role and actions to those in more senior positions can be an intimidating thought and a powerful motivator to make wise decisions. Because mediators often lack impartiality in Lao conflict resolution, this is a very important part of ensuring fair treatment of parties in conflict. Any perception of bias will make the resolution less fair and more difficult to fulfill and will be noticed if the conflict moves into higher levels of mediation. This will only add to any loss of face for the families and mediators involved. Clearly, this is meaningful for mediators, who almost always have close family connections to those in conflict, motivating them to make decisions in the best interest of resolving a conflict and not favouring one side or the other. This is like a built-in mechanism for ethics in conflict resolution.

Transparency and accountability are the two major pieces that control corruption. Corruption can occur by controlling information and preventing appropriate responses to decisions made by those in positions of authority. It is regulated through a circle of oversight – a system where any individual's actions are answerable to those in authority, and where those in authority are equally answerable to those for whom they have taken action. When methods of transparency and accountability are unable to prevent that circle of oversight, corruption becomes possible and leads to a growing sense of cynicism that undermines conflict resolution.

It is important to stress, however, that just as transparency does not mean publicity, accountability does not mean democracy. There are big governmental decisions that affect large populations of people, and these situations often demand an avenue for public critique. On the other hand, smaller decisions that affect fewer people are in less need of full democratic review. Essentially, the mandate to critique is defined by the conflict resolution process, not by an overly public system that invades privacy. Movement from small to large processes of conflict resolution defines who is accountable and the built-in mechanism by which accountability occurs.

Reparation/settlement

In Chapter 2, conflict in Laos was defined as a situation where one or more people are involved in an incident or perceive a set of actions that contribute to a "loss of face and eyes." Conflict resolution was defined as a process in which one or more people are engaged in actions that help to "rebuild face and eyes." In other words, its goal is to repair the status of conflicting parties, both victim and offender, bringing them back into a healthy relationship in the family and community. Reparation in Lao conflict resolution applies to everyone affected, including the victim, the offender, and the community. In rebuilding "face and eyes," reparation takes different forms for these different parties and takes shape as part of a settlement.

Reparation for victims includes repairing harm and providing compensation by recognizing that they may have been physically, emotionally, or financially victimized and that they may feel less secure with their community status and may need help in recovering from that loss. Often, this will require more than words and a symbolic ritual. Many conflict situations involve other losses, such as property, harvests, and possessions. In these instances, agreements will likely involve compensation or restitution as discussed through *op-lom* in early levels of mediation or defined by the *Neoy Gai Geer* in later levels. In any conflict resolution system, upholding the terms of a resolution, including compensation, is often the most difficult aspect of an agreement. Unfortunately, not everybody is capable of the same level of reparation. Finding the perfect amount of compensation that satisfies a victim's ability to regain his or her losses, while at the same time being an amount that is possible for an offender to pay, can take repeated trips back to mediation for help in renegotiating agreements. All too often these goals are not compatible. Although compensation may sometimes be incomplete, genuine attempts are a very important part of a community's perception of social justice. Sometimes, a genuine apology can be an act that helps to repair harm and contribute to compensation in non-monetary ways. Literature on forgiveness states that "[p]erfection isn't necessary in order to seek to forgive or be forgiven. It is a journey hobbled by vices and foibles. The important thing is that we try" (Briggs, 2008, p. 21).

Still, we must recognize that there are cases where no amount of compensation can undo losses. In those cases, support networks will be paramount. One sad story involved the accidental death of an employee at a construction site. Although an investigation cleared the business owner of any fault, a village leader negotiated with the owner to provide a large, funeral-style *soukhouan* to the family and community, as well as contributing monetary restitution. The village leader recognized that the family would need a large support network to help them cope with their loss, as well as assistance in recovering some of the lost wages and resources provided by their deceased son. In committing to a large *soukhouan*, the owner was not admitting blame, but was rather trying to redeem any loss of "face and eyes" by providing a format where the community could support each other and grieve together. Although I would not consider this situation a win-win in the sense that the son could not be brought back to life, its use of ritual helped to make the most of a situation where compensation for the death of a loved one was not truly possible.

Reparation for offenders involves rehabilitation by finding support to encourage changes to behavioural problems, by fixing structural inequality, and by fostering accountability for those individuals or businesses that need to be reminded of their responsibilities to a larger group. Different justice systems have focused on hugely varied techniques in trying to address this – from retributive justice's use of punishment and skills development programs in prisons, to restorative justice's endorsement of reparation, community reintegration programs, and forgiveness. Furthermore, different techniques are often employed for different kinds and levels of conflict. For example, restorative justice might be used for individual first-time offenders and retributive justice for violence in the workplace. On an international scale, countries and other international bodies try to transform each other on a regular basis through the media, travel restrictions, trade sanctions, and war crimes tribunals. Part of rehabilitation, particularly in restorative justice, involves remorse, apology, and forgiveness. Apologies are powerful ways to acknowledge offender responsibility and guilt and acknowledge the moral status of the victim (Govier & Verwoerd, 2002). In many cases, reparation for offenders must also come with the recognition that they may be victims as well and that a number of root causes of conflict behaviours must be repaired before complete rehabilitation is possible. As a key component of a social justice system, rehabilitation is seen as a way of reducing the load on conflict resolution systems, and many settlements include referrals to social services or support networks dedicated to drug and alcohol rehabilitation, community services, probation, incarceration facilities, and other organizations.

Reparation for the community requires addressing any safety or security concerns that arise from the conflict, ensuring that there are no ongoing threats to the continued physical, emotional, and economic sustainability of the larger community. Conflict resolution plays a vital role in community protection by guarding against justified threats and in calming perceived fears. This is an important reason why the larger community needs to be involved in the conflict resolution process, especially as the conflict increases in scope. As a key player in the assistance, encouragement, and support of parties in finding a satisfying resolution, implementing an agreement, and maintaining its terms, the community is protecting itself by rehabilitating others. Through its efforts, the community contributes to repairing harm from conflict and to re-establishing a safe and secure environment. And in that contribution, the community is justifiably involved in the celebration of an end to conflict and rebuilding of relationships between the conflicting parties and their respective families.

In Laos, compensation and rehabilitation are part of the reparation process, and in more complex cases, a written settlement might guide a path to maintaining or re-establishing social harmony. Different conflict examples in Laos show just how creative rehabilitation can be. Nang Piew, in the story of "Wrapped-Ash Delight," was rehabilitated through her own inner guilt and shame, the son who fought with his parents was rehabilitated through his relationship and new living arrangements with the village leader and his family, and the man who assaulted his wife was rehabilitated through the intervention of friends and family who interceded and separated the couple. In the last situation, the husband was not punished for his crime against his wife, but the intervention kept her and the rest of the family safe from abuse. He was, however, shamed by the community for his actions. Still, he continues to provide monetary compensation to her and has not re-offended.

The *soumma* and *soukhouan* ceremonies are a very important part of reparation as a way of rebuilding relationships between parties and within the community. These ceremonies are important for the victim, the offender, and the community. As part of an agreement and compensation package, the offender is often required to pay for the *soukhouan* celebration or even host the ceremony for the victim and his or her family. Depending on the scope of the conflict or crime, the *soukhouan* may be private or public. To the victim, the *soukhouan* represents the acknowledgment of the conflict, the reparation for harm done, and the compensation needed to make things right again. For the offender, the organizing and hosting of the event shows that he or she is taking responsibility for the conflict and desires to become a part of the community again. The effects of such ceremonies in relationship building and community well-being are very positive. It is a concrete demonstration of reparation and fulfills an aspect of compensation, rehabilitation, and community welfare as mandated by a resolution settlement. As part of full reparation, these rituals are an important part of a resolution agreement that includes compensation, rehabilitation, and protection for those affected by the conflict in a way that stabilizes relationships for the health of all.

Flexibility/litheness

According to conflict resolution scholar, Morton Deutsch (2000), there are four different kinds of justice: distributive justice, procedural justice, retributive justice, and restorative justice. Distributive justice refers to getting a "fair share" of the benefits and resources, and can be evaluated based on equity (rewards equal the amount of contributions), equality (everyone gets the same amount of resources), and need (those who need it more, get more). Procedural justice describes fair processes and treatment. Fair procedures, representations, and impartial decision-making process are important in procedural justice. Retributive justice refers to appropriate punishment for the wrongful acts in order to create balance. Punishment is proportional to the crime. When rules are broken, penalties are administered in order to deter the perpetrator from committing those acts again and to discourage others from engaging in destructive behaviour. Crime is seen as a violation against the state. Processes that define retributive justice include court systems, international legal proceedings, and other judiciary structures. Restorative justice values reparation, restitution, and making things right. Crime is seen as a violation against individuals and communities. Restorative justice is concerned with giving a voice to the victims, offenders, and community, while focusing on healing the individual, restoring offenders back to the community, and repairing harm. Community involvement can help prevent conflict from recurring in the future. Restorative initiatives include victim–offender mediation, community justice forums, and truth-reconciliation commissions.

Often, both academics and practitioners compare these different formats for justice in dichotomous categories: retributive versus restorative justice. Although these dichotomies are useful for comparisons across systems, they are also limiting in the separations they support. As evidenced by many different national bodies, including New Zealand, Canada, South Africa, Laos, and so forth, more complete conflict resolution systems are beginning to incorporate both of these elements into their justice systems. Increasingly, there is recognition that different conflicts, offenders, victims, and communities need different approaches to justice. Justice is a complicated concept, one that is deeply rooted in cultural interpretation, creating various understandings and explanations. As the New Zealand government recognized, a certain segment of their population was not responding well to its retributive-style justice system, and the government began considering a more restorative approach that might better suit this group's needs. Even within a single culture, justice remains on some level a subjective idea, one that means different things to different people. A successful conflict resolution system must be capable of dealing with the variances that are inevitably part of conflict. Parties in conflict have different skills, different financial means, different values, and different needs, which play a constant role in any conflict situation from its inception to its resolution. This is especially true in multi-cultural settings and will require flexibility or litheness from all sides to address conflicts in ways that satisfy different needs and interests.

For example, in most formal legal systems, the impartiality of procedural justice requires legal professionals to remove themselves from any situation in which they may have a vested interest or conflict of interest. In the Lao conflict resolution system, mediator neutrality or impartiality is not considered an advantage. Preference is given to mediators who are not outsiders, to those who the parties know and have connections with. Many in Laos believe that using mediators who have an "inherent bias" will help guide a more flexible resolution which will meet the needs of the individuals and communities in conflict. These third-party "insiders" know first-hand the needs of the conflicting parties – a definite advantage in developing flexible resolutions that are satisfying for the parties. Their personal connection will be important in guiding agreements that have a strong chance of success, because they recognize the social justice needs of the particular microculture in conflict, whether that be within a single larger cultural group or in a cross-cultural situation.

Recognizing that justice takes different forms for different people and understanding those individual needs is only the beginning of finding flexibility in agreements. Obtaining an agreement that bridges the conflict is equally important, and requires tact and delicacy in negotiation between the parties. *Op-lom* is a significant part of that process. As a tool for negotiation, *op-lom* is used throughout the conflict resolution process to discover the details of the conflict and to negotiate the terms of agreement. We have seen how the details of *soukhouan* arrangements are determined by the scope of the conflict and in cross-cultural situations, how *op-lom* is used to arrive at satisfactory arrangements based on the requirements of different ethnic traditions. *Op-lom* is the means by which flexibility is implemented to address the values and requirements of different individuals. Just as human interaction is constantly lithe (flexible, supple, and nimble), so must our *op-lom* also be. Successful *op-lom* must take into consideration distributive justice, procedural justice, retributive justice, and restorative justice as principles in finding mutually satisfying resolutions.

Litheness is also found in being open to adjustments and fine-tuning agreements. If the terms of the resolution for one or both parties prove too difficult to maintain, changes must be made to ensure adherence is possible. In the event that an individual's life situation changes and maintaining an initial agreement is impossible, there must be an opportunity to hone a new arrangement. After all, if the resolution falls apart entirely, justice will fall in its wake. As mentioned, in the Lao Conflict Resolution System, there are opportunities for the parties to return to mediation three times at each level in order to fine-tune the agreements and ensure that people follow through with the terms. This allows the parties to be involved in continual evaluation of the resolution until they create the best resolution possible in that situation. The parties are not stuck with an agreement that is not working once the implementation process begins, but are able to make constructive changes along the way.

Flexibility in the Lao conflict resolution system addresses various kinds of justice, whether it is distributive, procedural, retributive, or restorative. Through mediation and the *op-lom* process, there is a great deal of flexibility in reaching an agreement and fine-tuning the arrangements within the Lao conflict resolution system. Maintaining flexibility by providing an opportunity to keep resolutions healthy and sustainable is an important part of maintaining peaceful relationships and communities.

Creativity/originality

Much of the discussion of the tenets so far has centered on balance. We have discussed how the Lao people value individual privacy that is balanced with community-oriented living. The need for transparency and inclusivity must be balanced with the requirements of privacy. Accountability and reparation must be balanced with the scale and scope of the conflict. Accessibility and flexibility are an important part of opening doorways to conflict resolution processes, but must be balanced with the need to eventually settle disputes, find closure, and move forward. Clearly, these concepts are all evident in the Lao conflict resolution system, and they all have checks and balances to ensure that meeting the needs of one party does not impede meeting the needs of another party. Knowing when and how to be flexible in finding an appropriate balance for the different individuals involved in a conflict resolution process requires creativity.

Creativity, in terms of the process of mediation, is evident in the Lao conflict resolution spectrum. The way in which the spectrum has developed to incorporate transparency, accountability, inclusivity, reparation, flexibility, and other qualities in an entirely informal, non-professional system is original. There is creativity in selecting mediators from the many individuals available to choose from, especially in the early levels where family members can be parents, older siblings, and/or relatives from either the maternal or paternal side.

Many of the conflict resolution techniques, strategies, and agreements employed by those mediators are also creative, both in process and in reparation. The story of "Wrapped-Ash Delight" demonstrates the degree to which theatrical events can be creatively employed to provide public teaching experiences while still ensuring anonymity and saving face for all involved. Saving face through a public, yet anonymous conflict resolution process seems like a contradiction in terms, but in Laos it is employed with strategy, originality, and apparently, with frequency. Farmers working together to define a cost–benefit analysis, weighing individual profit against collective sustainability, shows creativity and flexibility. Engaging the farmers in *op-lom* through informal and formal discussions was likely not an easy task, and finding ways to encourage them to remember "gaining together and losing together" undoubtedly required deft and creative handling of individual personalities and community cohesion.

The resolution and reparation of many conflicts in Laos are also creative. Much of the creativity comes from the people who are directly involved in the conflict, and is based on their traditional values and customs. Several of the resolutions discussed in Chapter 3 demonstrate this creativity. The village leader who took in another family's son with behavioural problems showed creativity in resolution. It provided a healthy separation, a support network for the family, and mentorship for the young man. In the family undergoing an inheritance dispute, elders reminded the family that what is fair for one is not fair for another and that flexibility was required in distributing inheritance in spite of the explicit instructions in the will. They could still honour the will of their father by giving the inheritance to the daughter, and in return the daughter could meet the need for distributive justice by paying for education and building homes for her siblings. Coming to an agreement that served the needs of all the family members showed creativity.

Another aspect of creativity is found in the conflict resolution rituals of *soukhouan* and *soumma*. As discussed, the *soukhouan* is used for many different events in Lao life, from weddings to funerals, significant rites of passage, and conflict resolution. Earlier in this chapter we discussed the accidental death of a construction worker at the work site. This example demonstrates a truth about conflict and conflict resolution that can often be difficult to account for. We often describe conflict in terms of victims and offenders. In reality, this distinction is not always clear. In this case, the business owner is also a victim of this event. He lost a valuable employee, the training and resources given to that individual, and some degree of community credibility in owning a company where an individual died, accidental or otherwise. This accidental death is a conflict that does not have an identifiable offender, but only victims, specifically, the deceased son, his family, his employer, and his community. Navigating the boundaries between an individual who could be considered an offender and a victim will always require creativity, and the delicate act of restoring "face and eyes" to someone who straddles both areas will require imagination. In this case, we saw the creative use of a ritual that encompassed both conflict resolution and funeral as a way to begin the process of healing.

Cross-cultural *soukhouan* rituals that employ different cultural traditions and customs based on restoring "face and eyes" show creativity in a conflict resolution process. As stated in previous chapters, a *soukhouan* is done according to the injured party's traditions as part of restitution to the family. This is particularly meaningful for conflicts involving different ethnic groups, as it shows respect and honour for the culture of the victim and sincerity in resolving the conflict. Through negotiation and *op-lom*, the creativity in arranging rituals helps to bridge cultural gaps by educating each other on different cultural customs and repairing harm through concrete actions, demonstrating willingness to rebuild relationships, and restoring peaceful relationships within and across communities.

Finding balance will always be an important part of obtaining social justice through conflict resolution processes. Balance will be required for people with different or opposing cultural needs, and creativity will be key in finding balance between the needs of the victim and the offender and settling on terms that will maintain relationships. Just as every conflict involves many differences in nuance, so, too, will the resolution require originality. Balancing the different aspects of Lao culture with conflict resolution is not a simple task, but being creative in the process and resolution has provided interesting avenues with which to resolve issues.

Support networks

Having a strong support network can be the difference between success and failure in a conflict resolution process and maintenance of a conflict resolution agreement. The Lao conflict resolution system has several excellent internal mechanisms for developing strong support networks. As we have seen throughout this book, the natural progression from private to public serves multiple uses as a conflict resolution mechanism. Conflict resolution at lower levels of mediation is generally less complicated and involves fewer people. Correspondingly, conflict resolution at higher levels of mediation is more complex and includes more people. In terms of support networks, the size of the conflict resolution process has the added benefit of generating appropriately sized support systems, involving people who have an interest in seeing resolutions maintained.

The inclusion of previous mediators in later levels of mediation inherently makes family an important part of the extended mediation process because they are the first mediators in most conflicts. The more involved a family becomes in a conflict, the more they can rely on each other for support in the mediation process and any future processes. We have already noted how conflict is like lice, contagiously spreading from one person to another. Family and friends involved in any aspects of conflict resolution become increasingly motivated to ensure agreements are upheld, lest any harm to "face and eyes" spread to them personally.

Accountability also plays an important role in generating support networks. Mediators who are held accountable for bringing disputants back into a healthy relationship with each other and their community are going to have significant interest in helping people maintain agreed-upon resolutions. It is not uncommon for village leaders or the *Neoy Gai Geer* committee to appoint people involved in previous mediation sessions to act as overseers of agreements, ensuring that appropriate efforts are made to fulfill obligations. The mediators' accountability gives them a vested interest in supporting conflicting parties to the best of their abilities.

One of the most important aspects of the *soukhouan* and *soumma* ceremonies is to celebrate the closure of the official conflict resolution process and to solidify a support network for the parties. Families are responsible for helping the offender adhere to a settlement, organize a *soukhouan*, and pay for the rituals essential for relationship building. Clearly, those people invited to the ritual have already played some kind of role in the conflict resolution process, and their involvement in the ceremony is part of their duty to provide continual support in meeting the terms of the agreement, witnessing the re-establishment of the parties into healthy relationship, and guiding them towards reconciliation. At the ritual, they bear witness to the agreement, offer blessings to the honoured guests, participate in the spiritual health of those in conflict through their participation in restoring *khouan* and by showing *boon koon*, and otherwise demonstrate their personal commitment to supporting the conflict parties.

Further, support networks are extremely valuable in those circumstances where the required level of compensation to restore a victim's personal losses is not possible for the other party to pay. Here, support networks need to play a role in helping victims recover their losses and take a significant responsibility in helping perpetrators provide the necessary compensation. In the example of broken dams in the rice fields causing destruction of various farmers' crops, the compensation needed to be addressed by an entire community of people in order to heal relationships and reconstruct farms required for the subsistence agriculture that they all relied on. If reparation is one of the more difficult aspects to maintaining a resolution, support networks can be the means to uphold or break agreements.

Relationship building

A significant amount of time has been dedicated to restoring "face and eyes" as a Lao metaphor for conflict resolution. We have noted that this metaphor is representative of an individual's relationship to his or her community as seen by the individual and by others. Restoring "face and eyes" is an important overarching theme and goal of conflict resolution in Laos. Specifically, conflict resolution seeks to bring people back into relationship with their respective families and communities.

Relationship building is an integral part of conflict resolution. This is evident in the Lao people's interpersonal discussion, reliance on mediators to help in conflict situations, and conflict resolution rituals of the *soukhouan* and *soumma* that are geared specifically to rebuilding relationships. The Lao conflict resolution system is centered on maintaining healthy communities, which are the essential lifeblood of their cultures. Having healthy "face and eyes" provides an individual with access to all parts of the community, which in turn strengthens the community itself. This concentration on relationship building seems to be successful even as Laos continues to develop and grow. Its conflict resolution system remains in spite of continued efforts to "modernize" it. Personally, I do not think that a more modern, formal system will replace it anytime soon. The relationship-building *soukhouan* and *soumma* rituals have become an important part of the overarching Lao identity, and they will continue to focus on the art of relationship building for as long as that identity remains.

The importance of relationships in conflict transformation and peacebuilding has been discussed by many scholars in the conflict resolution field (see Boulding, 1988, 2000; Bush & Folger, 2004; Lederach, 1995, 1997, 2003). Boulding (2000) describes a culture of peace as one that requires the constant examination of our relationships with all living things, including creatively dealing with differences and conflicts, and listening to one another. Lederach (1997) stresses relationship building as a key part of reconciliation. Reconciliation is an idea that generates some controversy in conflict resolution literature. Assumptions underlying reconciliation include a long-term relationship between parties, encounter and engagement with each other, and innovation in mechanisms to create peace. An environment in which reconciliation is possible calls for rebuilt relationships based on apology, forgiveness, and trust, and space for truth, mercy, justice, and peace (Lederach, 1997). Considering all that we have looked at, I think that it is fair to say that the goal of the Lao conflict resolution system is to build relationships that lead to the ultimate goal of reconciliation between parties.

However, we have already studied a story that adds a level of complexity to the idea of reconciliation and why an ultimate goal of reconciliation is controversial. The spousal abuse case that ended up with the couple separating never achieved reconciliation. In fact, some experts would argue that complete reconciliation should not be a goal in such abuse cases. The family violence dictated a need for separation, and its potential to become chronic meant that any steps toward full reconciliation should be taken with great care. The separation in this case was a very important and necessary step – one that provided a platform for the families to begin a process of redefining their communities and building healthy relationships that supported their places in them. There are times when an optimal scenario is the acceptance of peaceful co-existence without reconciliation, where people exist in mutual tolerance or respect, live with difference, and commit to not using violence (see Chayes & Minow, 2003; Kriesberg, 1998; Kumpesinghe, 1999; Weiner, 1998).

With this in mind, we should recognize that restoring "face and eyes" does not always mean building or rebuilding relationships between victims and perpetrators. However, it does mean that balanced conflict resolution will provide ways for both victims and perpetrators to find healthy communities and, when necessary, separate ones. Ensuring safety and protection is part of a healthy community. Resolutions and support groups are important in providing and maintaining that commitment. In this sense, restoring "face and eyes" is something that is seen through the lens of community. Reconciliation may be a noble goal, but Laos demonstrates that it is not always a requirement. Nevertheless, building relationships within the community is. In the story of spousal abuse, the respective support networks of each party helped them build a relationship within the boundaries of maintaining distance from each other and living their separate lives. They continued to have a relationship that was based on the children. They did not reconcile, but are living in co-existence, comfortable with their new, more distant relationship.

That said, rebuilding relationships can happen in even the most difficult and incomprehensible crimes. The 2006 shooting of ten schoolgirls (five of whom were killed) in the Amish school in Nickel Mines, Pennsylvania, shocked the world by its brutality. However, equally astonishing was the Amish community's response of forgiveness and reconciliation with the dead gunman's family, the Roberts, in the midst of this terrible tragedy. This story of mercy, compassion, grace, and forgiveness led to healing of families, communities, and hope for the world. Kraybill, Nolt, and Weaver-Zercher (2007a, 2007b) noted that the Amish culture deeply values the biblical teachings of Jesus, who taught and demonstrated forgiveness, and of Dirk Willems, an Anabaptist martyr, who in his escape from prison turned back to save the life of a guard chasing him over an icy pond, only to be burned at the stake when the very guard whose life he saved turned him in to the authorities.

Within hours after the shooting, Amish neighbours comforted the Roberts and offered forgiveness. The community set up a charitable fund for the Roberts family so they could support themselves without their husband and father, who was the murderer of the Amish children. Through their own grief, the Amish comforted the Roberts, attended the gunman's funeral, and invited the widowed Marie Roberts to attend one of the Amish girls' funerals. As Briggs (2008) states, "[T]he Amish enfolded their grief within their normal circle of prayer and daily communion. They didn't speak out. They looked within. They did it together" (p. 9). Marie Roberts stated in a letter to her Amish neighbours:

> *Your love for our family has helped to provide the healing we so desperately need. Gifts you've given have touched our hearts in a way no words can describe. Your compassion has reached beyond our family, beyond our community, and is changing our world, and for this we sincerely thank you.*
>
> (McElroy, 2006)

This story is a great example of the importance of support networks and relationship building in times of overwhelming crisis, pain, and sorrow. The grace and compassion offered here demonstrates the potential to deal with devastation in a way that continues to bring a powerful hope for peace.

Relationship building is an essential, overriding piece of conflict resolution. The desire, will, and courage it takes to embark on this relationship-building journey are not easy. Looking at the protracted international conflicts in our world, we can see how difficult this path is in undoing the many years of hatred, distrust, and violence. However, Laos is a strong example that demonstrates its potential even in very difficult situations. Through *op-lom* and rituals that have been the backbone of fostering peace, one relationship at a time, Laos shows us that peace is not found in politics, but it is found in everyday relationships. Lederach (1997) says, "The greatest resource for sustaining peace in the long term is always rooted in the local people and their culture" (p. 94). Building those grassroots relationships is the key to peace in Laos and other cultures around the world.

RESOLUTION

Familiarity, accessibility, inclusivity, transparency, accountability, creativity, flexibility, reparation, support networks, and relationship building all exist in successful conflict resolution systems. If even one of them is threatened, so, too, is effective conflict resolution. Still, Laos shows us that conflict resolution systems are both robust and resilient, and can survive small- and large-scale violence, discrimination, displacement, and other disruptions to cultural bonds.

I present these tenets, not as a new theory that claims all conflict resolution systems are inherently the same, but as a framework with which to understand that many groups share similar underlying needs and that those needs are satisfied in very different, culturally defined ways. These tenets have been repeatedly demonstrated in the Lao conflict resolution system and other conflict resolution structures around the world. For me, the biggest difficulty in using them came in trying to remember them all as a list of principles. Therefore,

- **R**elationship Building
- **E**xplainability/Accountability
- **S**ettlement/Reparation
- **O**pportunity/Accessibility
- **L**itheness/Flexibility
- **U**nderstanding/Familiarity
- **T**ransparency
- **I**nclusivity
- **O**riginality/Creativity
- **N**etworks/Support Networks

Figure 7.1 RESOLUTION

I developed an acronym for ease of remembering and discussing (see Figure 7.1). RESOLUTION was an obvious choice. It further clarifies the relationship of these tenets to conflict resolution by implying that effective resolution is composed of these ten elements.

Knowing that these principles exist will make it easier to understand conflict situations in our world, from the small-scale interpersonal conflicts of the family or workplace to the large-scale international conflicts involving political unrest and security threats. There are so many situations where we need better ways to understand, predict, and implement conflict resolution systems that will lead to peacebuilding between individuals and groups.

Over and over again, the world has shown us that conflict is cyclical in nature. Formal theorist and mathematician Lewis F. Richardson concluded in his statistics and patterns of large-scale conflicts that there are cycles of intensity that correspond to frequency of wars, and if we know the natural patterns of human conflict, then we can prevent violence (Schellenberg, 1996). If a conflict goes unresolved, it is doomed to be repeated, with each action fuelling an ever-degrading and explosive situation. And this is further complicated by a world made up of nations, communities, businesses, social groups, families, and individuals, all of whom interpret conflict differently and have different culturally based approaches to conflict resolution. In identifying the tenets of conflict resolution that emerged from the Lao case study, I am proposing that they are instrumental in resolving the needs of conflicting parties in many cultures, even though different cultures and evolving cultures shape the conflict resolution process. These approaches to conflict resolution address common problems differently, but what they share are the basic principles identified in the ten tenets.

The processes of conflict resolution are not necessarily interchangeable. As noted, interchanging conflict resolution systems has proven extraordinarily difficult because different cultural worldviews interpret the same actions in remarkably different ways. Around the globe we express our emotions, experience conflicts, and conduct conflict resolution in different ways, but we have basic human needs for love, community, and security. Human needs theorists identify a number of essential needs, including safety/security, love/belonging, self-esteem, personal fulfillment, participation, freedom, identity, and cultural security (Burton, 1990; Galtung, 1996; Maslow, 1954; Max-Neef, 1991; Nussbaum, 2000, 2001; Sen, 1999). I am proposing that effective conflict resolution also has basic needs and they are found in relationship building, explainability/accountability, settlement/ reparation, opportunity/accessibility, litheness/flexibility, understanding/ familiarity, transparency, inclusivity, originality/creativity, and support networks.

It is important to be able to simplify complex cultural conflict resolution processes into a manageable set of principles. In doing so, we create a tool for understanding the mechanics of conflict and the basic qualities of conflict resolution – "building from the ground up" so that we can objectively examine different processes used to resolve conflicts. In the analysis of conflict, design of resolution process, and the ultimate resolution of conflict, these principles allow us to look at the individual parts to determine if anything is missing and which needs are unmet. This exercise can help us identify the strengths and weaknesses in our conflict resolution process and make necessary changes in order to develop successful resolutions and build positive relationships between people and communities.

Obviously, that leaves us with more questions, including how to apply these tenets to other conflict situations around the world while incorporating their cultural worldviews. Similar to the concept of a non-static culture, conflict resolution processes are continuously evolving. As we have seen, groups grow together through advantageous relationships, and conflict resolution must develop as part of maintaining those relationships, to support a healthy working and living environment. Peaceful communities require the development of infrastructures that support proactive changes in relationships through a vision of a shared future, as well as practical responses to conflict (Lederach, 1997).

Conclusion

Lederach's (1997) statement supports the idea that conflict resolution systems must continuously evolve to support dynamic relationships. It is the use of the word "develop" that provides a clue as to where more research into conflict resolution design must take place. Specifically, conflict resolution has a fundamental relationship to development issues. The interplay between development and conflict resolution goes two ways. Developing relationships for economic, social, political, or other purposes drives the need for effective conflict resolution. Equally, the development of positive conflict resolution systems will sustain the relationships needed for further development. Escobar (1995) states the importance of grassroots relationships in promoting sustainable development by taking an interest in local culture and knowledge, defending and promoting localized, pluralistic grassroots movements. Faure (1995) also encourages us to be creative in stimulating dialogue about conflict resolution and development, and to allow the wisdom from local communities to be heard. Imposing our own ways of doing things will only result in destruction. Through the transformation of local, traditional practices, groups will be put in a position to successfully address issues that will promote positive growth.

By recognizing the way in which conflict resolution evolves, from micro to macro, conflict resolution design will have to approach the problem from a development and growth perspective. Essentially, the tenets of conflict resolution suggest a framework, a blueprint, for a process where the individuals and groups involved can complete the details by choosing the players, symbols, and rituals that are meaningful and credible in their culture. The people who use such conflict resolution systems will be the ones to design, implement, and monitor them, not the political leaders, legislative bodies, and other leadership figures whose lives revolve around a different reality. It will be the grassroots relationships that either establish any lasting peace or condemn a conflict to a destiny of repetition.

Bibliography

Bercovitch, Jacob, & Jackson, Richard. (2009). *Conflict Resolution in the Twenty-first Century*. Ann Arbor: University of Michigan Press.

Bogdan, Robert C., & Biklen, Sari Knopp. (2007). *Qualitative Research for Education: An Introduction to Theories and Methods* (5th ed.). Boston: Pearson Education, Inc.

Boulding, Elise. (1988). *Building a Global Civic Culture*. New York: Columbia University Press.

Boulding, Elise. (2000). *Cultures of Peace: The Hidden Side of History*. Syracuse: Syracuse University Press.

Briggs, Kenneth. (2008). *The Power of Forgiveness*. Minneapolis: Fortress Press.

Burton, John W. (1990). *Human Needs Theory*. New York: St. Martin's Press.

Bush, Robert A. Baruch, & Folger, Joseph P. (2004). *The Promise of Mediation: The Transformative Approach to Conflict* (rev. ed.). San Francisco: Jossey-Bass.

Chayes, Antonia, & Minow, Martha L. (2003). *Imagine Coexistence: Restoring Humanity After Violent Ethnic Conflict*. San Francisco: Jossey-Bass.

Deutsch, Morton. (2000). Justice and Conflict. In Morton Deutsch & Peter T. Coleman (eds.), *The Handbook of Conflict Resolution* (pp. 41–64). San Francisco: Jossey-Bass.

Enright, Robert D., & North, Joanna (eds.). (1998). *Exploring Forgiveness*. Madison: University of Wisconsin Press.

Escobar, Arturo. (1995). *Encountering Development: The Making and Unmaking of the Third World*. Princeton: Princeton University Press.

Faure, Guy Olivier. (1995). Conflict Formulation: Going Beyond Culture-Bound Views of Conflict. In Barbara Bunker & Jeffrey Z. Rubin (eds.), *Conflict Cooperation and Justice: Essays Inspried by the Works of Morton Deutsch* (pp. 39–55). San Francisco: Jossey-Bass.

Freire, Paulo. (1990). *The Pedagogy of the Oppressed*. New York: The Continuum Publishing Company.

Galtung, Johan. (1996). *Peace by Peaceful Means*. London: Sage Publications.

Govier, Trudy, & Verwoerd, Wilhelm. (2002). The Promise and Pitfalls of Apology. *Journal of Social Philosophy*, 33(1), 67–82.

Kraybill, Donald B., Nolt, Steven M., & Weaver-Zercher, David L. (2007a). Amish Grace and the Rest of Us. *Christianity Today*, 15, 1–6. Retrieved March 1, 2009, from www. christianitytoday.com/ct/2007/septemberweb-only/138–13.0.html.

Kraybill, Donald B., Nolt, Steven M., & Weaver-Zercher, David L. (2007b). *Amish Grace: How Forgiveness Transcended Tragedy*. San Francisco: Jossey-Bass.

Kriesberg, Louis. (1998). Coexistence and the Reconciliation of Communal Conflicts. In Eugene Weiner (ed.), *The Handbook of Interethnic Coexistence* (pp. 182–198). New York: Continuum Publishing.

Kumpesinghe, Kumar. (1999). Coexistence and Transformation in Asia: Some Reflections. In Kumar Rupesinghe (ed.), *Culture & Identity: Ethnic Coexistence in the Asian Context* (pp. 3–37). Washington, DC: The Saskawa Peace Foundation.

Lederach, John Paul. (1995). *Preparing for Peace: Conflict Transformation Across Cultures*. Syracuse: Syracuse University Press.

Lederach, John Paul. (1997). *Building Peace: Sustainable Reconciliation in Divided Societies*. Washington, DC: United States Institute of Peace Press.

Lederach, John Paul. (2003). *The Little Book of Conflict Transformation*. Intercourse: Good Books.

Masina, Nomonde. (2000). Xhosa Practices of Ubuntu for South Africa. In I. William Zartman (ed.), *Traditional Cures for Modern Conflicts: African Conflict "Medicine"* (pp. 169–181). Boulder: Lynne Rienner Publishers.

Maslow, Abraham H. (1954). *Motivation and Personality*. New York: Harper.

Max-Neef, Manfred A. (1991). *Human Scale Development: Conception, Application and Further Reflections*. New York: The Apex Press.

McElroy, Damien. (2006, October 16). Amish Killer's Widow Thanks Families of Victims for Forgiveness. *The Daily Telegraph*, pp. 10–17. Retrieved March 27, 2013, from www. telegraph.co.uk/news/worldnews/1531570/Amish-killers-widow-thanks-families-of-victims-for-forgiveness.html.

Nussbaum, Martha C. (2000). *Women and Human Development*. Cambridge: Cambridge University Press.

Nussbaum, Martha C. (2001). *Capabilities and Human Rights*. St. Paul: Paragon House.

Rigby, Andrew. (2012). How Do Post-Conflict Societies Deal with a Traumatic Past and Promote National Unity and Reconciliation? In Charles P. Webel & Jorgen Johansen (eds.), *Peace and Conflict Studies: A Reader* (pp. 234–246). London: Routledge: Taylor & Francis Group.

Schellenberg, James A. (1996). *Conflict Resolution: Theory, Research, and Practice*. Albany: State University of New York Press.

Sen, Amartya. (1999). *Development as Freedom*. New York: Knopf.

Weiner, Eugene. (1998). *Coexistence Work: A New Profession*. New York: Continuum Publishing.

Conclusion

It is November 2014, and I have mostly finished my manuscript. I am in my home office, surrounded by a rather scattered collection of about 1,000 books, audio interviews, 100 large binders overflowing with notes and pictures, and everything else one would need to write a book. I work on a computer that faces a wall, with one picture drawn by my children when they were ages five and seven. I used to face the window, but in the summers I found the incessant activity of the birds and squirrels running around in the beautiful oak tree to be distracting. In the winters the fluffy, white snowflakes covering our streets would call me to go out and play in the snow with my children. My home in the Canadian Prairies is comfortable, and I feel truly lucky to be a part of this community. I am not a fan of the long and bitterly cold winters here, and I miss the heat of the tropical rainforests of Laos, but I'm fortunate enough to be able to travel on occasion and get my "fix" of tropical weather. Truthfully, the weather is the least of the differences between my life in Canada and my former life in Laos.

I realize that the difference for me is not so much the location. I love the people, food, way of life, and the multi-ethnic diversity here and in Laos. In these ways, Laos is as rich as any country in the world. What made Laos unendurable for our family at the time was the violence, ambition without boundaries, and foreign manipulation. That is what truly disrupts, displaces, and destroys people.

On one of my many trips to visit family in Laos, I had a conversation with a friend. A group of maybe eight people, including my family members and other friends, were sitting outside the friend's small wooden house, enjoying some fresh young coconut, sticky rice, dried meat, and Beer Lao. My husband asked him what he had done during the war, if he had fought or supported either side, and how he had earned a living. He told us the following story:

> *For my whole life I drove a boat up and down the river. Early in my life I transported goods between different urban and rural centers, sometimes to deliver to different people and sometimes to bring to the markets. Later in my life I transported tourists who wanted to go see different sights. I still drive sometimes for one of the hotels. During the war, I transported rice by boat up and down the Mekong and Nam Ou rivers. It was not in service to either army, but as transport and trade of food and goods. I did not fight for either side and*

tried to stay neutral. The rice would be packed in big sacks, sometimes up to 100 pounds. I had many different boats over the years, but during the war I had a solid transport boat, about thirty feet long and maybe eight feet wide. It was made of wood, and had a roof to protect the rice (and myself) from rain and water. During the war, it was very dangerous to be travelling on the river. I would stack the rice up very high and make sure to overlap each bag onto the next to make a strong "wall of rice" for protection. I would only leave enough space for my eyes to see where I was going and would drive very fast. Sometimes there would be soldiers hiding in the jungle along the riverbank and they would shoot at me as I passed by.

I asked my friend what safety the rice actually offered him. If they had really wanted to kill him, couldn't they have just sunk the boat and shot him when he was exposed in the water? I knew the answer even before I asked the question, but I was so sickened by what I knew to be the truth, I had to ask to be sure. He said, "The soldiers didn't care about killing me. They knew that the boat, especially a boat full of rice, was valuable. They could use the boat for their own transport, and they could eat the rice or sell it to obtain more weapons. They didn't want to damage the boat or the rice, but knew if they killed me that the boat would run ashore, and they could claim it and my transport for their own." This is the price of war – the devaluation of a human life, the life of a man, husband, father, grandfather, son, and uncle. He had less value than a cheap wooden boat full of rice.

I ask myself how these people who would shoot at my friend, these soldiers who are sons, husbands, and fathers themselves, could have possibly seen another human life in this light. After all, I have come to know some of these ex-soldiers, and they are good men – committed to their families and communities. Still, the answer is painfully obvious: the reason they did not value human life during the war was because their lives also had no value. Human life was a means to an end; therefore, their lives were a means to an end.

Still, I have spent the last few days reading and re-reading my manuscript, feeling encouraged by the truth and optimism it presents. After all, the Lao people's struggle to survive the brutality thrust upon them reminds us that peace is also part of the human condition. Today in Laos we see many people in positive relationships with one another at home, work, and community. Although conflicts continue as a natural part of human existence, the mechanisms to help them live in peace have largely been re-established. There has been political stability, economic growth, and relative peace over the last forty years.

One of the themes of this book is "peace persists." I do not need to be convinced of this truth; but at the same time, I believe the world takes advantage of this all too often. There are those who believe that violence is an inevitable part of the human condition. Over the last few days of editing and writing, I have been reading news reports on the Internet and local newspapers – reading the latest on the current violence in the Middle East, race issues in the United States, stories of torture committed by the Central Intelligence Agency (CIA) under orders from the US government, and missing Aboriginal women in Canada. The media today seems to be a mouthpiece for the official Western government position on the Islamic State crisis. Western forces are going overseas to train local troops, supply them with weapons and money, and give support to these troops with air power. The government is stressing that almost all ground fighting will be done by local military, minimizing the risk to Western lives. Deep-cover CIA military units will seek out and destroy specific targets of interest. Exceptional intelligence gathering and technical military precision will ensure that mistakes and civilian casualties are kept to a bare minimum.

I am half convinced that these articles are plagiarized from originals composed in the 1960s and 1970s. The only difference seems to be the substitution of Middle East for Southeast Asia, Iraq for Vietnam, and extremists or "radicalized people" in place of Communists. These current conflicts seem to have an eerie resemblance to ones that have already taken place.

If Southeast Asia is any indication, the results look to be fairly predictable. Western money and weapons are contributing factors in breeding corruption and warlords. Beyond training local troops, Western governments will quietly hire and supply weapons to guerilla military warlords, who have their own agenda. The intelligence will not be strong enough to prevent errors, and the supposed precision will still end up killing a few thousand innocent people, children, and probably entire villages when bombs go drastically wrong. Local resentment, fueled by mistakes, will turn 100 extremist leaders into 1,000. Inhumane interrogations, wrongful deaths, refugees and displaced people, and other realities of war will twist 1,000 followers into 10,000. A very brief search on the Internet, a few documentaries, and a little reading seem to suggest that this is already happening. Have we learned nothing from the past?

The end game is also predictable. Eventually the Western public will grow weary of the war games, the financial expense, and the danger to lives, and will demand that their governments withdraw their interests overseas and use the public purse to fund job creation, health care, and other services in their home countries. Governments will ultimately be forced to listen to their constituents (or be voted out). The resulting withdrawal of advisors, money, weapons, and troops will be a catastrophe to the Western-friendly forces. Hundreds of thousands will flee to refugee camps. Years of war and violence will have polarized political views into the extremist tendencies that we are currently witnessing. The new political reality will see others "re-educated" or killed, and the new government will likely take a very hard line against any who question their legitimacy or threaten their power.

Having lived through this personally, I am heartbroken at the chain of events that has been set in motion. Yet, Laos reminds me to stay optimistic and hopeful, because in this place and with these people; peace overtook violence; healing enveloped brokenness; and individuals, families, and communities were restored. This is not to say that the war in Laos has not created long-lasting trauma. The war hardened positions, entrenched attitudes, and created an impossible environment of fear in both the ruling Communists and the Lao population as a whole, leading to a mass exodus of financial and human capital. Even forty years after the war, there still is an appalling toll to pay. Unexploded ordinance (UXO) still ravages the population, and there are still forgotten groups, buried deep in the jungles, who struggle to survive the memory of a war that is still going on for them.

This is the dual truth in Laos. They are still struggling with their history, but at the same time are positive about their future. Today, Laos has positive relations with its neighbours, robust economic growth, a strong and growing business class, and development in many other areas. Thanks to the wisdom and strength of the "war generations" and their constant caretaking of traditions and rituals of peace, future generations of Lao people have much to look forward to and enjoy. Hopefully, these young groups will continue to oversee their culture with the same diligence and embrace the peace that is granted them.

Two generations of Lao people have focused on recovery from war and rehabilitating themselves, their families, and their communities. They are not lost generations, for they have struggled against the demons left from violence and created an environment that their children can cultivate from a position of health and strength. Their efforts should not go unnoticed, and the rest of the world would do well to heed their wisdom, because looking at the current state of world affairs, it will be needed again.

The intricacies of protracted, long-standing, systemic conflicts are incredibly difficult to fully grasp, whether that be in the family, workplace, community, or national and international theatres. On a global scale, our world has too often underestimated the complexities of intervening in violent and oppressive situations. Democracy is not a cure-all for the world's marginalized people, military intervention destroys people and infrastructures that cost billions of dollars to rebuild, rebuilding in a post-conflict environment takes much more time than foreign governments have been willing to commit to, and trade sanctions penalize the poor more than the rich.

But we should not be discouraged. Peace exists and continues to find its way into our world, regardless of our bungling. Laos is proof of that. Maybe it is optimistic to think that it is possible to take an old, simple, grassroots approach to conflict resolution and use it as a lens with which to view all the complexities of macropolitics and international conflicts. Some might think it is simply ridiculous to even suggest the idea of *Conflict Resolution and Peacebuilding in Laos: Perspective for Today's World*. But clearly, the Lao people have a great truth to offer, because peace is persistent in finding its mark there, and their rich culture is thriving again. Above all, Laos shows us that peace is not found in politics – it is found in relationships. Those relationships have come together one at a time, growing in numbers and in diversity. As they grew, their conflict resolution systems evolved with them, feeding a social connectedness that links their diversity together.

There are countless millions of people in the world who have few recognizable means for obtaining social justice. Poverty, war, violence, religious fundamentalism, corrupt political regimes, and many other inequalities control the lives of the world's most marginalized people, preventing them from improving their circumstances. As a global society, we have often been incapable of understanding how to effectively address these situations beyond hoping for positive political change and, in some circumstances, using military options to produce that political change.

Governments, non-governmental organizations (NGOs), and other practitioners need new evaluative tools to measure peace potential and to assess reconstruction efforts in these conflicts. They need fresh ideas to help design conflict resolution systems in situations of human persecution, displacement, forced migration, and other forms of social oppression. The people of Laos offer perspective on these issues, helping us understand conflict resolution in both detailed and general principles and why these principles are important in today's global world. It is my hope that *Conflict Resolution and Peacebuilding in Laos: Perspective for Today's World* contributes to the study of peace and conflict at large, providing a forum for discussion on conflict resolution processes and rituals in working towards social justice among all of the world's marginalized, oppressed, and displaced people.

Glossary of Lao words and expressions

There may be regional differences in pronunciation and meaning of the terms identified in this glossary. Sometimes different regions will use different terms to describe the same thing. Also, as the Lao language evolves, new terms are being developed to describe similar concepts. The terms used in this paper are ones that I grew up with and are more characteristic of the Luang Prabang region in Laos.

Achaan	Teacher, professor
Ai na	"Embarrass face," embarrass
Ban	Village
Baci	*Soukhouan*, conflict resolution ritual or ceremony
Boon koon	Respect, gratefulness
Boon sep sern	Katdu's celebration, akin to *soukhouan*
Boon tan koon pa mer	Respect festival for parents
Bong gun	Police representative
Bong loon	Military representative
Bor mee bunha	Avoidance, "I don't have conflict"
Bor sear na sear tda	No loss of face and eyes
Bpak	Speak
Bpeng na, bpeng tda	Repair face and eyes
Bunha	Conflict, problem
Chai (hua chai)	Heart
Chai hawn	"Hot heart" as in hot temperament
Chai hi	"Strong heart" as in being angry
Chai yen	"Cool heart" as in calm temperament
Dee chai	"Good heart" as in being happy
Dok mai took tien	Small floral bouquets wrapped in banana leaf
Ethnic Lao	Majority ethnic group in the Lao Loum grouping
Fei pouk (mut) khene	Threads for *soukhouan* and *soumma* ceremonies
Gai	Chicken
Gai geer	Informal mediator
Gern	Money
Got mai	Customary laws, laws, regulations
Hei	Swidden rice farming

Hei pon	Blessings
Hmong	Minority ethnic group in the Lao Soung grouping, Meo people
Hor	Ethnic group from the Lao Soung grouping
Hrooi	Khammu house spirit, house guardian
Kao poon	Traditional Lao soup made with coconut milk and red curry
Katdu	Ethnic group from the Lao Teung grouping
Kha	Slaves, traditionally associated with the Khammu population, derogatory term
Khammu	Minority ethnic group in the Lao Theung grouping
Khouan	Spirit or soul
Khuan ban	Village leader, village chief
Kow chai gun	Understand each other
Kun ha	Set of five items for *soukhouan* and *soumma* ceremonies associated with Buddhist Dhamma
Kwang	Province
Kwai	Buffalo
Lan xang	Million elephants
Lao	All the people in Laos, Ethnic Lao language
Lao Loum	Majority population in Laos (e.g., Ethnic Lao), "Lao of the Plains" or "Lowland"
Lao Soung	Minority population in Laos (e.g., Hmong or Meo), "Lao of the Mountain Tops" or "Highland"
Lao Theung	Minority population in Laos (e.g., Khammu), "Lao of the Mountain Slopes" or "Upland," indigenous people
Lkuun	Ritual leader in Khammu villages
Lom	Talk
Makbeng	Central floral arrangement in *soukhouan* ceremony
Meo	Minority ethnic group in the Lao Soung groups, Hmong people
Mer tdu	Mother (non-biological), used as an honorific
Moo	Pig
Muang	City
Na	Paddy rice farming, wet rice farming
Naga	Protective deities, spirit of the rivers, snake-like water dragons
Nei ban	Village leader, village chief, sub-division leader
Neoy Gai Geer	Village mediation committee
Ngeuak	Fearsome spirit of the rivers, snake-like water dragons
Ngoor	Cow
Nop	Palms pressed together, hand greeting
Nup ter gun	Respect each other
Nup ter tow gua	Respect elders

Oh	Ethnic group from the Lao Theung grouping
Op-lom	Discussion, problem solving
Ot	Refrain from, abstain from
Ot gun bai	Having tolerance, remaining calm
Ot ow	Just taking it, tolerance
Ot tone	Having patience and endurance
Ow na tda kern	Bring back face and eyes
Pa biang	Traditional Ethnic Lao scarf
Pa kao samakee	Communal meal
Pa khouan	Serving table in *soukhouan* ceremony
Pah loong	Relatives, aunt/uncle
Pathan ban	Village president
Paw ban	Village leader, village chief, sub-division leader
Paw-mer	Parents, father/mother
Paw tdu	Father (non-biological), used as an honorific
Pee nong	Relatives
Phi	Spirit, ghost
Phi ban	Protective village spirit
Phi hern	House spirit
Phi khouan keert	Disruptive spirits
Phi khoun wat	Monastery spirit, temple spirit
Phi pba	Forest spirit
Phi then	Earth spirit
Pi Mai	New Year
Por bpeng chit chai	Reparation according to one's heart
Por chai	Satisfied, satisfied according to one's heart
Sa tan tot	Monk
Sahaphan Maenying Lao	Lao Women's Union
Samakom Poo Nying	Lao Women's Union
San ban	Village court
San kwang	Provincial court
San muang	District court
San soung	Supreme court
Seur chai	Trust
Sin	Traditional Ethnic Lao skirt
Sin bor luck/sin a tit na	Do not steal (Buddhist Dhamma)
Sin ga may	Do not have affairs or behave in sexually inappropriate ways (Buddhist Dhamma)
Sin moo cha	Do not lie (Buddhist Dhamma)
Sin pa na	Do not kill (Buddhist Dhamma)
Sin su la	Do not use drugs or intoxicants (Buddhist Dhamma)
Son ta na	Speak
Soot hern	Bless the home
Soot mon	Meditation chants
Soukhouan	Baci, conflict resolution ritual or ceremony

Soumma	Forgiveness or reconciliation ritual or ceremony
Sow noom	Young people's representative
Tai Deng	Red Tai ethnic group from the Lao Theung grouping
Tai Maen	Ethnic minority group, part of the Tai speaking group
Tdat sin (*chai*)	Decision
Terk bap terk vein	Bad luck, bad omen, shame, disgrace, humiliation
Terk tot	Punishment
Tien	Candles
Txiv neeb	Shamans, fortunetellers
Tow gua	Elder
Tow gua neo hom	Village or community elder
Tuk tuk	Lao taxi, truck with long benches
Wat	Temple
Wao	Talk
Yun	Knots in thread as used in *soukhouan* and *somma*

Index

CPSIA information can be obtained
at www.ICGtesting.com
Printed in the USA
BVHW071956090119
537472BV00009B/77/P